Understanding
AMERICAN FOOTBALL

Understanding AMERICAN FOOTBALL

The Simplest, Clearest, and Most Detailed Guide for Spectators

Ed McCorduck

NTC Publishing Group

Library of Congress Cataloging-in-Publication Data

McCorduck, Edward Scott.
    Understanding American football : the simplest, clearest,
and most detailed guide for spectators / Ed McCorduck.
       p.   cm.
    ISBN 0-8442-0572-9
    1. Football.   I. Title.
GV950.6.M33   1998
796.332—dc21   97-50063
                                         CIP

Cover design by Todd Petersen
Interior design by Scott Rattray
Graphics/images courtesy of ClickArt® Incredible Image Pak™
© 1995–1996 Broderbund Software, Inc. All rights reserved. Used by permission.
ClickArt, Incredible Image Pak, and Broderbund are trademarks and/or registered
trademarks of Broderbund Software, Inc.

Published by NTC Publishing Group
A division of NTC/Contemporary Publishing Group, Inc.
4255 West Touhy Avenue, Lincolnwood (Chicago), Illinois 60646-1975 U.S.A.
Copyright © 1998 by NTC/Contemporary Publishing Group, Inc.
Printed in the United States of America
International Standard Book Number: 0-8442-0572-9

18   17   16   15   14   13   12   11   10   9   8   7   6   5   4   3   2   1

For Tracey, my beloved wife

Contents

Acknowledgments   xi

Chapter One: Introduction   1

Chapter Two: What's Needed to Play Football   5

The Football   6

Football Fields and Stadiums   9

The Parts of a Football Field   15

Markings   15

Goalposts   23

Pylons   26

Benches and Sideline Areas   27

Players   29

Uniforms   29

Equipment   38

Helmet   39

Shoulder Pads   42

Gloves   42

Shoes   43

Other Equipment   45

Coaches   48

Officials   50

Chapter Three: How Football Is Played   55

Object of the Game   55

Length of the Game   56

What Happens During a Football Game   60

Pregame   60

Introduction of Players, National Anthem,
and Coin Toss   62

Kickoff   65

Offensive Series   69

Offensive Positions   70

Defensive Positions   74

Huddles   77

The Down Position, the Quarterback
Count, and the Snap of the Ball   78

Running Plays   81

Passing Plays   88

Kicking Plays   101

Punting   101

Field Goal Attempts   109

Extra-Point Attempts   114

Safeties   116

Officials and Penalties   117

Some Fundamentals of Playing Football   138

Tackling   138

Blocking   141

Player Conduct   144

General Offensive Strategies   148

General Defensive Strategies   152

Late-Game Strategies   156

Close Games   158

Chapter Four: The Organization of Football   165

*Organizational Aspects Common to
All Types of Football*   165

Team Names, Leagues, and Schedules   165

Practices and Training   168

Game Statistics   171

Football Championships   172

Team and Individual Player Statistics   173

Exhibition Games   175

Media Coverage of Football   176

Fan Attendance at Football Games   177

Cheerleaders and Mascots   183

High School Football   185

College Football   188

Who Plays College Football   188

The College Football Season   196

Professional Football   213

National Football League (NFL)   214

The Teams and Organization of the NFL   214

NFL Players   218

The NFL Season   227

NFL Europe   240

Canadian Football League (CFL)   242

Chapter Five: Other Kinds of Football   245

Semiprofessional Football   245

Arena Football   247

Youth Football   252

Flag and Touch Football   255

Glossary   261

Acknowledgments

would like to acknowledge the contribution of certain people to the creation, production, and completion of this book. The first people I would like to thank are Richard Spears and Sharon Sofinski of NTC/Contemporary Publishing Group, Inc. I want to thank Sharon for her help, especially in the final stages of writing the book. And I'd like to express my appreciation to two other people who are indirectly responsible for my writing this book. One is my first football coach, Roger Abraham, who probably would be very surprised to learn that one of his worst players wrote a book about the game. And then there's my dad. It was he who introduced me to football at an early age, which led to my becoming a life-long fan of the game. Because of this, he can be forgiven for still rooting for the New York Giants when all good residents of Upstate New York ought to support the Buffalo Bills. At the same time, I would like to thank my long-suffering mom for putting up with two football and sports maniacs like us. The same goes for my own wife, and perhaps I should apologize in advance to my daughter, Brittany—unless I can turn her into a football fan also.

Understanding

AMERICAN

FOOTBALL

Chapter 1

Introduction

This is a book about the sport that in the United States and Canada is called *football*. Unlike most of the rest of the world, English-speaking Americans and Canadians do not refer with any form of the word football to the international sport known by the full name of *association football*; that game they call *soccer*. So from now on in this book, the term "football" will be understood to describe the particularly North American game, which in recent years has begun to be played and watched in other areas of the globe, such as Europe. And though football as played in the United States is a little different from the game played in Canada, the similarities are so great that in this book I freely use "football" to refer to both national versions of the game.

Even people who don't pay a lot of attention to sports are aware that football is more than just a game. Football is a firmly rooted part of American popular culture, occupying a place that used to be held by baseball. While baseball is still popular and historically has had the greatest influence on American culture, it is no longer the national pastime as football arguably is (though to claim that there is one dominant sport in the United States, with its great diversity of people and forms of recreation, is probably folly). This is not to say that most Americans participate in playing the game of football, but rather that among sports that capture the attention of a great many Americans, football is probably supreme—primarily because of its extensive coverage by that oracle of American popular culture, television. Therefore, *anyone who wants to understand the contemporary United States ought to know something about American football.*

Yet there are many Americans who know almost nothing about football, or who may be casual observers of the game but not understand much of why it's played the way it is. And of course all over the world there are millions of people who may have heard of the American game of football but know little about it, even if it's played in some form in their countries. It is for these two audiences that I have written this book, and this purpose has shaped many of its aspects. For example, I have tried to write the text so that non-native speakers of English can follow it well enough to learn from it, phrasing the explanations of the game as simply as I could.

For the benefit of non-native speakers and native speakers alike, I have also highlighted the key terms of football and other words and phrases likely to be heard in a discussion of the game. These key terms are set in **bold type** and the definition of each is given in the Glossary. Parentheses are used around optional parts of a term; for example, where I write "**(quarterback) sacks**," this means that the term occurs as either *quarterback sacks* or *sacks*. And because this book may be read outside of the United States, when measurements of the football field and other items are given in the English system of feet, yards, etc., the metric equivalents are also included in parentheses. This is done even though the game and its rules are based on the English system, and it is also followed in Canadian football in spite of the fact that Canada officially uses the metric system.

Since I intend this book to be used by people who are not Americans or Canadians, I have paid some attention throughout to some of the cultural aspects of the game and how they relate to American and Canadian life. Readers who are North Americans may find these discussions overly simplistic, but I hope they will tolerate them for the sake of readers from different countries. I have included cultural information in the main text and also in the short sections throughout the book that have the title "Time-Out"; these digressions discuss minor but nevertheless interesting aspects of the game, and many of them point to the impact of football on the larger culture, or vice versa.

For North Americans and others who are not knowledgeable about sports in general, I have included some rudimentary explanations of what is involved in team athletic competition, and for non-native speakers I have supplied basic English vocabulary on this topic, especially concerning scores and winning and losing games. Again, these discussions may come off as too simple for many readers, but I hope that the terminology I use in describing these things will be useful for readers whose native language is not English.

As I discuss in later chapters, many more men than women actually play the game of football, but female players are not unknown at some levels of the game. As a result, in this book both masculine and feminine pronouns (for example "he or she") are used when referring to a generic football player or someone else associated with the game. This occurs when I talk about participants at any level of football where women have been represented; thus, since women have played high school and college football, whenever I discuss individual players at these levels I feel I must refer to them as "he or she," though both in the current game and especially throughout its history female players have been very scarce. Similarly, because some women have been owners of professional football teams and some have been sports journalists, when I refer to these positions generically I also use both pronouns. On the other hand, since to my knowledge no women have ever played professional football in leagues featuring male players, I use only masculine pronouns in referring specifically to NFL, NFL Europe, or CFL players.

I have tried to keep a neutral tone in this book, but occasionally readers may perceive some of my biases shining through. I have played football (though not very well) both at an organized level and in many informal, backyard games, and I have been a follower of the game most of my life. In spite of this, I have purposely tried not to ignore the negative aspects of the game in this book; I mention things such as injuries to younger players, the exploitation of players at the college level, the overcommercialization of the game at the professional levels, and football-related illegal activities such as drug abuse and gambling. I also do not shirk from the indisputable fact that football is a violent game, but I disagree with those who think the game is only about violence and is therefore senseless or even silly (grown men throwing each other to the ground, etc.). I am no fan of the excessive violence in the sport, but to me the challenge of the physical demands of the game are a part of its appeal. Speaking as a former player, there is something exhilarating in being tired, battered, and dirty after a game but having the satisfaction of coming out of it uninjured and victorious, or at least having performed well. The main fascination of the game for me, however, is its complexity: the complicated strategies, the precise execution, the teamwork and discipline, and the sheer athleticism that are necessary for success in the game. I am also interested in the business and organization of football and its impact on the culture, and these things I discuss as well.

This book is my personal view of the wonderful and wacky world of American football. As such, it may have its imperfections, but I hope that what I have presented here will enhance knowledge and appreciation of the game of football and its place in American life.

Chapter 2

What's Needed to Play Football

To play an informal game of football, just a **football**, players, and a place large enough to play (a **field**) are needed. But to play organized football—that is, football played competitively in established leagues—other things are necessary: **equipment, uniforms, coaches**, and **officials**. This chapter will describe each of these essentials. The focus of the discussion will be on organized football and on the kinds of organized football most familiar to people who have heard about the game: professional football as played in the National Football League (NFL), the Canadian Football League (CFL), and NFL Europe (formerly the World League of American Football); **college football** played under National Collegiate Athletic Association (NCAA) rules; and high school football, played under the rules of the National Federation of High School Associations (NFHSA). (Note: Except where noted, everything that is said in this book about the NFL also applies to NFL Europe.)

The Football

A **football** is a ball made from four sections of leather that are sewn together over an inner rubber tube called a bladder. The bladder is filled with air to a pressure of between 12½ and 13½ pounds per square inch (0.78–0.94 kilograms per square centimeter), making the total weight of the ball between 14 and 15 ounces (392 to 420 grams). Air is put into a football from an air pump through a thin needle that goes through a small rubber tube built into the football. If footballs aren't damaged they usually remain fully inflated, but they may lose small amounts of air from being used in games.

The leather on the outside of a football is usually a natural tan or dark brown in color. (The CFL specifically requires that

 the leather be "Horween Red.") In high school and college games, a football with a rubber or plastic case is sometimes used. When a football is fully inflated, it has the shape of a prolate spheroid—it is round around the middle with two ends that come to a point. From one end to the other, a football can be between 10⅞ inches and 11⁷⁄₁₆ inches (27.62 and 29.05 centimeters) long, and its circumference around the middle, its widest part, may be between 20¾ and 21¼ inches (52.7 and 53.98 centimeters).

Because it is filled with air a football will bounce on the ground, but because of its shape it will not bounce straight up

like a round ball. Its shape also does not permit the football to roll straight forward on the ground like the round ball of soccer. But a football is not meant to be moved forward by rolling or bouncing it on the ground. It is advanced by being carried or thrown by players, and for these purposes a football has small bumps on the leather that help players get a better grip on the ball. A football also has eight large white laces (and as many as 12 on a high school football) that tie together two of the leather sections. To **pass** a football, a player holds it in one hand with the fingers between the laces and throws it with a motion that makes the ball roll off the fingers. This makes the football go forward while spinning on its long axis with one end cutting through the air, and it will travel farther as a result.

A football may also have one-inch-wide white stripes around both ends. These stripes (which may be yellow in high school

---

T I M E · O U T

If a player doesn't throw the football with the right motion, it will wobble and possibly go end over end, and it will not go very far. This kind of throw is often referred to as a **wounded duck**.

---

football) are placed 3 to 3¾ inches from the tip of each end of the football. NFL footballs, however, do not have stripes (see the illustration of an NFL football at the beginning of this section).

In the NFL and CFL, footballs are made by a single manufacturer, Wilson, whose name appears prominently on the footballs. NFL and CFL footballs also have printed on them reproductions of the signature of the commissioner of the respective league.

During a game of organized football, several footballs are kept available on the sidelines, but only one can be used in the game in progress. Sometimes footballs are kicked or thrown into the **stands**, and in a game played outdoors during bad weather a ball may become too wet or muddy to be thrown, caught, or held on to. In such cases a new ball may be put into play, sometimes after every down in very bad weather (a ball can be wiped with a towel but cannot be dried by any mechanical means during a game).

In the NFL, the home team must provide 24 balls to the referee for his approval (which includes making sure they are properly inflated) one hour before the official start of the game. During the game, **ball boys** assist the officials in keeping footballs on both sidelines and putting new ones in play when needed. In the CFL, a minimum of seven footballs are kept available on the sidelines. In college football, each team must supply six footballs to the referee for testing 60 minutes before the start of the game. Since both teams supply the balls, each team has the option of choosing to use only the balls it supplied while on offense. In high school football, the home team must supply at least one legal ball for the game, but either team may choose any legal ball to use on a kickoff or when it starts an offensive series.

TIME·OUT

Footballs are not cheap; a new official NFL ball, for instance, can cost more than $100. Therefore, football teams and officials try to keep balls from leaving the field. Just before a field goal or extra-point attempt, for example, a net is raised behind the goalpost to catch the kicked ball and keep it from going into the stands (the net is lowered after the attempt so as not to obstruct the view of the spectators sitting behind the goalpost). And if a ball is thrown or kicked into the stands, stadium personnel try to get it back from any spectator who recovers it. Sometimes players throw a ball into the stands deliberately, perhaps in celebrating a touchdown, and for doing so they are usually fined by their league.

> # T I M E · O U T
>
> There is a tradition in football that when a game is over, a **game ball** is awarded by a team to a player or players who performed especially well during the game or who were especially responsible for the team's win. And sometimes players who make a special play, such as scoring their first touchdown or making a score that wins a game, may want to keep the ball they used on the play and not let it be used again in the game.

Football Fields and Stadiums

Organized football is played on a very large, rectangular field that is a little smaller than a field for soccer. A field for American football is 360 feet (109.73 meters) long and 160 feet (48.77 meters) wide, and in Canadian football the field is even larger, 450 feet (137.16 meters) long and 195 feet (59.44 meters) wide. A football field can be laid out on any athletic field, or it can be located inside a stadium with seats for thousands of spectators. The only requirements for a football field are that the ground be level and that the surface of the field be covered either by natural grass that is mown short or by **artificial turf** or **AstroTurf**. Underneath artificial turf, which is

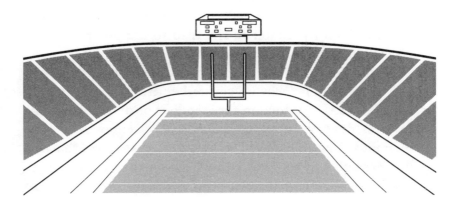

colored green to make it resemble natural grass, is a layer of asphalt or some other hard surface. One or more layers of padding separate this hard surface from the artificial turf to cushion players who fall down or are tackled on the field. However, many players complain that an artificial surface is harder than a natural grass field and causes more injuries to them when they hit the ground. They also complain about injuries unique to fields with artificial playing surfaces, such as *turf burn* and *turf toe*. For these reasons, many football players dislike artificial surfaces and prefer to play on natural grass fields, and in recent years many stadiums have had their artificial surfaces removed and replaced with a natural surface.

There are two main reasons a football field may have an artificial surface. One is that in areas such as the Northeast or Midwest regions of the United States and in all of Canada, football is played in outdoor stadiums in the months of November, December, and January when the weather is cold and there is a lot of precipitation. Under these conditions, fields with a natural surface often become very muddy and playing the game becomes difficult. Artificial surfaces, on the other hand, are not affected by adverse weather conditions (except for becoming a little more slippery) and remain playable throughout the year; even if a lot of snow falls on the field, it can simply be shoveled or plowed off the surface. In addition, the surface of most outdoor artificial turf fields—and of some fields with a natural surface also—slopes about a quarter of an inch (about half a centimeter) per each foot (30.48 cm) from the center of the field to the outer edges so that water from rain or snow will drain off the field.

The other reason a football field may have an artificial surface is that a stadium may be covered entirely by a dome. An artificial surface is needed in these indoor or domed stadiums since grass does not grow where it is never exposed to sunlight. Football can be played in any domed stadium that has a large enough playing field and whose dome is high enough above the field so that thrown or kicked balls don't hit it. In fact, football doesn't need as big a stadium as baseball does, and several indoor stadiums exist that were built only for football and other events and are too small for baseball; examples of these are the Silverdome in Pontiac, Michigan; the RCA Dome in Indianapolis, Indiana; and Syracuse University's Carrier Dome in Syracuse, New York.

T I M E · O U T

In some places, both baseball and football—and possibly other sports such as soccer—are played in the same stadium. Very often, the seasons of these sports overlap; the first football games may be played before the last baseball games, and parts of the field will still have the dirt surface of the baseball infield (except for the pitcher's mound, which is always leveled out for a football game). Traction is often difficult for football players when they cross this dirt surface, so after the baseball season ends, the infield is covered with sod or the artificial surface.

Since baseball requires a larger field than football, the stands for spectators in stadiums where both sports are played end up being far away when the football field is laid out (though in some stadiums, such as San Francisco's 3Com Park, some of the stands are on rollers and can be moved closer during the football season). This is one of the reasons football leagues prefer that games be played in stadiums built especially for football, and often the existence of or the promise to build a football-only stadium is a requirement for a city to get a new team.

If a football game is played in a stadium or at a field with bleachers, there will be an area on top or in the middle of the stands called the **press box**. This area, which is usually enclosed, is where members of the media—for example, newspaper reporters and TV and radio personnel—are located while they cover the game. Coaches and officials from both

---

T I M E · O U T

The style of announcing used by the public-address announcer at a football stadium is different from that of an announcer on a television or radio broadcast of a football game. What a public-address announcer says is limited to a few basic formulas—for example, "Carry by number thirty-two, John Smith, tackled by number fifty-five, Bill Williams. Loss of two, second down and twelve." In contrast, a broadcast announcer speaks more freely and naturally, and there is the important difference that a broadcaster can—and, especially on the radio, is expected to—describe the play of the game as it is happening; a public-address announcer, on the other hand, does not speak until each play is over.

---

teams may also be in the press box during the game, usually in separate compartments; they are usually in communication with the coaches and players on the field and assist them in many ways (see "Coaches," below).

The press box is also where the stadium's public-address announcer is usually located. Almost all football fields have a public-address system in which loudspeakers are placed in different spots around the field. The public-address system is used for giving spectators information about the game in progress. This information may include the names, numbers, and positions of starting players and, after each play, the player or players most involved in the play and the result of the play; for example, the offensive player(s) who carried, passed, and/or caught the ball and defensive player(s) who made the tackle are announced to the crowd, as well as the current down and yardage to go for a first down. Any penalties called and any scoring resulting from the play are also announced. Besides information related to the game, the public-address system may also be used to give public-service or commercial announcements or even to play music for entertainment or to lead the home-field crowd in cheering for their team. Music can be played only during breaks in the action of the game, not while the game is in play.

Almost all football stadiums and fields have a scoreboard. Scoreboards are large structures that can stand by themselves or are built right into the interior walls of the stadium. Using displays built from small lights that alternate between on and off to create different numerals, football scoreboards provide the following information for spectators and players: the current scores of both teams; the current **quarter** and **down**; and the time remaining in the quarter in minutes and seconds. The time remaining is given by a digital clock, but unlike a conventional clock the time on a scoreboard clock runs backward; that is, at the beginning of each quarter the clock shows 15 minutes and 00 seconds, then after one second the clock reads 14:59, and the clock counts down in this manner until it reads 00:00, at which point the quarter ends. Some scoreboards provide additional information, such as the number of yards the current team on offense needs for a first down, which team currently has the ball, and the time remaining on the play clock (see "Length of the Game" in chapter 3), though in professional and college football there are usually separate scoreboards for the play clock, placed where they can easily be seen by the players on the field. Smaller scoreboards, giving only the current score and quarter and the time remaining in the quarter, may be placed in other parts of the stadium.

Scoreboards at some football stadiums, especially at the professional level, are quite sophisticated. They can display letters and whole words as well as numerals, giving, for example, public-address announcements or the scores of other games. Many stadiums also have large video screens that are connected to a television broadcast of the game so that spectators inside the stadium can see replays of action that has just

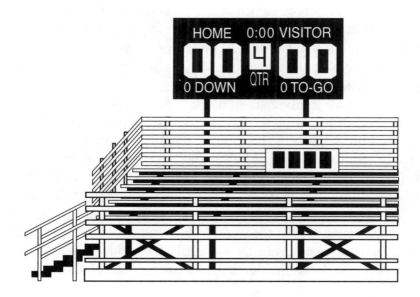

occurred (but video of game action that is happening at the moment cannot be shown).

A scoreboard is controlled by personnel in the press box. The scoreboard operator pays attention to the officials on the field and follows their signals, such as those that indicate when to start or stop the game clock. The officials must also be able to communicate directly with the scoreboard operator, since in some cases they may determine that the scoreboard shows incorrect information about the game. (An inaccurate time on the game clock most commonly results when the scoreboard operator doesn't start or stop the clock as directed by the officials.)

Most fields for organized football have artificial lighting that is turned on for games played at night or in bad weather. All indoor stadiums have lights, of course. The lighting may be built into a stadium's structure or, especially around smaller fields, the lights may be at the top of very high poles. Lights that are part of a stadium's structure are usually placed at the topmost levels of the stadium. Also found around the tops of stadiums are flagpoles. On the days when games are played, flags with the colors and insignias or names of other teams in the same league as the stadium's home team are flown from these poles.

Finally, almost every football field and stadium has an indoor area called a **locker room**. The locker room is where players put on and take off their uniforms and equipment that are stored in their **lockers**. It is also where teams meet immediately before and after games and during the halftime intermission. Many locker rooms also have physical training equipment and facilities, and most have medical supplies and equipment for treating players' minor injuries; in addition, all NFL stadiums are required to have x-ray equipment for immediate diagnosis of any severe injury to a player.

The Parts of a Football Field

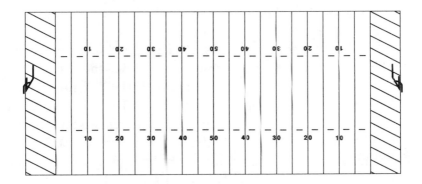

Markings

A football field is marked in specific ways. Most of the divisions of a football field are indicated with 4-inch-thick (10.16 cm) lines that are laid on the surface of the field. The material for the lines, most of which must be white in color, is usually made from powdered gypsum or calcium carbonate (both commonly referred to as chalk). On fields with a natural surface, the grass of course grows and has to be mown, so the lines frequently have to be reapplied. On fields with artificial surfaces, however, the lines are often sprayed on the field with a type of aerosol paint, which is much less likely than chalk to disappear and in fact is virtually permanent. Whatever material is used to make the lines, it must not be harmful if it comes into contact with a player's skin or eyes, which is common in a contact sport like football in which players are very often knocked to the ground.

Perhaps the most important lines on a football field are the ones that set off the outer boundaries of the field. The two parallel lines that run the whole length of the field are called the **sidelines**, and the two lines extending the width of the field at both ends are called the **end lines** (in Canadian football these are called **dead lines**).

A football field is divided lengthwise by lines, placed every 5 yards (4.75 meters), that extend the entire width of the field from one sideline to the other. In the NFL, these lines do not intersect with the sidelines but end 8 inches (20.32 centimeters) from them. At both ends of the field, however, there is a section that extends 10 yards (9.14 meters) out from each end line before the first lengthwise yard line; these two sections of the field are called the **end zones**. (In Canadian football, these areas are called **goal areas** and extend 20 yards [18.29 meters] from the dead lines.) The lengthwise yard line that marks the inner border of the end zone is called the **goal line**. This is one of the most important lines on the field, since crossing it with the football results in a score and is the ultimate aim of every offensive series (see chapter 3). For this reason, the two goal lines on the field often have special markings. In the WL the goal lines are yellow. In other kinds of football, especially high school football, the goal lines may also be a different color than white or there may be colored borders along both sides of the white goal lines. In the NFL, the goal lines are twice as wide (8 inches) as other lines on the field.

Between each of the long 5-yard lines are much shorter lines in the middle of the field and along the sidelines. These markers occur at one-yard intervals between the 5-yard lines (in other words, there is a marker for each of the yards between the lines) and are parallel to them. The markers along the sidelines begin 4 inches from the sidelines, and in the middle of the field there are two rows of these markers that extend the length of the field and are called **hash marks**. Like the yard markers along the sidelines, each hash mark is just 24 inches (2 feet, or 60.96 cm) long, and every 5-yard line is bisected in two places by a hash mark perpendicular to it and the other hash marks. In the NFL, the inner edges of the hash marks are 70 feet 9 inches (21.56 meters) from the nearer sideline, but in college and high school football they are only 53 feet 4 inches (16.26 meters) from the sidelines. This means that NFL hash marks set off a narrower area, 18 feet 6 inches, than those of college or high school football, where the distance between the rows of hash marks is the same as the distance from the inner edges to the sidelines. In Canadian football, the hash marks are 24 yards (21.95 meters) from the sidelines.

T I M E · O U T

Some stadiums may host both college and professional football games. In these stadiums, college and professional hash marks may both appear in the middle of the field, especially if the field has an artificial surface and the lines are permanently painted on.

Besides marking off the yards of a field, hash marks set the boundary of the area from inside which each play of the game must start. If a play ends with the ball downed in an area outside of the hash marks, an official must move the ball inside the hash marks parallel to the spot on the field where the ball ended up before the next play can start.

TIME·OUT

The area outside of the hash marks is referred to in football rules and officials' manuals as **out of bounds**, while the area between the hash marks, from which the ball must be put in play, is said to be **in bounds**. However, in the less technical usage of most fans, broadcasters, and even players, in bounds refers to any area of the field within the sidelines and end lines, and a ball or a player with the ball that goes outside of these, causing a stoppage of play, is out of bounds.

Thus, each of the 100 yards of a football field from one goal line to the other is marked, and this is why people usually say that a football field is 100 yards long when the actual total length of the field is 120 yards. Each of the 100 yards also has a number. From both goal lines to the middle of the field, each yard is numbered from 1 to 50. This results in the field being divided into two sections at the 50-yard line, and the lower the yard number, the closer the yard is to one of the goal lines. The midpoint of a Canadian football field, however, is the 55-yard line, since the field between the goal lines is 110 yards long. During a game, the 50 yards extending from the end zone defended by one team (i.e., the end zone that the other team must enter to score) is its **territory**. Referring to the two sections of the field in this way makes it possible to state the exact location of the **line of scrimmage**. For example, there are two 30-yard lines on the field, each 30 yards from one of the goal lines. In a game between two teams called the Warriors and Wildcats, if the Warriors have possession of the ball and are defending the end zone that is 30 yards behind the line of scrimmage they are starting at, it is said that the ball is "on the Warrior 30-yard line" or just "on the Warrior

30," or it can be said that "the Warriors have the ball on their own 30-yard line." If the Warriors have the ball on the 30-yard line and are only 30 yards away from the end zone defended by the Wildcats, the ball is said to be "on the Wildcat 30-yard line" or "the Wildcat 30," and so on.

The numbering of the yards of a football field is indicated on the surface of the field by numerals that straddle the yard lines extending the length of the field. The numerals are 6 feet (1.83 m) high and 2 to 3 feet (0.61 to 0.91 m) wide. They are put on the field with the same material that is used to make the lines, so they are solid white in color and may have colored borders. On most fields only the 10-, 20-, 30-, 40-, and 50-yard lines are marked, though some fields also mark the 5-yard lines that occur between these lines. In Canadian football all the lengthwise lines are numbered. On some fields a large "G" parallel with the line numbers is also placed in front of the goal lines. Numerals are placed on both sides of the field, with their bottoms 12 yards (10.97 m) from the sidelines in the NFL and 9 yards (8.23 m) from the sidelines in college and high school football. The bottoms of the numerals are set next to the sidelines so that they are correctly positioned for observers on each side of the field. The numeral representing the tens digit is put on what to observers on the nearer side of the field would be the left side of the line, and the 0 or 5 is put on the right. The numerals cannot touch the lines and can be no closer than 1 foot (0.305 m) to them. As for the two 5-yard lines, the 5 may be placed either on the right of the line or it may be centered on the line itself.

In addition to the on-field numerals, small upright signs made from flexible material are often placed perpendicular to the lengthwise yard lines several yards beyond the sidelines. The signs give the yard line number (usually only for those ending in "0") and are mainly for the benefit of players and officials on the field who may not always be able to read the on-field numerals.

T I M E · O U T

On many fields, small triangular arrows are placed no closer than 6 inches next to either the tens digit or the "0" or "5" of a yard number marker, depending on the direction of the closer goal line, to which each arrow points. These arrows are primarily for the benefit of people watching football on television. The action of each football play usually starts and finishes in just a portion of the field that television cameras focus on, so TV viewers see only a small part of the entire field on their screens, but the arrows help to indicate to them in which part of the field the action is taking place. For example, say you are watching a football game on TV and the team on offense is advancing toward the left of your screen. If you see the 20-yard line marker near the sideline that's at the bottom of your screen and the arrow is to the left of the "2" and pointing left, you know that the offense has only 20 yards to go for a touchdown (and it also means that the team is within range to attempt a field goal). But if the arrow is to the right of the "0" and pointing to the right, the team on offense is just 20 yards away from the end zone it's defending and has a long way to go for a touchdown.

The first part of this section has described the markings on the inside of a football field. There are also marks outside of the field. While these marks may not govern a football game as the interior lines do, they are still important. As mentioned above, football fields are bordered by 4-inch-wide sidelines and end lines, but in the NFL the entire field is surrounded by a white border area that is 6 feet (1.83 m) wide. The purpose of this large border is to set off an area in which only officials can stand during a game. Any part of the white border is considered out of bounds (in other words, the sidelines and the end lines are considered to begin at the inside edge of the border). In the WL, the entire field is surrounded by an 8-inch (20.32 cm) orange border. And in high school football, a broken line may go around the entire field 2 or more yards outside the sidelines and end lines to set off an area in which the officials may work.

Farther outside any of the borders described above are other lines, called **limit lines** or **restraining lines**. These lines, which may be yellow in color, actually are 12-inch-long segments placed 12 inches apart. These lines go around the field at a distance of 12 feet (3.66 m) from the sidelines and end lines, at least in stadiums where room permits; in smaller stadiums, the limit lines must be at least 6 feet (1.83 m) from the sidelines and end lines. In the NFL, the lines go 6 feet behind the white borders. The purpose of these lines is to limit how close persons other than players, coaches and other team personnel, or game officials may be to the playing field during the game. The people who must stay outside of the area between these limit lines and the field borders may include photographers, security personnel, and even—in smaller stadiums—fans.

On college football fields, there is also a 6-foot-wide solid white border just outside of both sidelines that runs between the two 25-yard lines. This is called the **coaching line** or **coaching box**. During a game no coaches, team officials, or substitute players can stay in this area; only the team's head coach and game officials or chain crew personnel are allowed. Similarly, in the NFL there is a yellow line that runs 6 feet behind the white border area between the 32-yard lines on both sides of the field. Between this yellow line and the border area only a team's coaches and one player who is recording game information may stand during the game.

Football fields also mark the areas along the side of the field where the coaches and personnel of both teams, including players of both teams who are not playing in the game at the moment, must remain during the game. These are called the **team areas**, and their dimensions vary somewhat in each type of football. On almost all fields the team areas are on opposite sidelines, but occasionally a field in a very small stadium may have both team areas on the same side of the field. In outdoor stadiums with a natural grass surface, large mats or rugs are often placed over the team area; otherwise, the ground of the area would become a muddy mess in wet weather with all the players, team personnel, and other people walking around in it.

On many football fields, there are other markings that have nothing to do with the game itself but are put on the field only for decoration. These may include a large insignia of the league or of the home team placed at the center of the field, and messages or symbols on the field near the sidelines. Examples of these messages or symbols might be the name of the stadium, the logo for the United Way (a charitable organization that has a special relationship with the NFL), or holiday greetings. Occasionally, even commercial advertising may appear on football fields (except on high school fields), especially during preseason games or in college bowl games sponsored by a corporation; for example, in recent years the Orange Bowl has been sponsored by Federal Express, and the logos of the company appear on the field during this game.

The most noticeable decorations on the field are in the end zones. The end zones of most fields feature a name, either the name of the school or city of the home team or the team's nickname, written in very large letters covering most of the area of the zone, often accompanied by an enlarged team insignia. (In games like the Super Bowl that are played in neutral sites, the names and/or insignias of both teams may be put in the end zones.) And all or part of the area of the end zone may be in a color different from the green of the field; if so, it's usually one of the colors of the home team.

Decorations on a field are allowed as long at they do not cover or cause any confusion with the required markings of the field. Other sports such as soccer, lacrosse, and field hockey may regularly be played on fields where football is also played, and lines marking the field for these sports may be visible on the field along with the football markings, especially on fields with artificial surfaces whose markings are more or less permanent. Generally, these lines for the other sports are a different color (usually yellow or red) from the white football lines.

Goalposts

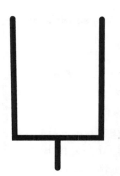

One of the most recognizable parts of a football field are the two **goalposts**, one located near each end zone. These structures, usually made from metal, consist of a base (or pedestal) that supports a horizontal **crossbar**. Extending vertically from both ends of the crossbar are two poles called the **uprights**. The goalposts are important in football scoring, since points are awarded when the football is kicked from a spot on the playing field over the crossbar and between the two uprights (see "Field Goal Attempts" and "Extra-Point Attempts" in chapter 3).

The base of the goalpost is anchored into the ground a few yards outside of the end line and exactly halfway between the two sidelines. The base is thus outside of the playing field, but since it is still close to the field it is padded from the ground up to a height of 6 feet to protect players who might run into it. In the NFL, the base is anchored just outside the white boundary area and is thus still outside the playing field, but in Canadian football bases are centered right on the goal lines (as in fact they used to be in the NFL and in American college football).

The padding is covered by a material that usually features the name and color(s) of the home team. The top of the base curves toward the playing field, and the point at which it meets the crossbar is 10 feet (3.05 m) above the field and directly over the end zone line. From each end of the crossbar, an upright 3 to 4 inches (7.62 to 10.16 cm) in diameter extends straight up 30 feet (9.14 m) in professional football, 20 feet (6.1 m) on college fields, and 10 feet (3.01 m) in high school football (though goalposts with college or professional heights are permissible at this level, especially where high school games are played on pro or college fields). The uprights are 18 feet 6 inches (5.64 m) apart in professional football and 23 feet 4 inches (7.11 m) apart in college and high school football.

T I M E · O U T

Even though the highest football goalposts are thus 40 feet from the ground to the top of the uprights, a kicked ball doesn't have to go directly through the uprights for points to be awarded. If the officials judge that a ball kicked higher than the top of the uprights would have gone directly through them if the uprights extended higher in a straight line, the kick is ruled good.

There is an older kind of goalpost that is still found on some football fields, especially high school fields. In this style, sometimes called the "H" type (the kind described above is often called the "Y" or "slingshot" type), the goalpost consists of two upright poles 20 feet high and 23 feet 4 inches apart that are connected by a crossbar that extends horizontally from the center of one upright to the center of the other (the crossbar is thus 10 feet above the ground). The two vertical poles are based directly on the end line, and both must be padded at least 6 feet up the pole.

Except in indoor stadiums where of course there is never any wind, small orange or red flags called streamers or ribbons may be put at the top of each upright of a goalpost to show the direction of the wind. The streamers are long and thin, 4 inches (10.16 cm) wide and 42 inches (106.68 cm) long, so that the slightest wind will make them flatten out and point in the direction of the wind. Knowing the direction of the wind is important for a team in deciding whether or not to attempt an extra point or field goal or which end zone of the field to defend at the beginning of the game. A team will want to be able to kick or throw with the wind—that is, with the wind blowing in the same direction as the flight of the football—and not against the wind because the resistance of the wind would slow the ball. The direction of the wind is also of interest to kickers, some of whom are such specialists that they can alter their kicking styles to adapt to slight changes in wind direction.

T I M E · O U T

Sometimes the wind blows so strongly in an outdoor stadium that parts of the goalposts, especially the uprights, actually sway. But goalposts are so sturdy that they rarely collapse.

Goalposts are painted white or a bright yellow or gold to make the crossbar and especially the uprights easier for the kicker to see. Kickers need this visual aid because the crossbar and uprights are not extremely thick to begin with, and on most kick attempts the kicker has to put the ball over the crossbar and through the uprights from several yards away, usually 20 yards or more. Kick attempts must also be made from inside the hash marks, so kickers face the goalpost directly and do not have much of a side view to help their depth perception. And in games played in a stadium that surrounds the entire field, including both end zones, the goalposts are viewed against the background of a crowd wearing clothing of different colors, so the uprights need to be brightly colored to stand out.

T I M E · O U T

There is a tradition in football for fans to run onto the field and try to take down the goalposts at the conclusion of a game in which their home team wins a championship. Security personnel at stadiums usually try to prevent this, since over the years many fans have been seriously injured by falling crossbars or uprights. However, the security forces are often greatly outnumbered by the fans who rush onto the field, and when that happens, they can do little to prevent the goalposts from being taken down.

Pylons

At the eight points on the field where the sidelines intersect both goal lines and end lines, there are little red or orange four-sided tubes sticking up out of the ground. These are called **pylons,** and they are made from a soft material and placed on short, flexible posts. Since players often run into or fall over these pylons, they are designed to collapse under a player but pop back into their original shape after the player gets off. The pylons are 18 inches (45.72 cm) high and each side is 4 inches wide. In college football, two additional pylons are placed 1 yard (0.91 m) behind each end line at the spot where the hash marks, if they continued into the end zone, would meet them. In high school football, these additional pylons are placed right on the end lines parallel to the hash marks.

The purpose of the pylons is to help players and officials determine whether a player, especially one carrying the ball, has crossed the goal line in bounds or is still in bounds in the end zone. If the player's body passes by the side of a pylon that faces the field, he or she is in bounds (and has scored a touchdown), but going over the pylon or outside of it is out of bounds.

Benches and Sideline Areas

In the team areas marked off outside of the sidelines, there may be several items. The most common objects are benches for players who are not playing in the game at the moment to sit on. The benches can be made of wood or metal, and they may have back supports, especially in college and professional football. There are also specially designed benches that are heated so that players can sit in them and warm themselves during games played outdoors in cold weather. Since benches are hard objects, they must be placed some distance away from the playing field to prevent players from colliding with them after they run out of bounds, though this still happens frequently; in the NFL, for example, the benches are placed 30 feet from the sidelines, near the outer border of the team area line.

T I M E · O U T

Usually, only players who have already played in the game and are resting sit on the benches. Substitute players usually stand in the team area near the sidelines during the game to show the coaches that they are ready and willing to be put into the game.

There may also be tables in the team area on which equipment or other items can be placed, such as large coolers containing water or other liquids for the players to drink. Headsets with microphones and earphones may also be put on these tables while coaches or players aren't wearing them. These headsets are connected to outlets in or near the bench area, and they allow players or coaches to communicate with other coaches and team personnel who are located in the press box (see "Football Fields and Stadiums," above, and "Coaches," below).

TIME·OUT

Another football tradition is for players on a team that has won or is about to win a championship game to dump the contents of a water cooler on their head coach. The players try to do this when the coach is not expecting it, and since the liquid in these coolers is usually chilled with ice (and many football championship games are played in the coldest months of the year in outdoor stadiums), the coach almost always reacts to the dumping with shock that quickly goes away in this time of triumph for his team.

Other objects in the team area may include crates and other containers with extra equipment and supplies, including first aid and other medical supplies and equipment; devices such as hand warmers or, in games played in very hot weather, large fans and/or devices that spray cool water on the players; and small nets attached to a frame into which kickers can kick balls for practice or to warm up. All items in the team areas must be placed far back of the sidelines to reduce the chance that players running out of bounds may crash into them.

Players

An informal game of football can be played with just a few players on each of the two teams, but in most types of organized football each team must have 11 players on the field during every play. A football team usually has many more than 11 members, however; professional teams have 45 regular players, high school teams may have nearly that many, and some college teams have double that number.

Most of the players on a football team play a specific position when they are in the game. Player positions are of two main types, **offensive** and **defensive**. There is also a third category, **special teams**, for kicking plays, but almost all special-teams players can also play **offense** or **defense** (indeed, very few players besides kickers play exclusively on special teams, except at the professional level). Most football players play only one position, or only a few closely related positions, on either offense or defense. This holds true most often on professional and college teams; it may be less true in high school, especially on smaller teams where many players may regularly play both offensive and defensive positions.

The specific football positions are discussed under "Offensive Positions" and "Defensive Positions" in the next chapter.

Uniforms

Football players have to wear special clothing called **uniforms**. A football uniform consists of a jersey worn over the top of the body and special pants and socks. Each player on a team must wear a jersey, pants, and socks of the same design and color as those of all the other members of the team.

A football **jersey** is a pullover shirt that must be large enough to fit over players' upper bodies when they also have shoulder pads on. The sleeves are of a medium length but appear short when worn over shoulder pads. The material of the jersey over the shoulders is usually reinforced, whereas the

material of the rest of the jersey is usually light, often with small perforations, to help keep the player cool (important when a football game is played in hot, humid weather conditions). Though the jersey material should be light, it must be strong enough so that it won't easily tear when grabbed while the player wearing the jersey is moving. Also, the jerseys must be long enough to reach the top of the pants and the bottom of the jersey must be tucked into the top of the pants at all times.

A jersey worn during a game cannot be cut or altered in any way, and it cannot have any attachments or projecting pieces to grab on to. If there were anything sticking out of the jersey, an offensive player would be at a disadvantage when trying to avoid being tackled by a defensive player, who could just reach out and stop the ballcarrier. But the NCAA and the NFL permit a towel to be attached to the jersey or tucked in at the waist so that players, especially skill players like quarterbacks, running backs, receivers, or punters who often handle the football, can dry their hands if they're wet from weather conditions or perspiration. The towels must be plain white in color, and if they fall off a player's jersey they must be picked up from the field before the next play. Another uniform attachment that is permitted is a hand warmer, which is usually just a covering sewn onto the front of the jersey into which skill players like quarterbacks can stick their hands to warm them during cold weather.

Nearly all football jerseys are one color all over. Most teams have two sets of jerseys, one that is white and one that is another color. The nonwhite jerseys are usually of a dark hue, but they may be a fairly bright color like the light orange jerseys worn by the football team of the University of Tennessee. In a game, one team wears its white jerseys and the other wears its colored ones. Except in high school football, where the **home team** is required to wear its dark jerseys and the visiting team its white, the home team has the first choice of wearing its white or its colored jersey. Most teams wear their colored jerseys at home, but some wear their white ones; perhaps the most famous team that always wears white at home is the Dallas Cowboys of the NFL. And a few teams do not have white jerseys but instead wear jerseys that are yellow, light gold, or light blue in color and that still provide a contrast with other teams' dark jerseys.

Whatever color they are, football jerseys have several kinds of markings. The most prominent are large numerals found on the back and front of all jerseys. These numerals give the player's identifying number on both the back and the front and, like the numerals on the field, they are often referred to as just numbers. The numerals may be cut from separate material and sewn onto the jerseys, or they may be simply screen-printed. The numerals on the backs of jerseys are at least 10 inches (25.4 cm) tall and those on the front are 8 inches (20.32 cm) tall, and on both the back and front the numerals are 1½ to 2 inches (3.81 to 5.08 cm) wide. The reason front numerals are usually smaller is that small numbers are more readable when players' arms are moving around in front of their jerseys.

On colored jerseys, the numerals on both sides are white or a light color (e.g., yellow or gold), and on white jerseys the numerals are one of the team's primary dark colors (usually the color of its dark jerseys). The numerals on either white or dark jerseys often have thin borders of one of the team's other colors. If there are two borders, at least one must contrast with the jersey color—that is, it must be a light color if the jersey is dark, and vice versa.

<hr>

T I M E · O U T

A new style of jersey that some teams in the CFL and the WL
have recently begun to wear features a very small numeral in
the upper right or left corner of the front of the jersey, where it
is perhaps even less likely to be blocked from view by the
player's arms. The team's insignia may also appear on the front
of the jersey in this style.

<hr>

As in other sports, the reason football players first started
to wear jerseys with numerals was so that spectators, officials,
coaches, and other players could identify the players; each
player on a team wore a different number. This is still the primary reason for wearing numerals, but the jerseys of almost
all professional football teams, many college teams, and even
some high school teams also have nameplates giving each
player's name. The nameplates are sewn or printed onto the
backs of jerseys above the numerals and give, in all capital letters, the player's last (or family) name. The last name is usually sufficient to identify a player, but if two or more players
have the same family name an initial standing for the player's
first name is included on the nameplate (for example, a team
may have a "B. WILLIAMS" and a "J. WILLIAMS"). Occasionally a player's full first name may be given, especially if
the name is short or if another player with the same last name
also has an identical first initial.

There is a system to the numbers football players wear on
their jerseys. A player's number can consist of one or two digits in the numerical sequence from 1 to 99 (and sometimes
players wear the number 00). The number a player wears
depends on his or her position. Players who play any position
in the offensive backfield wear numbers between 1 and 49;
quarterbacks wear any number from 1 to 19, and running
backs wear numbers between 1 and 49 but most commonly

between 20 and 49. Players on the offensive line wear numbers between 50 and 79. As a general rule, centers wear numbers between 50 and 59, guards wear between 60 and 69, and tackles between 70 and 79, but more often than not a center, guard, or tackle will wear any number in the range of 50 to 79, because linemen occasionally switch positions during a season or over their playing careers. Wide receivers wear numbers between 80 and 89, and they can also wear the same numbers as backs (i.e., 1 to 49). A tight end also usually wears a number between 80 and 89, but sometimes tight ends will have backs' numbers because they have been "converted" from running backs or wide receivers.

Defensive positions have assigned numbers also. Players on the defensive line can wear any number between 50 and 99, though usually they wear numbers between 70 and 99. Linebackers generally wear numbers in the 50s or the 90s, and in college football linebackers may wear numbers lower than 50. Defensive backs, like offensive backs, can wear any number between 1 and 49, though the usual range is between 20 and 49, especially in professional football.

Kickers and punters often wear numbers in the single digits, especially 1, 2, or 3, but they can also wear the numbers of backs, 1 to 49, or numbers in the 80s or 90s.

T I M E · O U T

Football players' numbers often signify more than just the players' positions. Numbers often come to be identified with famous players at a certain position, and new players often choose these particular numbers with this in mind. For example, 12 is a special number for quarterbacks because this number was worn by famous quarterbacks like Joe Namath, Terry Bradshaw, and Roger Staubach, and 32 is a desired number for a running back because this number was worn by backs such as O. J. Simpson and Marcus Allen. Sometimes wearing a particular number is a special honor for the player. For instance, the number 44 has been worn by illustrious running backs at Syracuse University such as Ernie Davis, Jim Brown, Floyd Little, and Larry Csonka, and the opportunity to wear this special number is offered to high school running backs whom the team is trying to recruit. But wearing a famous number can put a lot of pressure on a player; as an example, any linebacker for the NFL's Chicago Bears who wears the number 51 will find it hard to escape from the shadow of the Bears' great linebacker Dick Butkus, who wore this number.

Especially at the professional level, sometimes a team will honor a great player by retiring the number he wore. When a player's number is retired, no one else who ever plays for the team will be allowed to wear that number.

In addition to the large numerals on the front and back of jerseys, the same number may appear in smaller numerals on top of each shoulder or on both sleeves. These smaller numerals are required on jerseys worn by NFL and CFL teams.

Football jerseys may have other markings besides numbers and names. One of the most common is a stripe or stripes around the ends of the sleeves, and another is a colored band around the neck. Another common marking is the insignia of the team, which is often found on the sleeve or on top of the shoulder. In the past it was also common for teams, especially college and high school teams, to have their name printed in large letters above the numerals on the front of the jersey. While this is becoming less common, a trend has recently developed for NFL and college teams to wear jerseys with the team nickname written in very small letters (visible only in closeup, such as in television broadcasts) below the neck. In the NFL and in the CFL jerseys must have a small shield-shaped patch on the front of the neck opening giving the official insignia of the league. College football teams very often have a patch somewhere on their jerseys giving the name and/or insignia of the conference or league to which the team belongs.

Football jerseys are made by many manufacturers, and each of these usually puts a label with its name or trademark somewhere on the jersey. Football leagues generally restrict the size of these labels to make sure that they are not so large that, for example, they interfere with the identification of the player. Teams and leagues are generally quite careful to avoid over-commercializing football by displaying too many or too large corporate symbols. The NFL, in particular, strictly enforces uniform regulations, regularly fining players who wear apparel having the names or trademarks of companies that the league does not recognize as official equipment suppliers. However, semiprofessional football teams often accept corporate sponsorship in exchange for displaying prominently these businesses' logos on their uniforms.

Football jerseys often have markings that are placed on them only temporarily, perhaps for one game or just part of a season. One occasion on which a team's jerseys may carry a special marking is if the team is playing in a bowl game or a special exhibition game (like the NFL's annual American Bowl exhibition game, played outside of the United States). In such games, the jerseys of both teams usually carry a patch with the name and/or logo of the bowl or exhibition game. Also, a patch having small numerals or initials may sometimes be seen on jerseys. This kind of patch honors a person who has recently died, either a player of the team, in which case the numeral was his or her uniform number, or a member of the coaching or administrative staff of the team, with the initials standing for his or her name. These memorial patches are not permitted in college football.

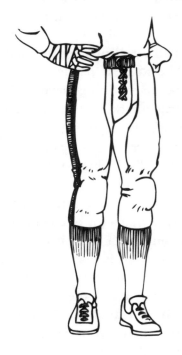

Football players also wear special pants. Football pants are made from heavy material and are tight-fitting, and they have short legs that extend only a few inches down from the knee. They also have inside pockets into which thigh and knee pads can be inserted.

Like jerseys, football pants can be white or any one of a team's colors. Some teams have two sets of pants, one white in color to be worn with the team's dark jerseys, and the other a darker color to be worn when the team is wearing its white jerseys. Very often football pants also have one or several parallel vertical stripes on the outside of both legs that extend down from the top of the pants around the waist section to the ends of the legs. Sometimes small numerals giving the player's number or other designs may also appear on the pants; for example, instead of vertical stripes the pants of the NFL's San Diego Chargers feature the image of a lightning bolt, which is the team's logo.

Football players can wear athletic socks that extend all the way up to the knee, covering the part of the leg left exposed by the short football pants, or they can wear shorter socks that leave much of the leg above the ankle and below the knee uncovered. Normally, the socks football players wear are white, but the longer socks may have colored stripes near the top. The NFL requires that players' socks extend all the way up to the knee and that the socks be solid white up to the mid-point of the lower leg, above which they may have bands of the team's color or colors.

T I M E · O U T

Some kickers prefer to kick the football with a bare foot, so they wear neither a sock nor a shoe on their kicking foot when they are in the game to kick.

Football players may wear clothing underneath their uniforms. In addition to underwear, which may include team-issued T-shirts, in cold weather players often wear under their uniforms a thin material that retains their body heat very well. This material can even be made into a covering for a player's head and neck and can be worn under the helmet. Some players also like to wear bandannas under their helmets; if a bandanna is worn, no part of it can show from under the helmet, and the bandanna must be one of the team's colors. Similarly, if players wear any kind of undershirt with long sleeves under their jerseys, all the players on the same team must wear the same color undershirts, either white or one of the team's colors.

Players who are not playing in the game but are in the team area on the sidelines can wear other clothing in addition to their uniforms. In cold weather particularly, they may wear large jackets or overcoats that fit completely over their jerseys even with their shoulder pads on. These overcoats or jackets may also have hoods that fit over the player's head when wearing a helmet. Players who have taken off their helmets can put on knitted caps, and many players wear baseball-style caps on the sidelines even in warm weather or in indoor stadiums. All these items of clothing, which coaches and other team officials on the sidelines may also wear, usually have the name and/or insignia of the team and are the team's color(s). This kind of apparel, identical or similar to that worn by college or professional players, has become popular with the general public and especially with young people (see chapter 4).

Equipment

Except in some variants of the game like touch football (see chapter 5), playing organized football involves vigorous body contact among players. Indeed, most football plays end when a player is **tackled**. For this reason, all players wear equipment designed to protect specific parts of their bodies in collisions with other players, other players' equipment, or the ground.

Amazingly, very little equipment was worn by football players in the early years of the game. It is true that football players of the past were not as big as current players—and therefore collisions between one player and another were less likely to result in injuries—but the game was just as physical, if not more so, than today's game. But now players on the youth, high school, and college levels are required to wear much protective equipment; professional players also must wear certain equipment, though the requirements are not quite as strict. Whatever equipment is worn, it must be manufactured to meet league standards and it must not be altered before being used. Since pieces of football equipment are fairly expensive, they and the players' uniforms are provided to players by the team.

Football players wear the following equipment:

Helmet

Worn on the head, the football **helmet** is made of hard, unbreakable plastic and has padding on the inside to help cushion blows to the head. The helmet covers all of the top of a player's head and most of the sides and back. It also comes down over part of the forehead, but the entire front, over the player's face, is open. Yet the player's face is not unprotected; all modern football helmets have **face masks** (also called **face guards**), which are metal or hard plastic bars about ⅝ of an inch (1.59 cm) in diameter that are joined to the sides of the helmet and curve around the open front roughly parallel with the player's mouth. Another bar may extend vertically from the forehead part of the helmet down to the horizontal bars. This vertical bar offers more protection to a player's eyes and nose by dividing the open space above the horizontal face

guard, thereby reducing the chance of another player's arm making contact with the player's face.

Some players wear helmets that have a clear or colored plastic shield that covers the entire open area between the top of the horizontal face mask and the forehead of the helmet. These shields may be worn for two main reasons: to offer greater pro-

T I M E · O U T

The number of bars on a player's face mask often depends on the player's position. Offensive and defensive linemen usually wear helmets having several horizontal bars and a vertical bar, because their positions involve the roughest play. In contrast, kickers, who are rarely involved in any contact during a game and who also need to have a clear view of the goalposts, usually wear helmets having just one horizontal bar.

tection for the eyes and, by reducing glare from the sun, to help the player see better when playing outdoors during daylight.

Helmets are kept in place on the player's head by an adjustable chin strap that goes from one side of the helmet to the other under the chin. The ends of the strap divide into two parts, each of which attaches to its side of the helmet by a snap-on type of button. The middle of the strap has extra support where it rests against the player's chin.

Though all the players on a team must wear the same style of helmet, football helmets can have a variety of colors and decorations; indeed, the design of a team's helmet is often the team's most recognizable symbol. The exterior surface of the helmet and the bars of the face mask can be white or one of the team's colors (and often the bars and the helmet are different colors). There may also be one or more colored stripes that go across the top of the helmet from the forehead to the back.

On both sides of the helmet, there is usually a decal featuring the insignia or the name of the team. On the helmets of some teams, the player's number also appears on the back or the front of the helmet, with one numeral on each side of the stripe (if there is one) or with both numerals on one side; some teams may even have the number on the side of the helmet in place of a team insignia. Occasionally, a decal may be placed near the back of the helmet giving the number or initials of a recently deceased player or some other person connected with the team, much like the memorial patches on jerseys mentioned above. And both in the middle of the front of the helmet and on the bottom of the back there is a small white plastic tab on which is printed the name of the helmet's manufacturer (e.g., Riddell) or the name of the team.

All football helmets used by U.S. high school, college, and professional teams must have on them a small label certifying that the helmet meets the requirements of the National Operating Committee on Standards for Athletic Equipment as well as a label warning of the risks of competitive play. The NFL also requires that a small decal bearing its shield be placed on all helmets used by teams in the league.

TIME·OUT

Often the insignia on the helmets of one team may be identical to that on the helmets of another. This usually occurs when the teams are in a different league or different level of competition. For example, a high school team with the nickname of "Lions" may have on its helmets the same logo, the image of a pouncing lion, used by the NFL's Detroit Lions.

Also, the Pittsburgh Steelers of the NFL are notable for having their insignia on only one side of their helmets (the right side). The other side has only solid black color.

Recently, helmets worn by quarterbacks in professional football have begun to be equipped with devices that enable the quarterback to hear a coach on the sidelines who speaks into a microphone and gives the quarterback plays or instructions. During a professional game, a quarterback may often be seen holding his hands over the sides of his helmet; he is not necessarily showing signs of stress, but rather he is pressing the reception devices in his helmet closer to his ears so that he can hear the coach, which is often not easy in a stadium with a large, noisy crowd.

Shoulder Pads

Shoulder pads are the heaviest piece of equipment worn by football players. Though the name of this piece of equipment is plural, it is a one-piece assembly with an opening in the middle that fits over the player's head and it is wide enough to rest on the player's shoulders. The pads that are joined together in the shoulder pads assembly are made from hard plastic and padded materials. The largest pads cover the top of the shoulders, and other parts of the shoulder pads hang down over the upper parts of the chest, back, and arms. Straps keep the pads in place on the player's body.

Gloves

Football players are also allowed to wear special gloves during a game. Gloves help protect players' hands and keep them warm in cold weather, but most players wear gloves even in warm weather or in indoor stadiums. The gloves are small, fitting tightly over the hands, and are worn often by players in all positions except quarterbacks, who like to be able to hold and throw the ball with their bare hands. Football gloves may be all black, black and white, or one of the colors of the team, and they often display prominently their manufacturer's logo.

In the NFL, players may wear gloves with a tacky surface, that is, one that helps players like receivers get a better grip on the football with their gloves, provided that the material of this surface does not come off on the football. But it should be noted that at all levels of football, including the NFL, adhesive material cannot be used on uniforms, nor can any slippery material that might be applied to players' uniforms to make it more difficult for them to be tackled or blocked.

Shoes

Players wear shoes that are specially designed for football. Football shoes are made from leather or canvas, or from synthetic materials like rubber and plastic. Whatever material is used, it must protect the player's feet and be durable enough to stand up to the rigors of the game. However, players often go through several pairs of shoes in one season, especially at the college and professional levels, where there are more games and teams have a higher equipment budget. Football shoes can be high enough to cover the ankles—which is preferred by linemen, who need extra support for their ankles due to the physical demands of their position—or they can have low ankles like those of athletic shoes worn in other sports. Most have laces, but some football shoes are fastened with Velcro straps.

The soles of football shoes are made from leather, rubber, or composition material, and they usually have small stubs called **cleats**. Cleats help players keep from slipping as they run on the football field by digging into the ground or artificial turf, giving the shoes and the players traction.

There are two types of cleats on football shoes: some are permanently attached to the soles, while others can be removed (usually by screwing them off small support stubs). Permanent cleats must be made from rubber or a similar material and not from any type of metal. Removable cleats, on the other hand, can have metal tips (usually steel) and they must be securely fastened to the soles of the shoes. Both permanent and removable—or detachable—cleats can be no longer than ½ inch (1.27 cm).

Moreover, some football shoes have cleats that are specially designed for play on certain kinds of fields or weather conditions. For example, some shoes are made specifically for playing on artificial surfaces, in which case smaller and more numerous plastic cleats are used, whereas on a wet and muddy natural-surface field a shoe with fewer but longer cleats would be preferred. When the weather is very cold, the field, be it a natural or an artificial surface, will freeze solid. In this case, players sometimes wear shoes with very short cleats or no cleats at all, since these kinds of shoes will give the best traction on a hard surface (just as basketball players wear cleatless sneakers on the floor of a basketball court).

T I M E • O U T

American sporting goods companies compete fiercely for the right to supply athletic shoes and other equipment to college and professional sports teams, including football teams. Having major college or professional football teams, whose games are frequently broadcast on television, wear equipment bearing their logos serves as effective advertising for these companies. Because of the high profile of the NFL in particular, this league has strict regulations governing the display of manufacturers' names and logos on players and their equipment. A company usually must get official approval from the league to have its logo displayed on uniforms and equipment during games. A player who wears equipment sporting the logo of a company that is not licensed by the NFL may even have to pay a substantial fine.

Football shoes are generally black or white, and they often have colored stripes in various places. Each player on a team must wear the same-color shoes, with the exception of kickers and punters; these players may wear shoes that have a different color from those of the rest of their teammates, but their shoes must still be either white or black. Kickers may even wear a different-color shoe on each foot. The reason punters and kickers may wear different shoes than their teammates is that their shoes may be specially designed for kicking the ball.

Other Equipment

Football players may wear other pads and other types of equipment in addition to those described above. Players wear knee, thigh, and hip pads that fit inside their pants (the hip pads may also include a tailbone protector), but in professional football kickers and punters don't have to wear these pads, since having these pads on their legs might interfere with their kicking abilities.

Players also may wear small arm, elbow, or wrist pads. Linemen especially, who generally have the most physical contact in a game, often wear pads on their arms. In the NFL and the CFL, these pads must be white or the official color of the team when worn by interior linemen. Besides offering protection from the rigors of the game, pads may be worn on the arm to cover an injury or even a cast; if the pad covers a cast, it must have enough cushioning both to protect players who get hit with the cast and to protect the cast and the player's injured body part under it.

Some players, particularly skill players like quarterbacks, running backs, and receivers, may also wear wristbands that help keep perspiration or precipitation from dripping down their arms onto their hands or gloves. Some quarterbacks at the high school and college levels may even wear large wristbands that have written on them the names or codes for the plays that can be run by the offense; the quarterback, after getting instructions from the coach, can read the right name or code off the wristband and call it in the huddle (see "Huddles" in chapter 3).

Players can also wear pads around their abdomen that offer protection to parts of the body—the ribs in particular—that are not protected by the lower shoulder pads. These pads are called **rib pads** or sometimes **flak jackets**, and they are popular especially with quarterbacks who take many hits to their midsections from onrushing defensive players.

Some players, particularly linemen, wear padding or braces around their necks either outside of their jerseys or under them. These are worn to help keep the player's head from being jolted too far back or to one side, which might result in a neck injury.

Another piece of equipment, which is optional in professional football but mandatory in college and high school, is a **mouthguard**. A mouthguard is an item made from clear or colored plastic that is molded to fit between a player's teeth; players keep mouthguards in their mouths while playing. Wearing a mouthguard helps to prevent players from biting down on their tongues when being hit or tackled and protects against other injuries to the mouth and teeth. Mouthguards have a length of plastic that attaches to the face guard of a helmet so that players can take them out of their mouths while not actually involved in the game.

Playing football, which involves running and collisions with other players, presents special risks of injury to players' legs, and especially their knees which can be bent in unnatural ways. In recent years, as players have become bigger and faster and the force of impact when players tackle or run into each other has thus increased, there has also been a rise in the number of knee injuries. As a result, new ways to protect players' knees have been sought and developed. It is common now for players—especially offensive linemen, who don't have to move around as much as other players—to wear braces around their knees to help keep the knees from bending too far in the wrong direction. The braces can be made out of firm substances like metal or hard plastic, and they are worn under the pants as long as they are not exposed. Players who have to run a lot, like backs, may choose to wear lighter, more flexible knee braces, or bandages made from firm fabric that also offer protection for the knee.

To protect their legs, ankles, and other parts of their limbs from being bent too far out of place, football players may have parts of their bodies wrapped tightly with a kind of adhesive tape. This taping, which is usually done before games but can be done while a player is on the sidelines during a game if needed, helps to keep the wrapped parts from bending or twisting too far. And if a player does twist his or her ankle or some other body part but the injury is not too severe, wrapping the area tightly with tape usually lessens the pain enough that the player can still play. The tape is usually applied to the skin under the uniforms, but sometimes players have tape wrapped all around the outsides of their shoes and ankles (ankle sprains are quite common in football). This external tape must be either white or one of the team's colors.

Equipment football players wear must meet league standards, including the general rule that no equipment should be intended to confuse or injure other players. Usually, the umpire judges whether or not a player's equipment is acceptable, especially where equipment becomes damaged and therefore illegal during a game, as when a jersey is torn. Generally, a player wearing illegal items or without legal ones will not be allowed to enter the game. When the infraction is minor, such as when a player's pads become exposed from under the uniform, an official needs only to tell the player to fix the problem and the player may remain on the field.

One type of illegal equipment that officials especially look out for is a hard object protruding from a player's body or uniform. Any kind of metal is generally disallowed (though professional players may wear jewelry), except where it is a part of uniforms or equipment, but even in these cases it must not be sharpened. In 1996 in Albuquerque, New Mexico, a high school player wearing a helmet whose metal buckle had been sharpened inflicted cuts on several players on the other team before officials stopped the game and ejected him.

T I M E · O U T

High school football tries to accommodate players with disabilities. The National Federation of High School Associations (NFHSA) allows its member associations in each state to permit persons with artificial limbs to play in games as long as the limbs pose no danger to other players. Also, state associations may allow teams having one or more deaf players (and sometimes an entire team if it's from a school for the deaf) to use a drum to substitute for the signals of the officials given by whistle or the voice signals of the quarterback.

Coaches

Every organized football team has at least one **coach**. Most teams have more than one coach, and professional and major college teams have very large coaching staffs consisting of several **assistant coaches**. Unlike other sports, football usually doesn't have player/coaches (coaches who are also available to play in a game for their team), since coaches at all levels of

football are usually a great deal older than their players, although most coaches were at one time players themselves.

The **head coach**, as he or she is called when the team has more than one coach, has the final say on all the important decisions a team has to make during a game, such as offensive play selection, defensive and special-teams strategies, and the acceptance of penalties. But very often, especially in the professional and major college ranks where a team has many assistant coaches, the head coach doesn't make every decision but instead delegates authority to one or more of the assistant coaches.

If a team has more than one coach, there is usually an **offensive coordinator**, who is responsible for the team's offensive unit and often calls the offense's plays, and a coach responsible for the defensive unit called the **defensive coordinator**. There may also be a coach who works just with the special-teams unit (see chapter 3). A team with a larger coaching staff may have coaches who specialize even further. Most college and all professional teams have coaches who work just with the team's quarterbacks, running backs, offensive linemen, receivers, tight ends, defensive linemen, linebackers, defensive backs, or kickers. And most college and professional teams have a strength and conditioning coach who is responsible for developing players' bulk, size, and stamina through weight lifting, exercises, special diets, and the like.

During the play of the game, coaches are not allowed on the field of play inside the sidelines and end lines. Instead, they must remain in the team area with the extra players and other team personnel. However, some coaches do not spend the game in their team's area on the field but rather work in the press box or some other area high in the stands. From these locations, they can see the entire field from above and, more important, the positioning and movements of all the players on the field, which coaches on the sidelines may not get a good view of. The coaches in the press box or stands can relay information to the head coach, other coaches, or even players on the sidelines through communications devices (most coaches on the sidelines can be seen wearing microphones and headphones).

Coaches in the press box may do more than just communicate through electronic devices. Especially at the professional level, coaches or other team personnel in the press box often use devices like computers for analysis of game statistics or for calling up plays, or they take photographs of offensive or defensive formations on the field and send them to the coaches and players on the sidelines. These photographs can be examined during a game.

Coaches at almost all levels of football also have at their disposal a great amount of film or videotape that is taken of the action of games (not including the separate film or videotape taken by journalists covering the game). Most of the film and tape is taken from cameras placed in the press box or in areas high in the stands or at both ends of the field so that all the players on the field can be seen at the same time and their movements and actions can be followed. Coaches and players review the films and tape extensively in the days after a game to analyze the team's performance in order to find ways to improve it, and film of a team's future opponents is also acquired and examined to study the other team's personnel, strategies, and performance.

Officials

Football **officials** (who are all sometimes referred to as referees, even though the term "referee" properly applies only to the chief official) usually preside over games as a crew, with each official having specific responsibilities. Chapter 3 provides more detailed information about football officials and their duties.

Like players, football officials also have distinctive clothing and equipment. An official's **uniform** consists of a shirt that has black and white vertical stripes, white pants, long socks—usually with black and white horizontal stripes—and black athletic shoes, usually with cleats. The front of the shirt usually has a small insignia of the league, and the back may have a patch with small letters giving the official's position (e.g., "BJ" for back judge). There may also be a number that identifies the official. Officials also wear baseball-style caps with bills; the chief official, namely the referee, usually wears a white cap, and those of the other officials are black with thin white stripes that come down from the top of the cap. In cold weather officials, like players, may wear gloves or extra clothing under their uniforms and hoods under their caps.

Officials carry equipment to help them control football games. Each official has a whistle, which he can blow to call the ball dead, meaning that the current play is officially over. An official blows his whistle for three main reasons: (1) to signal that a play is complete (i.e., when the player carrying the ball has been tackled, an attempted pass falls incomplete, or points have been scored); (2) to stop a play from continuing for some reason (e.g., an illegal formation or other violation before the play or when the official thinks that a player has been downed and the play is thus over); or (3) when players begin to fight during or after a play.

All officials also carry small yellow pieces of cloth called (**penalty**) **flags**. These flags, which are also called "markers," especially by broadcasters (as in "There's a marker down on the play"), are carried by officials in their pants pockets or loosely attached to their uniforms at their hips.

When an official observes a player committing a penalty during the play of the game, he tosses the flag high in the air; the flag returns to the ground fairly quickly and not far from where the official threw it, because one end of the flag has a small weight attached to it. When the play is over, the presence of one or more flags on the ground is the signal that an official has seen a penalty. The game clock is stopped and the official who threw the flag reports the violation to the referee (unless the referee threw the flag himself); the game cannot continue until the penalty is announced to both teams and to the crowd and the penalty yardage is marked off or the referee announces that the penalty has been refused. Then the flags are picked up and taken back by the officials before the start of the next play. (For more about football penalties, see "Officials and Penalties" in chapter 3.)

Some officials also carry other equipment. They may have a small piece of plastic or some other marker, often blue in color, that they throw on the ground to mark the farthest forward progress of the ball in case the player carrying it is knocked backward, or to indicate where a kickoff or pass was received in case there is a penalty that requires marking off the yardage from that spot on the field. One official, usually the line judge, also carries a timing device on which he can keep track of the official time left in the game in case the clock on the scoreboard malfunctions. And at professional and most college football games, the referee carries a microphone and a transmission device linked to the stadium's public-address system. At all levels of football, the referee indicates penalties through hand signals (see chapter 3), but by using this device he can announce to the crowd the specific penalty and the number of the player who committed it. The referee turns on this device only when he is announcing penalties; he keeps it turned off at all other times not only so that it will not interfere with the public-address system but also because the language players use is often not decent enough to be picked up by the microphone and heard throughout the stadium! (In fact, by rule players must remain a few feet away from the referee when he has his microphone turned on to address the crowd.)

There are other persons who help control a game of organized football from the sidelines. They wear distinctive clothing, usually a large vest with special markings (e.g., a fluorescent X in the NFL or the name of the conference in college football), but not the black and white stripes of the on-field officials. These people operate such equipment as the **chains** that measure the length needed for a **first down**, the **down indicator**, and the **line-to-gain indicator**. One pole is moved before and after each play, with its bottom end touching the ground at a spot on the sidelines parallel to the **line of scrimmage**—that is, the position of the front end of the ball. The other pole is held at a spot parallel to the point on the field beyond which the ball must be advanced to get a first down. On the first down of every series, the chain between the poles is stretched its full length to measure the 10 yards necessary for the ball to be advanced in order for the team on offense to earn another series of downs. (See "Offensive Series" in chapter 3 for more on downs.)

TIME·OUT

There are two exceptions to this general procedure for managing the chains. One is when the line of scrimmage is more than 10 yards *behind* the yard necessary for a first down. In this case, the second pole remains on the first down yard and the other end of the chain is stretched out to the maximum 10 yards but it does not reach the line of scrimmage. And if the situation is **goal to go**, the second pole is placed on the goal line no matter where the line of scrimmage is (that is, the chain is not stretched out), and the first pole follows the scrimmage line for each play.

The chain operators also have other pieces of equipment. There is the **down indicator**, which is usually operated by the official holding the pole parallel to the line of scrimmage and may occasionally be combined with this pole. The official holding the pole showing the point to be reached for a first down is usually also responsible for placing the **line-to-gain indicator** on the ground outside of the sidelines.

The chain operators work on the sidelines just off the field of play (in the NFL, in the 6-foot white boundary area; see "The Parts of a Football Field: Markings," above). The sidelines where the chain operators stand must be on the side of the field opposite the press box—that is, when the operators face the field they face the press box as well, so that the chains and down indicator will be visible to anyone in the press box. There may be another set of officials operating another down indicator, line-to-gain indicator, and chains on the other sideline, but the indicators facing the press box are considered the official ones; the chains brought onto the field to measure for a first down always come from these sidelines (see "Officials and Penalties" in chapter 3).

This chapter has discussed everything that is needed to play the game of football. The next discusses *how* the game is played.

Chapter 3
How Football Is Played

This chapter will describe what happens at a football game. Topics discussed include the rules of football, player positions, the length and scoring of a game, some common plays, general strategies, and football penalties and the officials who enforce them. Also, some attention will be paid to what goes on immediately before and after a game.

Object of the Game

Football is a game played between two teams of players, a **home team** and a **visiting team** (or **visitors**). Each team tries to score as many points as it can during the fixed length of the game. The team with more points at the end of the game is the winner or the winning team, and the other is the loser or the losing team. A game may also end in a **tie**, but most playoff or championship games cannot end in ties because one team must win; usually an overtime is played until one team scores and thus wins the game (see "Length of the Game," below).

Football has a system for scoring points. The highest number of points, 6, is awarded when a team scores a **touchdown**.

A touchdown is scored when a **ballcarrier** crosses the opposing team's goal line, when a player catches a **pass** while standing in the other team's end zone, or when a defensive player recovers a ballcarrier's fumble in the end zone defended by the ballcarrier's team. If a kicker on a team kicks a **field goal**, 3 points are given to the team. In Canadian football, 1 point is also awarded when the ball is kicked past the dead line in a field goal attempt. Two points are awarded when a team forces a **safety** or when it makes a successful **two-point conversion** (see below). And 1 point is given when a team kicks the ball through the uprights after a touchdown; this is called an **extra point** or a **point after touchdown** (PAT). These different ways of scoring will be discussed further below.

T I M E · O U T

If a team scores points on a play but a penalty was called against the scoring team on that play, the points are not counted unless the other team declines the penalty, which teams rarely do in this situation (see "Officials and Penalties," below).

Length of the Game

It is usually said that a football game is 60 minutes long. However, this does not mean that football games are completed in one hour. The 60 minutes are counted on the game clock, which is frequently stopped and restarted during a game. In fact, a football game usually takes two to three hours, and sometimes longer, to play.

Football games are also divided into four **quarters**. Each quarter is 15 minutes in length on the game clock (in high school football, quarters are 12 minutes long). At the end of the first and third quarters, when the game clock is down to

0:00, the clock stops for one minute during which time both teams on the field switch ends—that is, the team on offense now attacks the other end zone. The clock is then reset to 15:00 and begins to count the time down when the next play starts.

Football games are also divided into a **first half** and a **second half**; the first half is the first and second quarters, and the second half is the third and fourth quarters. At the end of the first half, an intermission called the **halftime** takes place. The halftime lasts for 15 minutes, and during this time both teams go back into their respective locker rooms for a meeting and for some rest, and there is usually some kind of entertainment on the field for the crowd. The entertainment is often marching bands, especially in high school and college football, but a more sophisticated show may take place during the halftime of professional games. Also, special ceremonies may take place to honor current or former players, team officials, members of the community, or the like. At the end of the halftime, both teams return to the field and the third quarter starts with another kickoff. The team that received the opening kickoff in the first quarter now kicks off, and once again the teams defend the opposite end zones from the ones they defended in the second quarter.

As mentioned above, even though a football game is 60 minutes long (48 minutes in high school football) the game clock is stopped and restarted frequently during a game. Among the reasons the game clock may be stopped are when a penalty is called, when there is a **change of possession**, when a pass falls incomplete, when a player with the ball steps out of bounds, when points are scored, or when a quarter ends. In college and high school football, the clock is also stopped after a first down has been gained so that the chains can be moved to measure the new first-down yardage; when the chains are in position, the clock is started again.

There is also a second clock used in football games, called the **play clock** (or **25-second clock**). After every play in which the game clock is stopped, this clock is reset to 25 seconds and then counts down the time left before the offense must begin its next play. (In the NFL, if there was no stoppage of the game clock after the previous play—for example, after a running play that ended inbounds—the play clock is set to 40 seconds.) If the offense has not started its play before the play clock reads "0," the officials stop the game and call a **delay of game** penalty on the offense. The purpose of this clock is to keep a team from deliberately holding up the game when it **has the lead** in the game and has **possession** of the ball.

A team can also stop the game and play clocks for various reasons, such as when it feels it is not ready to continue play or because it wants to preserve time left in a game in which it is losing and needs time to score more points. The clock is stopped by calling a **time-out**. Each team is allowed three time-outs per half, and any player on the offense or defense can call a time-out (but usually the quarterback is the only player on the offense who calls time-outs). Players can request a time-out by directly asking an official for one or by using a hand signal in which they stick out one hand flat and put the other under and perpendicular to it, making the shape of a *T*. An official then signals the clock operator to stop the game clock, and the clock stops for one minute. During this time, the quarterback and the captain of the defense usually go over to their respective sidelines to confer with their coaching staffs, and personnel of both teams go onto the field to give the players water or other liquids. (In the WL, head coaches can also go onto the field during a time-out.) Sometimes, especially late in a close game, the entire offensive or defensive unit may go over to the sidelines, not just to confer with the coaching staff but also to get a **pep talk**.

Not only the teams but also the officials may call time-outs for various reasons. They may call a time-out so they can get together to discuss a disputed play or ruling. The officials also call a time-out when a player is injured during a play and is unable to get up off the ground when the play is over. When an injury time-out is called, staff from the player's team run onto the field to help the injured player. In the meantime, the quarterback and the defensive captain may go over to their respective sidelines and team attendants may bring water out to the players on the field, just as during time-outs called by the team. If the player recovers after a short while, he or she must walk off the field; a substitute player enters the game, and the injured player cannot reenter the game until after the next play at the earliest. Sometimes players are so severely injured that they must be carried off the field by teammates and team personnel, and in some cases an injured player is taken off on a stretcher (with special precautions to avoid any risk of paralysis if the player is injured in the head or neck area) to the locker room for treatment, or perhaps even to an ambulance parked inside or near the stadium for transporting the player to a hospital.

TIME·OUT

When players who have been lying on the ground injured get up and start to walk off the field, or especially when they are carried off the field, many members of the crowd applaud politely as a show of sportsmanship and kindness, even if the players are from the visiting team. Nevertheless, some fans of the home team will boo an injured visiting player and some will even cheer when the player gets injured. The majority of football fans, however, regard this behavior as very **unsportsmanlike**.

In professional and major college football, where most games are broadcast on television, there are also several pre-arranged time-outs, called TV time-outs, during which commercials are shown on the television broadcast. These TV time-outs are one of the main reasons some games at these levels last for more than three hours. And in professional football, there is also a clock stoppage called the **two-minute warning**, which occurs during each half of a game. When the game clock reaches 2:00 in the second and fourth quarters, the officials call a time-out (or if a play is ongoing when the clock reaches 2:00, the clock is allowed to continue and the officials call the time-out as soon as the play is over). The two-minute warning is often an important part of the strategy of a game, since it makes an additional time-out available for a team to use at the end of a game or a half (see "Late-Game Strategies," below).

Some football games—especially playoff and championship games that cannot end with tied scores—have playing times of more than 60 minutes. This happens when the teams play an **overtime** quarter following four quarters of regulation play at the end of which the score is tied. An overtime quarter is also 15 minutes long but it—and the game—ends as soon as one team scores in any way (for this reason, the overtime is often called **sudden death**). If neither team scores, another overtime quarter is played, and this continues until one team finally scores.

T I M E · O U T

In the NFL, all regular-season games that have a tie score at the end of regulation play must be followed by an overtime period. If neither team scores during this period, however, no more overtime quarters are played and the game officially ends as a tie.

What Happens During a Football Game

Pregame

The pregame period is what happens before the football game actually begins. One thing that occurs is the **pregame warm-up,** which generally takes place an hour or two before the official starting time of the game. When both teams have arrived at the field or stadium and have put on their uniforms and equipment (at some levels of football, the visiting team might arrive already dressed), they go out onto the field. One team occupies half of the field from the 50-yard line to the end zone and the other team stays in the other half of the field, though it is not uncommon for players and coaches from both teams to meet with and talk to each other during this time.

The pregame warm-ups consist of two main activities. One is calisthenics, especially various stretching exercises through which players loosen their joints and muscles in preparation for the physical demands playing football puts on their bodies. The other activity is drills, in which players under the direction of their coaches practice for the final time some of the formations and plays they will use in the game. Often players work in groups based on position—for example, the linemen may go to one corner of the field to work out and the backs and receivers may go to another—and sometimes an entire offensive unit may practice plays against a defensive unit of the same team. After the pregame warm-ups, the teams return to their locker rooms until shortly before the official start of the game.

T I M E · O U T

Sometimes individual players come out for warm-ups before the rest of their team. Some players may appear wearing their football pants and shoes but no jerseys, shoulder pads, or helmets, and they do stretching or running before practicing with the rest of their team. Also, traditionally kickers and punters are the first to take the field and begin practicing during the pregame. These players, of course, work on their kicks, and for this they like to have a large part of the field open.

Introduction of Players,
National Anthem, and Coin Toss

When the teams return to the field shortly before the start of the game, most players go directly to the sidelines, but a few may engage in some last-minute calisthenics or drills before joining the rest of their team. Quarterbacks, in particular, like to throw a football a short distance to another player several times to loosen up their throwing arms.

In professional football and at most college and high school football games, the starting players (starters) and head coach are introduced to the crowd. All the nonstarting players of a team go onto the field first and (often accompanied by cheerleaders) line up in two rows that lead almost back to the locker-room entrance. Then the public-address announcer says the names, positions, and numbers of the players who will start the game on offense and defense. In college football, the announcer may also mention the city or town and state the player is from, and in professional football the announcer may tell the college the player attended. A typical player introduction may be like this: "At quarterback, from UCLA, number eight, Troy Aikman!" The player then runs out onto the field and receives cheers from the crowd if his team is playing in its home stadium, or silence or even boos if the player is part of the visiting team. The player runs through the rows of teammates and receives encouragement in the form of handshakes or backslaps or yells.

When all the players of a team are out of the locker room and on the field, the players, coaches, and all other personnel of each team go to their team areas along the sidelines and begin to line up. Any players wearing their helmets remove them, and other personnel remove any hats or headware. At about the same time, the public-address announcer asks the crowd to stand up for the playing of the national anthem. At this point, a military honor guard may march onto the field carrying the flag of the United States and/or Canada, possibly along with a few other flags, such as the one for the branch of the service the guard represents. More often, however, the only American or Canadian flag to be honored during the national anthem will be the one flying above the stadium (see "Football Fields and Stadiums" in chapter 2).

In the United States, the national anthem is "The Star-Spangled Banner," and in Canada it's "O Canada." In NFL exhibition games played outside of the United States, the national anthem of the country where the game is taking place is often played in addition to the American anthem. The anthem may be sung by a singer or singers before a microphone on the field, or a prerecorded anthem may be played. At the college and high school levels especially, the marching band that will perform at halftime may play the national anthem at this point.

T I M E · O U T

At the beginning of some games, the public-address announcer asks the crowd and the teams to observe a moment of silence in honor of a player, team official, or some other important football person who has recently died. After this request, all the players and team personnel and most of the crowd remain silent and motionless for a short time, and many bow their heads. A moment of silence may also be observed for the death of some prominent person in the community or nation, or for the victims of an accident or disaster.

After the playing of the anthem, the **captains** from both teams go to the center of the field at the 50-yard line for the **coin toss.** The referee goes out to the middle of the field with a large coin and, after the teams' captains have met at midfield and exchanged handshakes, asks the captains of one team (usually the visiting team) to call "heads" or "tails" while the coin is in the air. The referee then flips the coin into the air and lets it fall onto the ground. If the coin on the ground has its face side up and the captain had called "heads" before the coin landed on the ground, or if "tails" was called and the coin rests with its reverse side facing up, that captain's team wins the toss; if the correct side of the coin was not called, the other team is said to have won the toss.

The team that wins the toss gets to choose between receiving the opening kickoff and selecting which end zone to defend. Among the reasons a team may want the choice of end zones instead of receiving the ball first is if the wind is blowing strongly toward one end zone. This would be an advantage for whichever team was trying to score into this end zone, since any passes thrown or any kicks in this direction would go farther. Therefore, a team will often choose to defend *this* end zone in the first quarter so that it will be going toward it in the second quarter, which is often an important quarter for scoring since it occurs before halftime. At the start of the second half, the team that lost the coin toss gets to choose first between receiving the ball or defending a certain end zone, though nearly always a team chooses to receive a kickoff at the start of the third quarter, either to control the ball if it's **ahead** in the game or get possession of the ball to try to score if it's **behind**.

Whichever option is chosen by the team that wins the coin toss—to receive the opening kickoff or to choose the end zone to defend—the other team gets the second option. When this is decided, the referee has the captains of both teams stand facing each other in the direction the teams will be going in the first quarter—that is, toward the goal lines they will be trying to score over. The referee then uses hand signals to indicate to the crowd which team will **kick off** first and which team will receive the opening kickoff. He may also announce which team won the toss—and its decision—over the public-address system if he is equipped with a microphone and transmitter (see "Officials" in chapter 2). The captains all shake hands again and then head back to their sidelines. When the captains return to their teams, each team usually gathers around the head coach or one of the captains for a brief but spirited pep talk, which usually concludes with the whole team uttering a cheer to motivate themselves to play well in the game.

Kickoff

Each half of a football game begins with a **kickoff**, in which the **kicker** (or **placekicker**) of one team kicks the football toward the other team and a player on the other team tries to **receive the kickoff** and **return** it. As during all other plays in football, each team must put II of its players on the field during a kickoff. The players who are used on kickoffs—and

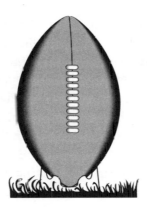

punts—are called a team's **special-teams unit,** which is composed of players who are not the **starters** but who may replace starters if they get injured or perform poorly in the game. Players are usually assigned to special-teams if they are not the best players on a team, but especially at the professional level some players play on special-teams not because they aren't good enough to be starters but because they specialize in kick returning, kick coverage, or other special-teams duties. The kicker is part of the special-teams unit that kicks off, but because kickers are typically not as big, fast, or athletic as other football players, they are usually replaced by another player on the special-teams unit when the team is going to receive a kickoff. In fact, many kickers at the college and professional levels are former soccer players from Latin America, Europe, or elsewhere who have little experience playing American football.

The 11 players of the kicking team go onto the field in their own territory—that is, in the half of the field at the end of which is the end zone they will defend in the first quarter. The kicker stands in the middle of the field near where the football is to be placed for the kickoff (see below). Five players line up between the kicker and the sideline on the right side of the kicker, and five players line up on the kicker's left.

The receiving team may line up in its territory in a variety of formations. Whatever formation is used, there is always at least one player who stands at or near the goal line of the end zone the player's team is defending (often there are two players back here). This player, called a **kick returner** or a **return man**, is the player who will try to receive the kickoff and return it. A kick returner is usually a running back or wide receiver by position, since this player has to be able to catch and run with the football. In all return formations, the players of the receiving team do not all line up on the same yard line but spread out in the territory between the kick returner and a point 10 yards from the kicking team's line. No member of the receiving team can line up closer than that. Usually at least two players line up on one line together, and there may be as many as five on a line. Five players are most likely to be placed on the line that is at least 10 yards from the kicking team to guard against an onside kick (see "Late-Game Strategies," below).

An official gives the kicker the football in the middle of the field. The kicker places the ball on a **tee** (visible in the illustration on page 65) on the yard line from which the kickoff is to be made; in professional football, this is the 30-yard line, and in college and high school football it is the 35. In weather conditions where the wind is strong enough to blow the football off the tee, a member of the kicking team may hold the ball as on an extra-point or field goal attempt (see "Kicking Plays," below).

The kicker then goes back several yards behind the ball and waits until the officials at the other end of the field, who are back by the kick returner(s), indicate by signals that the receiving team is ready. The kicker then lifts an arm to signal that he or she is ready to kick off and starts running toward the ball. The other players on the kicking team, lined up about 10 yards behind the line the ball is on, begin running forward almost as soon as the kicker does. They must be sure to stay slightly behind the kicker, however; if they cross the kickoff line before the ball is kicked, a penalty will be called. Reaching the ball on the tee, the kicker meets the ball with the front of the foot of his or her kicking leg, kicking the ball in its lower half to make it travel high in the air and farther downfield. At the moment the kicker kicks the ball, the game is officially under way and the game clock starts.

Whether the ball is kicked off from a tee or from the hold of a player, the football is upright as it is kicked and therefore flies in an end-over-end motion high in the air before it comes down to the receiving team. Most kickoffs travel deep into the receiving team's territory, and some are so deep that the ball travels beyond the end line of the end zone, either without hitting the ground or hitting the ground somewhere before the end line and then bouncing past it. A kickoff going out of the end zone is called a **touchback**, and the first play after a touchback begins on the 20-yard line of the receiving team.

The kick returner may catch the ball before it goes out of the end zone but may decide not to try to return it. The returner then kneels in the end zone while holding the ball, with one knee touching the ground. This is called **downing** the ball, and the result is the same as a touchback—that is, the next play will begin from the 20-yard line with the receiving team on offense. Kick returners often (but not always) down a kickoff when they catch it several yards behind the goal line, because from there they do not have as good a chance of getting past the 20-yard line before being tackled as they would if they caught the ball in front of the goal line. So when returners down kickoffs it doesn't mean they're afraid to run with the ball; it's just smart strategy.

T I M E · O U T

In Canadian football, if a ball enters the end zone on either a kickoff or a punt, the receiving team must return the ball past the goal line or the kicking team receives 1 point (called a **single**).

If the returner catches the ball in the field of play or in the end zone and does not down it, he or she runs with the ball as far up the field (i.e., toward the other team's end zone) as possible before being tackled. The other players on the receiving team run toward the returner while the ball is in the air, but as soon as the returner catches the ball and starts to run with it they turn and start to **block** players from the kicking team, often in a **wedge** formation.

The players on the kicking team run down the field as far as they can before they are blocked. While running down the field, the players try to stay spread out across the field as they were when they lined up for the kickoff so that they cover any part of the field that the returner might try to run toward. But the kicker, who as mentioned above is usually not as good an athlete as the other players, tends to stay back in order to be ready to tackle the returner in the rare event that the returner eludes all the other kicking-team players. If the returner gets by the kicker and outruns all the kicking-team members to score a touchdown, the return team attempts an extra point as usual after any touchdown.

Usually, though, the returner is tackled or forced out of bounds somewhere in the returner's own territory and the first series of downs will start from the yard line where the returner was stopped, with the team that returned the ball on offense and the kicking team on defense. Sometimes the returner will **fumble** the ball and a player from the kicking team will **recover** the fumble. In this case, the kicking team goes on offense and the return team is on defense on the next play. If a **runback** is fumbled and the other team gains possession, it is a bad break for the return team—and a good one for the kicking team—particularly if the fumble takes place in the return team's own territory, thus giving the other team the ball in **good field position**.

As on any play in football, a penalty may be called during the kickoff and the return. If the penalty is against the return team or against the kicking team while the ball was being returned, the yardage is marked off from the spot to which the ball was returned and the return team goes on offense as normal. However, if the penalty was on the kicking team during the kickoff the team will have to kick off again, this time five yards back from the usual kickoff spot. The most common penalties called against kicking teams are kicking the ball out of bounds so that it is not touched by a return-team player, and crossing the kickoff line before the ball is actually kicked.

During the time-out that follows the end of the kickoff play, someone from the kicking team's sideline (usually a ball boy or a team assistant) runs out onto the field and retrieves the kicking tee, which is usually yellow, orange, or red in color to make it easier to locate on the green field. It is important to remove the tee from the field, since even though a tee is made from plastic and is relatively small, it could injure a player who falls on it or a running player could trip over it during the game.

Offensive Series

After a kickoff (or a punt), the team having the ball goes on **offense** and the other team is on **defense**. The team on offense has possession of the ball, and the team on defense tries to prevent the other team from moving the ball forward and scoring. The defense also tries to gain possession of the ball for its team.

The offense gets four chances called **downs** (three in Canadian football) to run a play to advance the ball 10 yards from where it is at the start of the offensive series (i.e., at the first down of the series). As soon as the offense has moved the ball 10 or more yards past the original line of scrimmage, whether this happens on one down or as the accumulated forward yardage of two or more downs, a new **first down** is awarded and the offense gets a new series of four downs to advance the ball 10 yards from where the ball was at the end of the play on which the offense was awarded the first down. This continues, as long as there is time on the game clock, until the offense scores or it fails to advance the ball 10 yards in a series of downs. If a team doesn't get 10 yards in four downs, possession of the ball goes to the other team (that was on defense) at the spot where the other team's fourth-down play ended. But most of the time, if an offense has not advanced 10 yards by the end of the third down and thinks it probably won't get far enough on the fourth down, the offense will **punt** the ball away so that the other team will get possession much farther down the field and that much farther from the punting team's goal line (see "Punting," below).

Offensive Positions

As mentioned above, each team has a maximum of 11 players on its offensive and on its defensive units. (In Canadian football, there are 12 players on each unit.) On both offense and defense, football players play specific positions. The offensive positions are divided into three general groups: backs, linemen, and ends. There are two types of **offensive backs**: quarterbacks and running backs. The **quarterback** is the most important player on the offense. The quarterback begins every offensive play by getting the ball from the center lineman and has the choice of running with the ball, handing it off to another back, or passing it to a receiver. Thus, quarterbacks need to be fairly good athletes, able to handle the ball and run fairly well. Most important, quarterbacks need to have strong arms to throw the football so that it travels quickly to receivers short distances away, and also to throw **long** or **deep** passes. Quarterbacks must also be able to throw the ball accurately to their own receivers who are running patterns (see below) at nearly full speed. Football teams like to have quarterbacks who are tall so that they can see their receivers down the field over offensive and defensive linemen, who are usually the tallest players on the field.

The quarterback is the leader of the offense. Quarterbacks tell their team, in the **huddle** or with an audible (see below), what play they are going to run on each down. The play may be selected by the quarterbacks themselves or selected by their coaching staffs, who send in the play by various means (see below). Especially at the major college and professional levels, with the large amount of exposure these teams get in the sports news media, the quarterback is often identified with the whole team for good or bad; that is, if a team wins many games a lot of the credit is given to its starting quarterback, but the quarterback gets a lot of the blame on a losing team.

As their name indicates, the main job of **running backs** is to run with the football after being given the ball by the quarterback, but in the modern game of football that is certainly not the only thing they do. On any down, a team on offense may have as many as three running backs or none at all. The running backs line up behind the quarterback, and there are names for the backs based on their positions: **fullbacks** are running backs who line up directly behind the quarterback, while **halfbacks** may either line up in back of but not directly behind the quarterback or position themselves directly behind the fullback and quarterback. This last alignment is often called an "I formation," since the quarterback, fullback, and halfback form a straight line like the letter *I*. If there are three running backs with one halfback on each side of the full-back lined up behind the quarterback, it is called a "T formation." The T formation, however, is not commonly used except in short-yardage situations (see "General Offensive Strategies," below) where two of the running backs are run through the line of scrimmage first and block for the third, who gets the **handoff** from the quarterback. Another running-back formation is a **split backfield**, where two halfbacks line up in back of and on both sides of the quarterback. And in formations where there is only one running back, this back is often referred to as a **tailback**, especially if the back lines up far to one side of the quarterback to be in a good position either to get a handoff or to receive a pass.

Running backs need not be very tall or very big, but they need to be tough enough to stand the physical punishment of being tackled many times in a game by defensive players, who are often much bigger. Running backs should also be good runners, of course, fast enough to run away from defensive players and gain several yards before they are tackled, although fullbacks, whose usual assignment is just to block for other running backs, tend to be large and strong and not necessarily very fast. As mentioned above, modern running backs also need to be able to do things other than running, such as catching passes and blocking **onrushing** defensive players. Short passes to running backs coming out of the **backfield** are commonly used passing plays in modern football (see "Passing Plays," below).

Offensive linemen tend to be very large players, and they really don't need to be fast runners or skilled athletes. Their primary assignment is to block for running backs and protect the quarterback from onrushing defensive players on pass plays. This mostly requires strength and toughness, though agility is also useful since the defensive linemen they have to block can be quick as well as big and strong.

Each offensive play must start with five offensive linemen on the line of scrimmage. Like backs, linemen have names based on their positions. The **center** is in the middle of the line, and at the start of every offensive play the center **hikes** the ball to the quarterback. On each side of the center are the **guards**, referred to when necessary as the **left guard** and the **right guard** for the side of the center each is on. Next to the guards are the offensive **tackles**. There is a **left tackle**, who lines up on the left side of the left guard, and a **right tackle** on the right side of the right guard.

Aside from the hiking duties of the center, the duties of the offensive linemen are usually the same, and as a result the physical requirements of all offensive linemen are not very different (indeed, offensive linemen often play more than one of the positions in their careers). Tackles tend to be the tallest offensive linemen, followed next by guards and then centers; one reason for this is that it is easier for quarterbacks to see downfield to their receivers if their centers and guards in the middle of the line are not very tall.

One of the primary functions of ends is to catch passes, and there are two kinds of ends in football. One is called the **tight end**. The tight end lines up on the line of scrimmage next to a tackle, and very often the tight end is used for blocking, like an extra offensive lineman. For this reason, tight ends are usually both tall and large, but they also need to be fairly good runners and able to catch passes. When they are used as pass receivers, tight ends usually run short routes (see below); tight ends rarely **go deep** or **go long**, because they are usually not fast enough to run far downfield in a short enough time for the quarterback to pass the ball before being tackled, as wide receivers are. In most offensive formations, one tight end lines up on the right side of the right tackle if the quarterback throws with his or her right hand, or on the left of the left tackle for left-handed quarterbacks. Occasionally two tight ends may line up, one on the side of each tackle, especially in short-yardage situations where tight ends are needed to block for a rusher. Or an offense may use no tight end at all, substituting for the tight end another wide receiver or running back, this being a common formation in long-yardage passing situations.

The other kind of end is called a **wide receiver**. The reason the name of this position includes the word *wide* is that wide receivers line up several yards to the left or to the right of the linemen on the line of scrimmage. The primary assignment for wide receivers is to run downfield and catch passes, though wide receivers also block and are sometimes even used on running plays (see below). Because wide receivers mainly run and catch passes, they are usually slim and very fast, with good hands for catching the ball. Teams also like to have wide receivers who are tall, because a tall wide receiver has an advantage over a shorter defensive back when reaching or jumping in the air to catch a pass thrown high.

Defensive Positions

As offensive positions can be grouped into backs, linemen, and ends, the positions on the defense can be grouped into linemen, linebackers, and backs. The names of the positions of **defensive linemen** vary depending on how many linemen a defensive unit employs; some defenses have only three linemen, but most teams use four. All defenses have two **defensive ends,** who are the players on each end of the defensive line. Defensive ends are usually among the tallest players on the defense, but they are also quick, because they often need to **rush** the quarterback by going all the way from the end of the line to the middle of the backfield where the quarterback stands on passing plays.

T I M E · O U T

Rushing the quarterback is also called "putting pressure on" or just "pressuring" the quarterback. Quarterbacks are rushed so that they are tackled before they can throw a pass or so that they will attempt a pass before they are ready or before a receiver is open, which may result in an incomplete pass or an interception.

If a defense uses just three linemen, the player between the ends on the defensive line is called the **nose tackle**. Like all defensive linemen, nose tackles need to be big because they have to fend off the blocks of equally large offensive linemen, but nose tackles don't need to be as agile as defensive ends. If a defense uses four linemen, the ones in the middle are called **defensive tackles**. Like nose tackles, defensive tackles don't need to be as quick as ends because the offense's rushing plays are often toward one of the defensive tackles and also because when they rush, the defensive tackles tend to go straight forward through the line toward the quarterback.

T I M E · O U T

Nose tackles usually line up directly opposite the center. In some defensive formations, however, a defense with four linemen may still choose to have one lineman opposite the center and two others on one side of this nose tackle. This formation is used especially to put these two linemen opposite the **strong side** of the offense.

Just as the number of linemen on a defense can vary, so can the number of **linebackers**. Almost all teams have a basic defense of either four defensive linemen and three linebackers or three defensive linemen and four linebackers, though the former is much more common. These defenses are often referred to as the four-three and the three-four, respectively. Linebackers, as their name indicates, begin each play a few yards behind the defensive linemen, though on some plays they may line up on the line of scrimmage next to the linemen. If they line up behind the defensive linemen, they position themselves directly behind, especially in short-yardage situations, or several yards back of the linemen, especially in passing situations. If a defense uses three linebackers, one linebacker generally lines up a few yards opposite the offensive center and is called a **middle linebacker**. The two other linebackers line

up on either side of the middle linebacker and just a little to
the outside of the defensive ends and are called **outside linebackers**. If a defense uses four linebackers, the two linebackers in the middle are called **inside linebackers**.

Linebackers have the greatest range of responsibilities on
a defense, and mostly for this reason a linebacker is usually the
defensive leader or captain. Linebackers tackle running backs
who run through the line of scrimmage or around the end of
the line. Linebackers may also rush the quarterback, particularly on blitz plays (see "General Defensive Strategies," below).
And linebackers may even be used in pass coverage, usually to
cover relatively slow tight ends and fullbacks. To perform all
of these duties linebackers have to be among the best athletes
on a team, fast enough to chase down running backs and quarterbacks but large and tough enough to make several tackles
during a game while enduring the blocking of larger linemen.

There are two kinds of **defensive backs**. Two backs line
up close to the line of scrimmage but several yards to one side
of the line, directly opposite the wide receivers of the offense.
These defensive backs are called **cornerbacks**, and their primary responsibility is to cover the wide receivers on passing
plays. There are two other defensive backs called **safeties**.
These players line up 10 yards or more behind the line and
are primarily used to defend against passing plays by covering receivers who come that far beyond the line of scrimmage.
The safeties are also distinguished by their position; the safety
who lines up opposite the strong side of the offense is called
the **strong safety**, and the other is called a **free safety**. Thus,
a defense usually has four defensive backs in its basic formation, but more backs may enter the game in situations where
the offense is expected to attempt a pass.

Defensive backs need to be fast to cover equally fast wide
receivers. They should also be able to catch footballs about as
well as receivers, since a defensive back's goal is not just to
prevent a pass from being completed to a receiver but also to
try to **intercept** (or **pick off**) the pass. Defensive backs need
not be very big, but safeties are often fairly large, since they

often need to tackle offensive players running with the ball who have gotten by the defensive linemen and linebackers.

Huddles

Before each play, the whole offensive team gathers in a **huddle**. The huddle is formed far behind the line of scrimmage so that the defense will not hear the quarterback **call the play** the offense is going to run. Nevertheless, the quarterback usually announces the play in a code—not just for security but also to save time in the huddle. During practices (see chapter 4), players learn these codes and the plays they stand for, and now they must remember the code for the play and know exactly what they have to do during the play. More than play calling may go on in the huddle; players besides the quarterback may talk, suggesting plays, giving information about the defense, or complimenting or even criticizing the play of teammates.

The defense usually huddles too, in order for the defensive captain to tell them what formation they will use for the next play. Just as the quarterback on the offense often does not actually select the offense's plays, the defensive captain usually just relays instructions from a coach on the sidelines. These instructions are given to the captain through signals or are told to a player on the sidelines who then enters the game as a substitute player and relays the instructions to the captain (or to the quarterback for the offense). This is why the quarterback and the defensive captain can often be seen looking over to their respective sidelines immediately after each play.

After the players get their instructions from the quarterback or captain, the huddle breaks up and the players walk or jog into their positions before the play begins. (Often players clap their hands once in unison right as the huddle breaks up as a show of team unity and determination.) Defensive huddles should break up well before the offensive huddles do; defense needs to be in position and ready when the offense comes to the line of scrimmage since the offense, by **snapping** the ball, determines when each play starts.

The Down Position, the Quarterback Count, and the Snap of the Ball

Before the offensive huddle breaks up, an official will have made sure the football is on the ground between the hash marks, with each end pointing directly to an end zone (thus parallel with the sidelines). The tip of the ball pointing in the direction the offense is advancing will be exactly on the line of scrimmage. The center crouches down and puts both hands on the ball. The other offensive linemen, including any tight ends, must get into the **down position** (or **three-point stance**), which means they must bend over in a crouching position with one leg a little in front of the other, supported by one arm with the fingers of the hand or the knuckles touching the ground and the other arm bent over the knee of the leg that's farther back. The linemen must stay in this position and not move at all until the ball is snapped. If a lineman does move, a penalty will be called against the offense, since a moving offensive lineman can cause a defensive player to jump **offsides**.

T I M E · O U T

Defensive linemen may also line up in the three-point stance opposite the offensive linemen before the ball is snapped, but defensive players can move before the **snap** of the ball. They may also line up in a four-point stance, which means they bend down in a crouch but have both hands touching the ground.

The offensive linemen who line up on either side of the center cannot start the play with any part of their bodies—including their hands, fingers, and the tops of their helmets as they are crouched over in the down position (see below)—closer to the line of scrimmage than the length of the football held on the ground by the center. In other words, they must line up behind the tip of the ball that points back to their own end zone. This area set off by the line of scrimmage and the back end of the football is called the **neutral zone**; the defensive linemen and all other defensive players also cannot line up anywhere inside this zone. (In Canadian football, defensive linemen also cannot line up any closer than one yard from the line of scrimmage.)

After the linemen come to the line of scrimmage and get in the down position, the quarterback walks up behind the center, crouches down, and puts his or her hands between the center's legs. The quarterback then shouts signals to the players on the offense; this is called the **(quarterback) count**. These signals may be a combination of code words or numbers (e.g., "Blue, Fifty Two!") meant to communicate things like the quarterback's **read** of the defense, done as the quarterback walks up to the line of scrimmage and looks at the positioning and/or presnap movements of the defense. Sometimes the quarterback may become concerned that the defense's apparent strategy will be effective against the play called in the huddle. In this case, he or she may call an **audible**. Audibles are used not only to change a play called in the huddle but also to call plays toward the end of games, when teams often don't go into huddles in order to save time on the clock (see "Late-Game Strategies," below).

When the quarterback is ready to get the ball and start the play, he or she shouts the number or code that was called in the huddle to be the signal for the center to hike the ball. Traditionally, this has been the word "hut" followed by a certain

---

T I M E · O U T

Sometimes quarterbacks are so concerned about the defense that they call a time-out shortly after walking up to the line of scrimmage. In such cases, the quarterback may want different offensive personnel to come into the game for the next play or may just want to confer with the coaches.

number. For example, if in the huddle the quarterback says "on two" after announcing the play, this means the ball is to be hiked after the quarterback shouts, "Hut one, hut two." Another custom is for the quarterback to say "hike," sometimes more than once (in the huddle the quarterback might call for the ball to be hiked after the second "hike," for example). On the right

T I M E · O U T

The quarterback count can be used as an offensive strategy. Quarterbacks tend to shout the actual snap signal a little more loudly than the other signals of the count since they are naturally a little more excited knowing the play is about to begin. As a result, defensive players listen closely for the rise in the quarterback's voice that will indicate the ball is about to be snapped. Quarterbacks often try to take advantage of this by raising their voices at some point in the count but not on the actual snap signal. They hope the defensive players will jump offsides as a reflex to hearing this change in the quarterback's voice. This deception by the quarterback is called a **hard count**.

The count can also work against the offense. Especially when the visiting team is on offense in a stadium with a large and noisy crowd, the offensive players might have trouble hearing the quarterback. (Indeed, crowds often make more noise when their home team is on defense, and the players often encourage this; see "Player Conduct," below). In this case, offensive players may be late in moving after the snap because they didn't hear the quarterback's signal, or they may move before the snap, thinking they heard the right signal, which results in a penalty against the offense. (Of course, a player may also simply have misunderstood the snap signal called in the huddle.) In these situations where there is a lot of crowd noise, offenses may go to a **silent count**.

signal from the quarterback, the center hikes the ball to the quarterback, and at this moment the play officially begins. All the offensive players can now move, and the defensive players can cross the line of scrimmage. If the game clock had been stopped on the previous play, it now starts again with the snap.

Once the quarterback gets the ball from the center, the offense must run a play to advance the ball past the line of scrimmage and down the field enough yards to get a first down. There are two main ways for an offense to advance the ball: a **running play** and a **passing play**.

Running Plays

On **running plays** (also called **rushing plays** or **rushes**), the quarterback **hands off** the ball to a running back, who then runs with the ball as far as he or she can until being tackled, running out of bounds, or scoring a touchdown. On these handoffs the quarterback, after getting the ball from the center, turns either to the left or the right—depending on which side of the quarterback the running back is lined up on—and holds the ball out about waist level. The running back, who starts moving forward at the snap of the ball, approaches the ball the quarterback is holding out. The quarterback then puts the ball in the running back's midsection, and the running back usually covers it with both arms, especially if the back is going to run **up the middle**.

In another kind of handoff, called a **draw**, the quarterback drops back as if to pass but hands the ball off to a running back, who, unlike on most running plays, does not move toward the line of scrimmage at the snap of the ball. As on many passing plays, the running back stays behind the line as if to protect the quarterback during a pass attempt (see "Passing," below), but runs forward after receiving the ball from the quarterback coming back. This type of handoff is meant to fool the defense by making them think that the offense is going to pass, since the quarterback is dropping back and the running back is not moving forward as if to

pass-protect. Seeing this, the linebackers and defensive backs tend not to move forward as they would to try to stop a rushing play, but instead stay back to cover any receivers or offensive backs who might come out to receive the pass; because they are not moving forward, they are not in the best position to prevent the running back who gets the draw from gaining several yards.

On rushing plays, running backs usually don't run straight ahead but run toward a certain **hole**. In the huddle, it is announced which hole the running back will head for, so the offensive linemen on either side of the hole must be sure to block defensive players away to clear the path for the runner. If there's a fullback or other running back in the offense, this back will often run through the hole before the runner to **open the hole**.

Running plays do not always have to go through a hole in the offensive line, however, especially if the running backs are particularly fast runners. A rusher can try to run **off tackle**, or the offense may try a **sweep**. These kinds of plays are meant to utilize the speed of the running back and take advantage of the relative slowness of defensive linemen and linebackers, who must run a considerable distance across the field to catch the runner.

Especially on runs around the line, the running back may hold the ball differently than on a handoff up the middle. A running back usually cradles a football by holding one arm bent against his or her side and tucking the ball with one end resting against the inside of the elbow and the other covered by the palm of the hand. It's important that the ball remain in the runner's arm securely so that the runner doesn't fumble it, which can easily happen when a defensive player suddenly and unexpectedly makes contact with the runner and the impact jolts the ball loose. While holding the ball like this the running back has one arm free that he or she can use to cover the ball for extra protection against fumbling, but often the runner will keep the arm free to **straight-arm** defenders.

The side of the line the running back runs toward usually determines which arm the ball will be carried in; in a run to the right side of the line, for example, the running back will cradle the ball in the right arm, since most of the players on the defense will be coming at the runner from the left. And a good runner can switch the ball between arms without fumbling if it becomes necessary, as in **open-field running**.

Open-field running also requires skills different than those needed for running up the middle. Running backs who go through the line rely primarily on strength and power to gain yardage since there are so many defenders in this area (though being able to get through the line quickly is also an asset). In open-field running, however, the emphasis is on speed, on outrunning any defenders who might be near. When defensive players get close, a running back needs to be able to use moves that leave the defenders unsure which way the runner is going and make it harder for them to run directly at the runner. A good runner is also able to stop and start running again quickly to avoid defenders.

When the offense needs a few yards or less for a first down or a touchdown, special running strategies are required. Because a running play is very likely in this situation, the defense usually puts several players on or near the line of scrimmage, and the offense likewise puts several players on its side of the line to block. Since there are so many bodies on the line, it's sometimes very difficult for a running back to find any open hole to run through, and even if the running back does try to run through the line the chances of getting very far are not good with all the defenders on the line. Therefore, running backs in these situations are often called on to leap high in the air over any linemen fallen on the ground or in a crouching position.

Running backs are not the only offensive players who may advance the ball by running with it. Some quarterbacks are fairly good athletes and are fast, so an offense will purposely design plays that call for the quarterback to run with the ball.

Other quarterbacks are not very mobile, and when they attempt runs it is usually unplanned. The simplest type of run attempted by a quarterback is when he or she takes the snap from the center and instead of handing off, dropping back to pass, or doing anything else, merely starts going forward with the ball. This play, called a **quarterback sneak**, is usually attempted in situations where the offense needs only a few yards. A quarterback sneak usually results in a gain of a yard or two, since the quarterback can just follow the center moving forward.

Another running play featuring the quarterback is the **quarterback draw.** Like the draw play where a running back gets the ball from the quarterback going back as if to pass, on a quarterback draw the quarterback drops back but then suddenly runs forward with the ball. The strategy behind this play is the same as that for a regular draw play; it is hoped that the quarterback will catch the defense in a pass-defense mode and can therefore get several yards across the line of scrimmage before the defense realizes it's a running play and starts to pursue the quarterback (once quarterbacks cross the line of scrimmage, they cannot attempt a forward pass; see "Passing," below).

Another quarterback run is the **bootleg** (also called a **quarterback keeper**, but **keeper** is also sometimes used to describe a quarterback sneak). In this play, the quarterback, either after dropping back as if to pass or right after getting the snap, runs around one of the ends of the line. Often the quarterback will **fake a handoff** before running with the ball. An effective type of bootleg is when the running back to whom the handoff was faked and any other backs run toward one end of the line and the quarterback, after faking the handoff, runs around the other, hoping that the defense's attention will be drawn to all the players running around the opposite end.

The (**quarterback**) **option** is another running play involving the quarterback; it is used mainly at the college and high school levels and rarely in professional football. In this play, the quarterback runs with the ball around one of the ends of the line, but a running back follows closely behind. If by the time the quarterback reaches the line of scrimmage there are one or more defenders close by threatening to stop the quarterback's run, the quarterback can toss the ball backward—or slightly to one side and backward—to the running back, who can then continue to run with the ball. In a well-timed option play, the quarterback releases the ball just as one or more defensive players reach the quarterback, thus ensuring that at least these defenders will not be able to tackle the running back. If, on the other hand, the quarterback meets few defenders at the line of scrimmage, he or she has the other option of keeping the ball and trying to gain as many yards as possible by running past the line. The quarterback may also throw a pass before crossing the line of scrimmage.

As mentioned above, quarterbacks may have to run with the ball without planning to. Sometimes onrushing defensive players almost reach the quarterback before the quarterback can throw a pass (most often because the receivers the quarterback wants to throw to are well covered, so the quarterback has to wait longer for them to get open). A quarterback may then **scramble** behind the line of scrimmage until a receiver gets open to throw a pass to, or the quarterback may see an **opening** across the line of scrimmage and decide to run in that direction to pick up yardage.

Sometimes a quarterback will have to scramble because of a **busted play** (also called a **broken play**). For example, sometimes the running back for whom the handoff was intended will run to the wrong side of the quarterback or not even go near the quarterback, or the quarterback will not hand the ball off properly to the running back, causing a mishandling or drop of the ball. As a result, the quarterback will be left with the ball and usually with no receivers yet in a position to pass to, and there is little choice but to keep the ball and by scrambling try to pick up a few yards or at least avoid a loss of yardage on the play.

Particularly in the NFL, there are special rules to protect quarterbacks from injury when they scramble. These rules were established largely because of the great difference in size and strength between most defensive linemen and quarterbacks. In the NFL in particular, quarterbacks are regarded as "marquee" players—that is, players who get a lot of attention from fans and the media and who if they were injured and couldn't play would hurt the popularity of the game. One of these rules to protect quarterbacks, called **in the grasp**, is intended to keep larger offensive linemen from slamming quarterbacks down on the ground. Another rule allows a quarterback who has scrambled past the line of scrimmage and who is about to get tackled by a defensive player to slide down onto the ground. This action has the same result as a receiver downing the ball on a kickoff: the play is over and the ball is down at that spot, and no defensive player can now hit the quarterback.

Another offensive player who may attempt a rush is a wide receiver. About the only time a receiver is used on a running play is on plays called **reverses** and **end arounds**. In end around plays, at the snap of the ball the wide receivers do not go forward as normal but run backward from the line of scrimmage toward the backfield, where they receive a hand-off from the quarterback and then continue running around the end of the line opposite from where they started at the snap. A receiver does the same on a reverse, except that instead of receiving the ball from the quarterback, a running back who has just gotten the ball from the quarterback hands it off to the receiver. After getting the ball, the receiver will be going in the opposite direction from the running back— hence the name of the play. The purpose of these receiver running plays is again to confuse the defense: the receiver normally does not go into the backfield, and the specific purpose of a reverse is to get the defense to chase the running back, who gets the ball first, making them unprepared to go after the receiver running in the opposite direction. Against more sophisticated defenses that might be able to recognize a reverse as it is starting, the running back might even fake the handoff to the receiver and keep running in the opposite direction.

T I M E · O U T

Especially in short-yardage situations, some teams use a trick play in which an offensive or defensive lineman lines up in the backfield as a fullback or halfback. The lineman can then either block for another running back or get the handoff. This kind of play is designed to exploit the lineman's relatively large size to power over the defensive linemen.

What has been said above should not leave the impression that only quarterbacks and running backs have anything to do on running plays. Football is a team game, and on every play all the players on the field have roles. On running plays, wide receivers, if they are not directly involved in the play as on a reverse, either block the cornerbacks or run downfield as if they were going out for a pass. They do the latter so that the defensive backs will run back to cover them, thus drawing the defensive backs away from the line of scrimmage where they could help in tackling the runner.

And as they do on all offensive plays, linemen block defensive linemen or linebackers during rushes. Unlike pass plays, however, where the offensive linemen's primary responsibility is to protect the quarterback trying to pass, on running plays the offensive linemen try to block defensive players forward and away from the running hole; each lineman usually has a specific blocking assignment (see below). On running plays, tight ends are usually called on to block like linemen.

Passing Plays

On a **passing play**, the quarterback throws a pass to a receiver—who could be a wide receiver, a tight end, or a running back—who has gone past the line of scrimmage a few or several yards down the field. The quarterback normally throws the football with an overhand motion so that the ball will fly through the air above the heads of the defenders. The receiver must catch the ball before it hits the ground for the pass to be **complete**(**d**). If the pass is complete—in other words, if the receiver makes a (**pass**) **reception**—the receiver can run with the ball until tackled. If the passed ball hits the ground before reaching the receiver, if the receiver drops the pass and the ball hits the ground, or if the receiver is out of bounds when the ball is caught, the pass is **incomplete** and the play is over. (The next play will start at the same line of scrimmage as that of the play that resulted in the incomplete pass.) Another type of incomplete pass is an **interception** (also called a **pickoff**). The player who intercepts a ball can run with it toward the other team's end zone until reaching it or being tackled by one of the offensive players. If the player is tackled, the player's team goes on offense at that spot on the field on the next play.

Receivers try to catch passes by turning toward the quarterback with their arms nearly fully outstretched and with their hands close together but fingers spread out. When the passed ball gets to them, receivers try to catch it with their hands and then bring it in toward their chests. If they can still run with the ball at this point (i.e., if they aren't being tackled and are still in bounds), they tuck the ball into one arm as running backs do on running plays and start running. Sometimes receivers have to make more difficult catches. A receiver may have to catch a pass while running away from the quarterback, especially on deep pass plays. In this case, receivers catch passes in their sides or over one of their shoulders. The quarterback's pass may also not come directly to the receiver and the receiver may be forced to dive in order

T I M E · O U T

Interceptions and fumbles that are recovered by the defense are both called **turnovers**, since in both cases the offense **turns the ball over** to the other team. The number of turnovers that a team forces its opponents to make is reported as a statistic called **takeaways**, and the number of takeaways that a team's opponents get are often called its **giveaways**.

Not all fumbles become turnovers, however. Players may fumble the ball but recover their own fumbles, or someone on the same team as the fumbler may recover the ball. In both of these cases, possession of the ball remains with the offense. A player who recovers a fumble may even pick up the ball and try to advance it, but all players are taught that the safest thing to do when trying to recover a fumble is to fall on it and make sure of possession, since players on the other side are sure to go aggressively after any ball that has been fumbled.

Many fumbles result in a pile of players from both teams on the ground covering the ball. In such a case, it is not easy to determine immediately which player has the ball and, consequently, which team has possession. Usually players have to get off the pile—or be pulled off—one by one until the players on the bottom of the pile closest to the ball are showing. An official then determines which player has possession of the ball, which usually means deciding which player has the best grip on the ball. The official will then signal by stretching one arm straight out and pointing to one of the end zones (see "Officials and Penalties," below); the team that must reach that end zone to score is the one that has possession of the ball.

Finally, it should be noted that not every time a player loses the ball is it called a fumble. Under the rules of football, the ground cannot cause a fumble; this means that if a player hits the ground after being tackled and the ball comes loose, the player is not considered to have fumbled. But if the player drops the ball before hitting the ground, then it is a fumble.

to catch the pass; the receiver can even be lying on the ground while catching the ball, and this is legal as long as the ball does not touch the ground before it is caught. Receivers may be so well covered that they have to use one arm to fight off a defender and have only the other arm to catch the pass with, but skilled receivers often make spectacular one-handed catches.

Even though the ball must not hit the ground before the receiver catches it for it to be a completed pass, the ball may make contact with other players on the offense or defense before it is caught by one receiver. The receiver must also hold on to the ball for at least a few seconds after catching it to establish possession of the ball; if the receiver catches the ball for an instant but then drops it, it is an incomplete pass. Also, the receiver must have at least one foot in bounds (both feet in professional football) when catching the ball; if not, the pass is ruled incomplete even if the receiver catches and holds on to the ball.

A quarterback can attempt a pass only from behind the line of scrimmage. On most passing plays this is not a problem since at the snap the quarterback usually retreats backward. Most quarterbacks take a **five-step drop**, but on some passing plays—like a quick out (see below)—the quarterback may drop back only a few steps or sometimes not step back at all before throwing the ball. After dropping back, the quarterback can stay in the **pocket** or **roll out**. Rolling out often helps the quarterback elude onrushing defenders, but it also offers the quarterback less protection from the offensive linemen than staying in the pocket would. Sometimes quarterbacks are forced to scramble, and if they are not attentive (especially when rolling out), they may run past the line of scrimmage before throwing a pass. This is an **illegal forward pass**, and the offense receives a penalty for it.

On some plays, particularly in situations where it is obvious to both the offense and the defense that the offense needs to pass, the quarterback will not line up directly behind the

T I M E · O U T

Sometimes a player may toss the ball backward to another player. This is called a **lateral**, and it is a legal play anywhere on the field as long as the player to whom the ball is **lateraled** is behind the player who tosses the ball. Players lateral when they are about to get tackled and there is a teammate nearby who could run forward with the ball. One might wonder why more players who get tackled don't lateral the ball to a nearby player; the reason is that whenever the ball is in the air there is always the risk that a defensive player will grab it. In general, it is always safer to keep the ball than give it up.

Related to a lateral is what is called a **shovel pass**. In this play a quarterback tosses the ball with an underhand motion— and usually with both hands—to another player, usually a running back who is already in the backfield. Since most shovel passes are attempted behind the line of scrimmage, they can be thrown backward or forward.

center but will stand about five yards behind the line of scrimmage. The purpose of this formation, called a **shotgun**, is to give the quarterback more time to stand and look for a receiver instead of dropping back and then throwing. By having the quarterback stand farther back from the line of scrimmage, the shotgun also gives the quarterback more protection (at least for a few moments) from onrushing defensive linemen. In this formation, the center must hike the ball harder to make sure it gets back through the air to the quarterback.

On passing plays, the wide receivers and sometimes the tight end and a running back run down the field past the line of scrimmage after the snap. The receivers do not run just anywhere, though; each receiver follows a precise **pattern** or **route** that is called in the huddle. Here are some common basic pass patterns in football:

Out—the receiver runs straight down the field for several yards and then turns to the right or left and runs toward the sideline. A variant of this, in which the receiver runs only a few yards forward and then suddenly turns, is called a **quick out**; this pass is often attempted when there are only a few yards to go for a first down or a touchdown.

In—the receiver runs straight down the field for several yards, turns to the left or the right, and then runs toward the middle of the field.

Crossing pattern—the wide receivers lined up on either side of the line run patterns in which one receiver crosses the middle of the field a few yards in front of the other. The intent of this pattern is for any defenders covering these receivers (especially in man-to-man coverage; see "General Defensive Strategies," below) to get in each other's way chasing the receivers.

Come back or (**button**)**hook**—the receiver runs down the field, stops, then takes a few steps back toward the quarterback. It is hoped that the defender covering the receiver will keep moving backward even after the receiver stops and turns back (cornerbacks generally move backward when they first cover a wide receiver).

Post pattern—the receiver runs several yards downfield toward the middle of the field.

Fly (or **go**) **pattern**—except perhaps for a fake to the outside or inside shortly after leaving the line of scrimmage, the receiver runs as fast as possible straight down the field. A pass to a receiver running this pattern that is thrown high and deep down the field is called a **bomb**. If completed, bombs can result in gains of 30 yards or more and, in many cases, touchdowns.

Screen pass—this pass is usually to a running back who runs just a short distance out of the backfield to the left or right side. A screen pass is particularly effective when the defense blitzes the quarterback; the quarterback avoids being tackled by **dumping the ball off** or **unloading the ball** to a running back who is close by.

On most passing plays, each receiver runs a different pattern but one receiver is the **primary receiver** (or **go-to receiver**). Most quarterbacks have a receiver on their team that they feel the most confident throwing to, especially when they are **under pressure**. Even though there is usually a primary receiver on every passing play, the quarterback must be careful not to look at that receiver all the time from the snap of the ball; otherwise, experienced defensive players might pick up on this and move between the quarterback and the receiver that the quarterback is looking at, leading to an interception. On the other hand, experienced quarterbacks often keep looking at a receiver who is not the primary target and may even make a **pump fake**, then suddenly turn toward the intended receiver and throw the pass.

Though several receivers may go down the field on a passing play, the quarterback tries to throw only to a receiver who is **open** and not to one who is being **covered**. The closer a defender is to a receiver, the more likely it is that the defender will make an interception or at least **break up the pass**. When they run their patterns, receivers try to run past or away from defenders, often by using moves like those of running backs.

In spite of these efforts, sometimes each receiver will be so well covered by the defense that the quarterback will have no one to throw to. The receivers will keep running around trying to get open, and usually they head back toward the quarterback to make it easier for the quarterback to throw to them. As long as the quarterback is protected from onrushing defensive players by the offensive linemen, he or she can stay in the

pocket or roll out and wait for a receiver to get open. But usually quarterbacks are forced to scramble as defensive players get near, and if they are about to be tackled they try to **throw the ball away**. Throwing the ball away is counted as an incomplete pass and results in just a loss of down, and quarterbacks are taught to do this instead of holding on to the ball and being **sacked**, which results in a loss of yardage on the play. But quarterbacks must be careful to throw the ball somewhere near a receiver, even if the receiver has little chance of catching it; if they don't and throw the ball anywhere on the field just to avoid a **sack**, a penalty called **intentional grounding** will be called (see "Officials and Penalties," below).

Because receivers normally run at full speed or near full speed when they go out for passes and because quarterbacks usually do not have a lot of time (often just a few seconds) to throw the ball from the snap to the moment when a defensive player closes in, good timing between the quarterback and the receivers is essential. To this end, quarterbacks and receivers work a lot in practice on the timing of pass patterns. The quarterback wants to be able to develop a sense for throwing the ball not to where the receiver is at the moment the ball is thrown but to where the receiver is *going* to be when the ball gets to the receiver. Quarterbacks and receivers try to perfect their timing to the point that receivers don't even have to look at the quarterback until the instant they are ready to catch the ball, confident that the ball will be there when they turn around.

Despite their work on precision timing in practice, in the circumstances of actual games receivers often have to alter their patterns somewhat and quarterbacks also must adjust the timing of their passes. These changes may be caused by the defense using a pass-defense formation or strategy that forces a receiver to run a slightly different pattern to get open. Receivers also may run a few yards longer or shorter than usual on a pattern so that they are in position to receive a pass just beyond the

T I M E · O U T

Quarterbacks cannot throw a pass to just any player on the offense, even when they are in danger of being sacked. Passes can be thrown only to **eligible receivers**, who are the backs, wide receivers, and tight ends of an offense. Linemen are **ineligible receivers**; they cannot receive a pass and they cannot go past the line of scrimmage as if to receive a pass. If a quarterback throws the ball at an ineligible receiver just to throw the ball away, a penalty will be called.

Sometimes, however, linemen are used as pass receivers, especially in situations where the offense's line of scrimmage is only a few yards away from the defense's goal line. A lineman can become an eligible receiver just by reporting this intention to an official. A lineman having reported as an eligible receiver may run into the end zone after the snap to receive a pass from the quarterback. This play is risky because linemen are not used to catching the football, but at least the pass is not thrown from very far away and the lineman does not need to run after the catch (which is a good thing because offensive linemen are not noted for their speed). The intent of this play is to catch the defense off guard, since linebackers and defensive backs focus on covering running backs and wide receivers and a lineman can slip by them fairly easily. But much of the surprise of this play is lost when the referee, as he must do in this case, makes an announcement to the crowd whenever an offensive lineman reports as an eligible receiver. This clearly serves as an indication to the defense that a pass to a lineman might be coming, though frequently a lineman announces as a receiver but doesn't go out for a pass on the next play.

first-down marker; in that case, the quarterback only has to get the ball to them to earn a first down for the offense.

Passing plays are often more complicated than the quarterback just throwing a pass to a receiver, especially at the college and professional levels. An example of a more complex passing play is the commonly used **play action pass** (also known as a **play fake**). In this play, after getting the snap the quarterback fakes a handoff to a running back and then drops back and tries to throw to a receiver who has gone downfield— sometimes to the very running back to whom the handoff was faked. The purpose of a play action is to freeze the defense; it is hoped that the defenders, particularly the linebackers and defensive backs, will see the quarterback apparently making a handoff to a running back and will immediately focus on the running back coming out of the backfield and move forward, leaving receivers going downfield uncovered. Experienced defensive players are on guard against play fakes, of course, but occasionally a well-executed play action, especially one in which the quarterback fakes the handoff well and the running back charges forward with his or her arms in the usual position for carrying the ball, will fool the defense and result in a completed pass and maybe a big gain for the offense.

At the start of many offensive plays, a wide receiver, tight end, or running back may move out of his or her position in the formation and suddenly start running across the field toward—and usually past—the quarterback. This is called a **man-in-motion** play. Ordinarily, offensive players do not move from their positions before the snap of the ball, but as long as the **man in motion** does not step forward—and as long as only one player is in motion—it is a legal play. (In Canadian football, all offensive backs may be in motion before the snap of the ball.) There are two main reasons an offense may set a player in motion. One is to help reveal whether the defense is planning zone or man-to-man coverage of receivers (see "General Defensive Strategies," below); if a defensive back or linebacker moves along with the player in motion on the defense's side of the line of scrimmage, it will indicate to the quarterback that the defense is in man-to-man coverage, since the one moving defender is apparently assigned to cover the player in motion. Another thing the man-in-motion play can do is draw the defense's attention to one side of the field—namely, the side the man in motion runs toward. If one or more defenders shift their attention to this side of the field as a result of the player in motion heading that way, it makes it more likely that a receiver who runs into the other side of the field will get open (in other words, it will open up that side of the field).

Some offenses run what are known as **flea-flicker** or **gadget** plays. These plays involve unusual actions and are sometimes called "trick plays," because their primary purpose is to fool the defense in some way. One of the most common versions of these plays is one in which the quarterback hands off to a running back, who instead of running across the line of scrimmage with the ball may stop after a few steps forward and toss the ball back to the quarterback. The quarterback then tries to throw to one of the receivers downfield, who—it is hoped—will have gotten open if the defense immediately focused on tackling the running back after the handoff.

Another unusual play occurs when not the quarterback but a running back attempts a forward pass. This play is often called a **halfback pass**, even though the pass may be thrown by a fullback or even a wide receiver who gets the ball on an end around. Like the play described in the previous paragraph, this one also starts with the quarterback handing the ball off to a running back, who then usually begins to run toward one end of the line of scrimmage. The running back then stops and throws to an open receiver downfield, who ought to be on the same side of the field the running back is on to make it easier for the pass to be completed. If there is no receiver open, the running back can just keep running with the ball (for this reason, the play may also be called a "halfback option"). The strategy behind this play is once again the hope that the defense will focus on the running back, thinking that the play is just a run around the end, and break off coverage of the receivers. The play is risky, though, since running backs are not experienced passers and can easily make a mistake like missing the receiver or throwing an interception.

T I M E · O U T

A special kind of halfback pass is one where the intended receiver is the quarterback. This play capitalizes on the fact that after a handoff quarterbacks usually do nothing except watch the rest of the play develop. (Occasionally, a quarterback runs downfield and blocks after a run around the end or a short pass, but not very often since this puts the quarterback, the most important player on the offense, at risk of getting injured.) As a result, defenders do not pay much attention to quarterbacks after they hand the ball off, so a quarterback can easily slip past the defense and get open for a pass.

Though they may be ineligible receivers, offensive linemen still have important duties on passing plays, just as they do on runs. As mentioned above at the end of the "Running Plays" section, the primary responsibility of linemen on passing plays is to protect the quarterback, which means they must block onrushing defensive players long enough so that the quarterback can drop back into the pocket, find an open receiver, and pass the ball. As also mentioned above, offensive linemen generally do not block forward during pass plays but get up from their stance at the snap and either block from where they are standing or **backpedal** in order to meet defenders coming in from the side. Since on passing plays the defense may rush four or fewer defenders, there is often at least one offensive lineman who is available to help another lineman block a pass rusher, so this lineman (often the center) usually backpedals and looks around for a defensive player to block. On some passing plays, particularly ones where it is obvious to the defense that the offense needs to pass, the tackles and perhaps even the guards line up a yard or two in back of their normal position and face not straight ahead as normal but toward the outside of the defensive line. This puts them in a better position to block onrushing defensive linemen, particularly defensive ends, and since they don't line up on the line of scrimmage they often start the play in an **up position**, giving them a better view of the defense.

Kicking Plays

Besides the kickoff, there are three other plays in football in which the ball is moved not by being run with or thrown but by being kicked: a **punt**, a **field goal attempt** (or **field goal try**), and an **extra-point attempt**. A team may attempt a punt or a field goal on any down, but these plays are almost always tried only on fourth downs. And an extra point can be attempted only after a touchdown.

Punting

As mentioned above in the "Offensive Series" section, if after three downs the offense doesn't think it will get enough yards on the fourth down to keep possession of the ball by earning a first down, it may choose to **punt** the ball. On a punting play, teams bring in their special-teams unit, which for this play also includes a player called a **punter**, though on some teams one player performs both the duties of placekicker and punter. Like a placekicker, a punter usually plays only on punts and is usually not as big or athletic as other players. Mainly for this reason, punters, like placekickers, tend to stay behind the rest of the players on the punting unit as they run downfield during punt returns, and they attempt to tackle the punt returner only if he or she has evaded all the other players on the punting team.

T I M E · O U T

When it is used, the term *placekicking* is meant to refer to kicking attempts made when the ball is upright and in place either in a tee or in the grasp of a holder; these are kickoffs and field goal or extra-point attempts. Punting is the only other form of kicking in the modern game, but there used to be another kind called "drop kicking," where the ball was dropped in front of the kicker, as on a punt, but kicked only *after* it hit the ground and bounced upward. The drop kick is now rarely used in football, mostly because the bounce of a football is so uncontrollable and unpredictable.

In a punt formation, there are seven players on the line of scrimmage, and the punter lines up about 15 yards directly behind the center, who is often called a **long snapper**. The center puts both hands on the ball and leans his head over almost to the ground so he can see the punter behind him in order to make a more accurate throw backward. He must toss the ball with enough force to make it travel back to the punter, but he must not throw it too hard or it will sail over the punter's head. If the snap does go over the punter's head, the punter will have to run back and recover the ball; even if the ball is recovered, the punter will probably not have enough time to punt the ball before being tackled by the defense. Thus, a poor snap by the center could result in a huge yardage loss for the offense coupled with a loss of possession since the punt was attempted on fourth down.

Also in the punt formation, two players line up on each side of the offensive line and several yards away from the end of the line, like wide receivers. At the snap, these players run downfield in order to tackle the punt returner as soon as the returner catches the ball. In professional football, two players on the return team line up opposite each of the ends of the punting team and are allowed to block them to keep them from getting downfield. In other types of football, the punting team's ends must be permitted to run down the field from the line of scrimmage without being blocked.

Another player on the punting team lines up a few yards behind one of the guards. This player's main function is to block any onrushing defensive players who make it past the punting team's offensive line, but sometimes this player has a crucial role in fake punts (see below).

The receiving team on a punting play also brings in its special-teams unit, and all the players on this unit line up on the line of scrimmage except for the punt returner and the one or two players who are assigned to block each of the ends of the punting team. The punt returner lines up about 50 yards downfield from the line of scrimmage. Like kick returners, this player is usually a running back or wide receiver, and sometimes even a defensive back. After the ball is hiked to the punter, the receiving-team players on the line rush over the line of scrimmage and try to tackle the punter before the ball can be punted. Punters are rarely tackled, because most punters can get the punt off with the 15 yards that separates them from the line of scrimmage (though when teams have to punt when the line of scrimmage is inside their own 5-yard line, the punter, standing in the back of the end zone, is closer to the rushers and more vulnerable). Therefore, rushers usually concentrate on **blocking** the punt, which is making contact with the ball as it is being punted so that the ball does not go very far forward or doesn't go forward at all (and usually as a result of the contact the ball bounces and rolls backward). The rushers have to get past the blocking of the offensive players to do this, but some punts do get blocked. Once a punt is blocked and the ball hits the ground, it, like a fumble, can be recovered by a member of either team. In high school and college football, if the ball is recovered by a defensive player, it cannot be picked up and **advanced**, but in professional football a player can recover the fumble and carry the ball as far as possible toward the punting team's end zone.

Like most offensive plays, punting plays usually begin with a huddle of the punting unit in which little is discussed besides the snap count, though a fake punt may be called at this time (see below). After the players have left the huddle and gone into their formation, the punter calls signals with arms outstretched toward the center. The center snaps the ball to the punter, who catches the ball and holds it with arms still outstretched and with the pointed ends of the ball facing the end zones. If the punter kicks with the right leg, he or she holds the ball with the right hand on the right side of the football near the end that points back, and with the other hand near the forward end of the ball on the left side (a left-footed

punter holds the ball the opposite way). The punter then takes one step with each leg, beginning with the kicking leg, and just before taking a third step lets the ball drop a short way, as in the illustration at left. Then the punter swings the kicking leg upward and the instep of his or her kicking foot makes contact with the falling ball a few feet off the ground. The punter continues to swing the leg upward after kicking the ball in a full kicking motion, as shown at right.

With defensive players rushing the punter at full speed and the punter concentrating on punting the ball with a kicking leg high in the air, football has developed rules to protect punters in this exposed position. If a defensive player makes contact with the punter on purpose after the punter kicks the ball, a penalty called **running into the kicker** is called. (But if the defensive player was blocked into the punter or if in any other way the contact was accidental, it is not a penalty.) Furthermore, if a defensive player runs into the kicker and in the judgment of the officials it was done with deliberate and excessive force, the officials will call a **roughing the kicker** penalty. More serious than a running into the kicker penalty, roughing the kicker is a 15-yard personal foul and always results in an automatic first down for the offense, the punting team (see "Officials and Penalties," below).

TIME·OUT

Punters have a reputation for being overly dramatic when defensive players run into them. Punters are often scorned for this, but if a punter tries to make the slightest contact—or even a narrowly missed contact—by a defender look like a forceful hit by spinning around or falling to the ground right away, an official is more likely to call a running into or roughing the kicker penalty.

As soon as the ball is punted, all the players on the punting team can run downfield to cover the punt. All the members of the receiving team also start to run downfield at this point since they obviously have no more chance of blocking it. The ball sails high into the air as it travels downfield, usually without the end-over-end motion of a kickoff or a placekick because it is punted while being held lengthwise, as explained above. As a result, a punted ball usually goes through the air with its long axis parallel to the ground and with a slight rotation. A good punt will travel 40 or more yards from the line of scrimmage; this is the point from which the distances of punts are measured, even though punters actually kick the ball from about 15 yards behind the scrimmage line. Even if the punt does not travel a great distance down the field, it may still be effective if it is high enough. A punt kicked high in the air with a **hang time** of several seconds enables the members of the punting team to get so far downfield that they are very close to the punt returner before the returner catches the ball.

Three things can happen after a ball is punted: a return, a fair catch, or no return. If the punt returner catches the ball and decides to try to return it, he or she should catch the ball while it's in the air; letting the ball hit the ground first is dangerous because of the uneven and unpredictable bounces of a football, though the returner can still pick up the ball from the ground and run with it. After getting the ball, the punt returner runs upfield and tries to advance as many yards as possible before being tackled or forced out of bounds. The other members of the receiving team, who had run down the field while the ball was in the air, now block for the returner. Whatever point on the field the returner gets to before being tackled is where the returner's team will take over on offense.

Instead of returning the ball, the punt returner may opt for a **fair catch** by waving one hand in the air as the punt is coming down. This means that the returner will not run with the ball after catching it, and it also means that the members of the punting team must allow the returner to catch the ball (i.e., they cannot be so close to the returner that they interfere with the returner's catching the ball). If the returner catches the ball after signaling for a fair catch, the play is immediately over and the returner's team will take over on offense at the spot the ball is caught. A punt returner signals for a fair catch when members of the kicking team are getting very close while the returner is still waiting for the ball to come down—so close that the returner can see that he or she will not get very far trying to run with the ball after the catch and also will most likely get hit hard by one or more players on the punting team, possibly resulting in an injury or fumble.

A third thing that may happen on a punt is that the returner may not touch the ball at all, but this doesn't mean it's a free ball for the punting team to recover. If no one on the receiving team catches the ball, the ball is allowed to roll until it stops or goes out of bounds. If they get downfield in time, one or more punting-team players may surround the ball and follow it as it rolls backward, being careful to not let the ball touch any part of their bodies. As soon as the ball stops rolling, one player will touch the ball to down it there and the play will be over. The punting team lets the ball roll as far backward as possible so that the other team will have to start on offense that far back on the field. If a punting-team player does not down the ball, a receiving-team player could pick it up and run with it, but this usually doesn't happen because the player who picks up the ball probably wouldn't get very far with all the kicking-team players around.

TIME·OUT

Occasionally, the ball bounces not backward but forward after it hits the ground on a punt. In this case the punting team tries to down the ball right away since the farther forward the ball goes, the closer to the punting team's goal line the other team's offense will start on the next play.

When a returner doesn't try to catch a punt and lets it hit the ground, the reason is usually that the punt lands close to the returner's own end zone. The returner hopes that the ball will bounce into the end zone, resulting in a touchback, which means that the returner's team will start on offense from the 20-yard line instead of deeper inside its own territory. If the returner doesn't catch the punt, it is important that every member of the receiving team stay clear of the ball; if it touches any member of the receiving team, the ball is **live** just as if it had been fumbled, and the punting team can recover the ball and start a new offensive series from that place on the field.

On the other hand, on punts that fall close to the receiving team's goal line, the punting team tries to down the ball as close as possible to the line so that the other team will have to start on offense very deep in their own territory. For this reason, punting-team players race downfield after the bouncing ball in order to stop it from rolling into the end zone. Often players dive at the ball just as it is about to bounce over the goal line and knock it back, though their momentum takes them into the end zone; as long as the ball doesn't cross the goal line, players can knock the ball back to be downed while any part of their bodies is in the end zone.

Unlike on kickoffs, if a punted ball goes out of bounds without being touched it is not a penalty; the receiving team simply starts the next play on offense at whatever yard marker the ball went out of bounds. Punters often take advantage of this rule, when they are punting about 50 yards or less from the receiving team's end zone, by deliberately kicking the ball at an angle so that it goes out of bounds. When the punter tries to punt at an angle, the chances are good that the punt will go out of bounds deep in the receiving team's territory, possibly inside the 10-yard line. This kind of punt is often called a **coffin corner**, since its aim is to put the ball into the angle formed by the goal line and one of the sidelines. If the ball does go out of bounds in this area, the offense has to start out with field position that nearly "kills" its chances of moving all the way down the field and scoring.

Offenses sometimes line up on fourth down as though they're going to punt, but after the ball is snapped they try to run or pass the ball for a first down. This is called a **fake punt,** and a number of different plays may be tried to get the first down. After receiving the ball, the punter may hold his or her arms out as if to punt but then suddenly start running with the ball, usually around one of the ends of the line. The punter can also try to pass the ball to a teammate who has crossed the line of scrimmage; this is especially likely to be tried when the punter has played the quarterback position before or is actually a quarterback who performs the punting duties. Another common play on a fake punt is for the snapper to hike the ball not to the punter but to the player who lines up a few yards behind the line of scrimmage (see above), who then tries to run with or pass the ball. This play is often effective because the receiving team expects the ball to be snapped to the punter, as it almost always is, and normally focuses entirely on the punter while rushing in.

Fake punts are usually attempted only when there's a reasonable chance of getting a first down—that is, when the line of scrimmage on fourth down is only a few yards from the first-down marker. And because fake punts have no guarantee of success, teams rarely try to fake a punt in their own territory; if they do try and fail to get a first down the other team will have the ball on the next play with fewer than 50 yards to go to the punting team's end zone (meaning that the chances are good it will get a least a field goal during the next few offensive series).

Field Goal Attempts

Another kicking play is an attempt to kick a **field goal**. A field goal is scored when the ball is kicked from somewhere on the field so that it travels through the air over the crossbar and between the uprights of a goalpost (or through the area directly above them; see "Goalposts" in chapter 2). As mentioned above, kicking a field goal earns the kicking team 3 points. This is less than the 6 points scored for a touchdown, and teams usually attempt a field goal only on fourth downs when the line of scrimmage is so many yards from their opponents' goal line that they have no reasonable chance of scoring a touchdown on the next play.

On a field goal attempt, nine players form the offensive line for the kicking team. These players are mostly linemen because their primary responsibility is to fend off defensive players who will try to block the kick. As on passing plays, where the offense knows defensive players will be rushing hard toward the quarterback, the linemen on the outside of the line on field goal attempts often line up a few yards behind the line of scrimmage and at an angle to better block the defensive rushers, who are often speedy defensive backs.

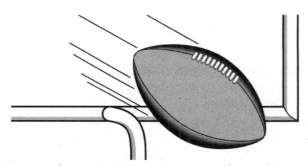

The other two players on a field goal attempt are the kicker and the **holder**. The holder kneels on the ground 10 yards behind the center, facing one of the sidelines but looking at and with one arm outstretched toward the center. The side the holder faces depends on which leg the placekicker kicks with: on the kicker's right side if the kicker is right-footed, and on the opposite side for a left-footed kicker. The kicker stands a few yards behind the holder, usually not directly behind the center but at a slight angle to the left or right, and faces toward the goalpost.

The holder calls signals with his or her arm still outstretched, and the center snaps the ball to the holder. As on punts, the center who snaps the ball to the holder is a specialist who must be sure to hike the ball through his legs so that it flies through the air to the holder. As soon as the holder catches the ball, the ball must immediately be put in place for the kicker. The holder places the ball upright, resting on one end, and puts just the tip of the index finger of one hand on the top end of the ball to hold it in place. The holder must also turn the ball so that its laces are not facing the kicker (the kicker doesn't want to kick the ball on this uneven part). Because these actions of the holder require a great deal of dexterity in handling the ball, the holder is usually a skilled player like a quarterback. Another reason holders are usually quarterbacks is that if the offense tries a fake field goal or if the kicker is unable to get the kick off for some reason, it is good to have the ball in the hands of a player like a quarterback, who can then pass or run with the ball. Holders can also be punters, since these players are experienced in handling balls hiked from a long snapper.

As soon as the ball is snapped the kicker starts to move toward the holder, which is another reason the holder needs to put the ball in place as quickly as possible. The kicker usually takes only a few steps and then kicks the upright ball held by the holder toward the goalpost. As on kickoffs, the kicker tries to make contact near the lower part of the ball so that it will travel higher and farther. On field goal tries, two officials are positioned on the end line on either side of the goalpost toward which the kick will be attempted. They watch to make sure the ball travels through the air over the crossbar and through the area inside or extending directly up from the uprights. If it does, the officials signal that the kick is **good**, using the same upraised arms signal they use to indicate touchdowns (see "Officials and Penalties," below). If the ball either lands on the ground without going over the crossbar or passes to the outside of one of the uprights, the kick is **no good**, and the officials indicate this by waving their arms in front of their midsections, a signal identical to that for an incomplete pass.

If the field goal is good, the kicking team is awarded 3 points and must now kick the ball off to the other team (see "Kickoff," above). If the field goal is no good, the other team gets possession of the ball where the line of scrimmage was when the field goal was attempted. This rule is something that teams have to consider when deciding on a fourth down whether or not to attempt a field goal instead of punting or trying to **convert**. If it's fourth down and the offense has the ball deep within the defense's territory, it makes sense to attempt a field goal, since the distance the kicker has to kick the ball will be relatively short. Even if the kicker misses the field goal, the other team will get the ball with poor field position deep inside their own territory. On the other hand, if the offense has the ball within the other team's territory but not really deep (between the 30- and the 50-yard line, for example), it may not want to risk missing the field goal and having to turn over the ball to the other team with fairly good field position. In this case, the offense will more likely decide to punt the ball and hope that it will be downed or go out of bounds deep in the receiving team's territory, or that the returner will not be able to get very far, putting the other team in bad field position.

Another factor in a team's decision to try a field goal is the weather conditions, if the game is being played outdoors. A team is much more likely to attempt a field goal if the wind is "at their backs"—that is, blowing toward the end zone with the goalpost toward which the kick will be aimed—since the wind ought to give the kick extra height and distance and thereby increase the chances that the field goal attempt will be good. But if the wind is blowing in the opposite direction or if there is a strong wind that is gusting or swirling all over the field, a team is less likely to attempt a field goal because under such conditions the wind might keep even a well-kicked ball from going through the uprights. Also, in very cold weather the ball is firmer and thus harder to kick a long distance, so teams don't try as many field goals in such weather.

As with punts, on field goal attempts the defensive team tries to block the kick. Usually all the players on the defense position themselves on the line of scrimmage, but some players may line up behind the line in the positions normally taken by inside linebackers. The reason for this—and for the fact that defensive players try to stick their arms in the air as they rush in toward the kicker—is that the trajectory of the ball is lower on field goal attempts than on punts. In fact, after the snap the defensive players behind the line sometimes actually climb up onto fallen or crouched linemen in order to be in a better position to block the ball as it sails over the line. If defensive players get their hands on the ball or if some other part of their bodies comes into contact with the ball in the air, the ball usually will not fly far enough to go over the crossbar, or it will be deflected so that it doesn't go straight through the uprights. When this happens, it is said that the kick is tipped or partially blocked. If one or more defensive players make such good contact with the ball that the kick doesn't go forward and even starts to bounce backward, the field goal attempt is said to be **blocked**. In high school and college football, the ball is declared **dead** as soon as the kick is blocked, and the team that was on defense then takes over possession of the ball at that spot on the field. In professional football a blocked kick becomes a free ball, and if it is recovered by a defensive player, it can be advanced. Any offensive player can also recover a blocked kick and try to advance it toward the defense's end zone. If the ball is advanced past the first-down marker, the offense gets a new series of downs; if not, and if the field goal attempt was made on the offense's fourth down, the defense gets possession wherever the ball is spotted at the end of the play.

TIME·OUT

A field goal attempt isn't always made on a fourth down. If it is late in the game and the team on offense needs 3 points either to tie the score or **take the lead**, the team may elect to attempt a field goal on a down other than the fourth. This usually happens when there are 10 seconds or less on the game clock, which is very little time to run a normal offensive play, especially a running play or a pass inbounds, after which the clock does not stop. Unless the offense is very near the goal line (about 10 yards or less), it usually decides to use the time remaining to try a field goal, even though it may not be the fourth down of the current series.

As mentioned above, offenses can fake a field goal attempt just as they sometimes fake punts. On a fake field goal try, the kicker approaches the ball held by the holder as on a normal attempt, but just as the kicker is ready to swing his or her leg forward to kick the ball, the holder takes the ball out of the kicker's way. The kicker, meanwhile, continues to swing the leg forward just as on a regular attempt. After picking up the ball, the holder tries to hide behind the kicker as long as possible, hoping that the kicker's motions will fool the defense into thinking that an actual kick was made. Then the holder, who as mentioned above is often a quarterback, can drop back and try to throw the ball to a player on the offense who has gone downfield (unnoticed, the offense hopes, and therefore uncovered by any defensive player). The holder can also try to run around one of the ends of the line to gain yardage, hoping that the defense still thinks that a real kick was attempted and is not defending against a possible run or pass.

Extra-Point Attempts

Every team that scores a touchdown is allowed to try to score at least one extra point immediately after the touchdown play. One means of scoring extra points is through a 2-point conversion, which, as the name indicates, can earn the team an additional 2 points if it is successful. In this play, the team's offensive unit lines up close to the goal line over which the touchdown was scored on the previous play (on the 2-yard line in the NFL, on the 3-yard line in college and high school football, and on the 5-yard line in the CFL) and tries to advance the ball into the end zone. The team can try to score through either a running play or a passing play. If the offense fails to advance the ball across the goal line, the next play will be this team's kickoff from its own territory (as would also happen if the team did score the 2 points). The defense, of course, tries to prevent the 2-point conversion from being successful, but a recovered fumble or intercepted conversion pass cannot be advanced toward the offense's end zone.

The other way a team can score points after a touchdown is through a kicking play known as an extra point or a point after touchdown (PAT). In this play, both the offense and defense line up on opposite sides of the line of scrimmage in pretty much the same formations as in field goal attempts, except that the holder kneels on the 10-yard line, closer to the center than for a field goal. Once again the snapper hikes the ball to the holder, who positions the ball for the placekicker to kick it over the crossbar and through the uprights. And once again the defensive team tries to block the kick. If the kick goes over the crossbar and through the uprights (as it usually does due to the short distance the ball has to travel), the team is awarded 1 point and kicks off on the next play. If the ball does not go through because it was not kicked right or because it was partially or completely blocked by the defense, no points are awarded and the team must still kick off on the next play.

T I M E · O U T

On rare occasions, because it is so risky, the kicking team might fake an extra-point attempt and try to run or pass the ball into the end zone, thereby earning 2 points. As on fake field goals, the holder is the key player in a fake; he or she is often a quarterback who can throw or run with the ball.

After they score a touchdown, teams usually try the 1-point kicking play instead of the 2-point conversion. The reason for this is that statistically the chances an extra-point kick will succeed are much higher than those for the success of a 2-point conversion. But there are times when a team will decide to **go for two**. If a team is **trailing** late in the game, it may try to get 2 points instead of 1 after a touchdown just to get closer to the other team's score. Since the team is already behind in the score, trading a fairly sure single extra point for the less certain points of a 2-point conversion is a worthwhile risk.

Sometimes teams who are ahead also try a 2-point conversion to protect their lead. As an example, say team A is leading team B by a score of 13 to 9 late in the fourth quarter. If team B scores a touchdown, the score becomes 15 to 13 in favor of team B. In this case, team B might choose to try a 2-point conversion, because if successful this would make the score 17 to 13 and would mean that team A would have to score a 6-point touchdown to win the game. Of course, the risk in this case is that if the 2-point attempt fails the score will remain at 15 to 13 and all team A has to do to win the game is get a 3-point field goal the next time it has the ball.

Safeties

Any offensive play can result in the offense losing yardage, which is what happens when offensive players get tackled on a spot of the field that is closer to their team's end zone than the line of scrimmage at the start of the play. In most cases, the line of scrimmage at the start of the next play will be that spot on the field where the player was stopped. But if an offensive player is tackled behind his or her own goal line, this is called a **safety**, and the team that was on defense earns 2 points. Getting a safety is a benefit for a team not just because it earns 2 points but also because the other team, which was on offense on the play that resulted in a safety, must now give up possession of the ball through a **free kick**. After the safety, the team that was on offense sends its special-teams unit onto its own 20-yard line. In the middle of the line is the punter, who is given the football by an official and must then punt the ball to the other team. The receiving team lines up as for a kickoff but of course closer to the other team's territory, since the punter is kicking from his or her own 20-yard line. As on kickoffs, if the free kick goes out of bounds without being touched, a penalty is called and the kicking team must kick again, but from its own 15-yard line. The player on the receiving team who catches the punt can return the ball, and when the play is over the receiving team takes over on offense.

Sometimes a team on offense will deliberately let the defensive team tackle one of its players in the end zone. This normally happens when the offensive team has the lead by several points late in the game and has the ball deep in their own territory. Instead of risking turning over possession of the ball to the other team so deep in its own territory through an interception or a fumble that may result from a normal play, the offense may have its quarterback or some other player allow himself or herself to be tackled with the ball in the end zone. To minimize the chance of injury, the offense can also have the player step over the end line out of the end zone, which also results in a safety being called against the offense; this often happens on punting plays from deep in the punting team's territory, when the punter is already positioned near the end line at the start of the play (see "Punting," above). The strategy behind this play is for the team on the offense to accept the 2 points given to the other team on a safety but to have the chance on the next play to free-kick the ball deep down the field; it is true that the other team will get possession of the ball, but the team will start much farther away from the kicking team's end zone than if it had recovered a fumble or intercepted the ball deep in the other team's territory, or even if the offense had punted the ball from its own end zone. Of course, the team that takes the safety hopes that it can keep the other team from scoring so that the 2 points of the safety aren't enough for the other team to win the game.

Officials and Penalties

Chapter 2 briefly mentioned football officials and the equipment they carry. This section will discuss in more detail the actions and duties of officials during a football game, including one of their most important functions: calling **penalties**.

In professional football, each game is controlled by a crew of seven officials. In college football, there must be at least four officials: a **referee**, an **umpire**, a (head) **linesman** and a **line judge**. A college game may also be worked by additional officials called **back judge**, **field judge**, and **side judge**. (These, along with the four mentioned above, are also the names of the officials in professional football.) At high school games there may be as many as five officials—a referee, an umpire, a linesman, a line judge, and a back judge—or there may be as few as three.

In any crew of officials, the **referee** has the ultimate control of the game. While any official can **call a penalty**, every penalty must be reported to the referee, who is responsible for announcing it to the teams and the crowd and for **walking off** the penalty yardage. The referee also makes the final decision in cases where there is disagreement among other officials on a penalty call or a rule. At the start of every play, the referee stands 10 to 12 yards behind the line of scrimmage on the offensive side.

Just as the referee is positioned behind the offensive line, the umpire stands four to five yards behind the defensive line at the beginning of every play. The umpire counts the number of offensive players to make sure there aren't more than the 11 allowed on the field during a play. The umpire watches for offsides penalties (see below), including making sure balls are not kicked or passed from over the line of scrimmage. The umpire also watches for offensive linemen who are not eligible receivers coming downfield.

T I M E · O U T

Since the umpire is positioned in the middle of the field on the defensive side of the ball, he is often in the area of the field where the most action takes place. As a result, he often has to scramble to get out of the way of onrushing ballcarriers and other offensive players, and sometimes he has to duck to get out of the way of a pass from the quarterback. In fact, umpires get hit by balls quite a lot, and as long as the ball doesn't hit the ground it is still live.

The **linesman** stands along the same sideline as the primary chain operators (see chapter 2) and moves throughout the game so that he is always facing the current line of scrimmage. He calls penalties for any illegal formations in the neutral zone, such as players lining up too close to the line of scrimmage.

The linesman also assists on actions called **measurements**. These occur when the ball has been advanced by the offense to a point on the field that is very close to the first-down marker but the officials on the field aren't absolutely sure the ball has crossed this mark. The officials on the field call a time-out, and the persons operating the chains on the sidelines (see "Officials" in chapter 2) jog onto the field with the chains accompanied by the linesman. Before coming onto the field, the carrier of the first pole carefully notes where the line of scrimmage was on the first down of the current series and puts the pole on that yard marker in the middle of the field, in a straight line on the ground directly behind the football and parallel to the sidelines. The carrier of the other pole stretches out the chain above the football as far as it will go, then lowers his pole to the ground next to the football. If the forward point of the ball (the end that points toward the goal line toward which the offense is advancing) touches or extends past the second pole, the referee, who stands by the second pole to observe the measurement, stretches out his arm and points to the goal line toward which the offense is advancing; this is the signal that the offense has gotten a first down (it is also the signal used to show which team has gotten possession of a fumble; see above). If the forward point of the ball does not reach the pole, it is not a first down and the official will note the distance between the point and the pole. He will then face the side of the field with the press box and hold up his hands or two fingers approximately the same distance apart as the distance between the football and the pole (as in the illustration above); this indicates the distance that remains for the offense to get a first down. After this procedure, the linesman and the chain operators jog off the field and back to their sideline.

The **line judge** has duties similar to those of the linesman. In addition to calling penalties for illegal formations in the neutral zone, the line judge works on the sideline with the operators of the second set of chains, which, as mentioned in chapter 2, are not the ones used to do measurements on the field. Like the linesman, the line judge always positions himself facing the current line of scrimmage.

While the umpire counts offensive players, the **back judge** counts the number of players on the defense to make sure there aren't more than 11. The back judge is also responsible for watching for interference infractions and other violations on passes far beyond the line of scrimmage, and also for calling penalties near the spot on the field where punts and kickoffs are caught and returned.

The **field judge** has responsibilities similar to those of the back judge; he is also able to call penalties on forward passes and on punts and kickoffs. The field judge, when present among the crew of officials, also indicates when the play clock should be started or stopped.

The duties of the **side judge** are similar to those of the field and back judges. Like both, the side judge watches for penalties on passes and kicks, and the side judge also counts the number of defensive players, as the back judge does.

There are many rule violations in football for which a penalty may be called, and several of these **infractions** have already been mentioned in this and the preceding chapter. In chapter 2, some of the basics of penalty calling were discussed, such as the tossing of penalty flags by officials and the referee's announcing the penalty to the teams and the crowd through a microphone. The discussion below addresses in more detail what is involved in the calling of penalties.

As mentioned in chapter 2, the calling of penalties starts with the tossing of a penalty flag by an official. When the play during which the flag was tossed is over, the officials signal for the game clock to be stopped and the official who threw the flag (if it wasn't the referee himself) reports the penalty to the referee. The referee then walks a few steps toward the sideline nearer the press box and signals with his hands, arms, and/or body what the penalty is. Below are the signals referees use to indicate the most commonly called penalties, along with an explanation of the penalty and the number of yards that are assessed against a team when it is enforced. (Note: 15-yard penalties always result in an automatic first down for the offense if the penalty is called against the defense; 10-yard penalties called against the defense *may* result in a first down if the offense has 10 yards or less to go for a first down at the end of the play on which the penalty was called; the same is true for 5-yard penalties.)

signal

penalty: delay of game

explanation: the offense did not start a play before the play clock **expired**

penalty yardage: 5 yards

or

penalty: illegal substitution

explanation: a team tried to put substitute players into the game while the ball was in play, or the players substituted for were not completely off the field when the ball was snapped

penalty yardage: 5 yards

or

penalty: excess time-out called

explanation: a player on a team tried to call a time-out, but the team had none left

penalty yardage: 5 yards

signal

penalty: false start

explanation: an offensive player moved in a way that indicated the start of the play before the ball was actually snapped (usually called because a lineman, running back, or man in motion moved forward)

penalty yardage: 5 yards

or

penalty: illegal formation

explanation: an offensive player was lined up in an illegal position, usually a lineman inside the neutral zone

penalty yardage: 5 yards

 signal

penalty: personal foul

explanation: a player used force in an unsportsmanlike manner toward another player—for example, by punching another player or making contact with another player after the whistle or when the other player was already out of bounds

penalty yardage: 15 yards

 signal   *followed by*

penalty: personal foul: roughing the kicker or holder

explanation: in the opinion of the officials, a defensive player deliberately ran with excessive force into a punter, placekicker, or holder for a kicker during the kick or immediately after the kick was made

penalty yardage: 15 yards

 signal | *followed by*

penalty: personal foul: roughing the passer

explanation: in the opinion of the officials, a defensive player deliberately ran into a quarterback throwing the football or immediately after the pass was thrown

penalty yardage: 15 yards

 signal | *followed by*

penalty: personal foul: clipping

explanation: an offensive player (or a player on the receiving team of a kick) blocked a player on the other team from behind

penalty yardage: 15 yards

signal

penalty: running into the kicker

explanation: a defensive player ran into a punter or placekicker during the kick or immediately after the kick was made

penalty yardage: 5 yards

signal

penalty: holding

explanation: a player kept another from moving freely by grabbing and holding on to part of the player's body

penalty yardage: 10 yards and, if called against the defense, an automatic first down for the offense

signal

penalty: illegal forward pass

explanation: a quarterback or other offensive player attempted a pass illegally, usually because of being past the line of scrimmage

penalty yardage: 5 yards

signal

penalty: pass interference

explanation: a player used illegal contact (holding the other player's arm, for example) to keep a player on the other team from catching the ball (usually this penalty is called on a defensive player, but it is possible for an offensive player to interfere with a defender who is trying to make an interception)

penalty yardage: in professional football, an automatic first down at the spot of the infraction (unless it was in the end zone, in which case the ball goes on the 1-yard line); in college football, an automatic first down and a 15-yard penalty from either the spot of the foul if it was less than 15 yards from the line of scrimmage or from the line of scrimmage if the infraction occurred more than 15 yards downfield; in high school football, 15 yards from the line of scrimmage and an automatic first down; and if this penalty is called against an offensive player, 10 yards from the previous line of scrimmage and a loss of down

or

penalty: interference with a fair catch

explanation: a punt returner signaled for a fair catch, but a punting-team player made contact with the returner before the catch of the ball

penalty yardage: 15 yards from the spot of the foul

signal

penalty: intentional grounding

explanation: in the opinion of the officials, a quarterback or another player on the offense deliberately threw the ball so that it landed on the ground for an incomplete pass in order to avoid being tackled behind the line of scrimmage; this penalty is more likely to be called if no receiver is close to the spot where the ball lands

penalty yardage: 5 yards

(*Note:* It is permissible for a passer to throw the ball out of bounds, which is also ruled an incomplete pass, to avoid being tackled.)

signal

penalty: ineligible receiver

explanation: a player on the offense, almost always a lineman who has not reported as an eligible receiver, went past the line of scrimmage as if to receive a pass, or a pass might have actually been thrown at him or touched him (usually by accident, but if in the officials' opinion the pass to the lineman was intentional, this penalty will be called)

penalty yardage: 10 yards

or

penalty: ineligible member of the kicking team downfield

explanation: a player on a punting team (not one of the two players who are allowed to do so) went past the line of scrimmage before the ball was punted

penalty yardage: 5 yards

signal

penalty: offsides

explanation: at least some part of a player's body was over the line of scrimmage at the moment the ball was snapped

penalty yardage: 5 yards

or

penalty: encroachment

explanation: at least some part of a player's body was over the line of scrimmage at the moment the ball was snapped and contact was made with a player on the other team

penalty yardage: 5 yards

or

penalty: neutral zone violation

explanation: at least some part of the body of a lineman (except the center) was in the neutral zone at the moment the ball was snapped

penalty yardage: 5 yards

TIME·OUT

Players on the defense often jump over the line of scrimmage when they think the ball is being snapped. As long as they get back behind the line of scrimmage before the snap of the ball, no offsides penalty will be called. But skillful quarterbacks often take advantage of a defensive player's eagerness by immediately calling for the snap; if this is done quickly enough, the defensive player will be caught on the offensive side of the ball and a penalty will be called. But the play may continue, resulting in what is called a **free play**. If the offense knows that an offsides penalty is going to be called against the defense because the officials threw penalty flags right after the ball was snapped, they may try a more daring play—like a long pass—realizing that even if the pass is incomplete or intercepted, the offsides penalty against the defense will result in the offense still having the ball, and 5 yards farther upfield from the line of scrimmage where they started. And if the play is successful, resulting in a gain of more than 5 yards, the offense can simply refuse the penalty (see below).

signal

penalty: pushing or helping the runner

explanation: a player tried to push or otherwise help the ball carrier advance the ball farther through physical contact

penalty yardage: 5 yards

signal

penalty: illegal motion

explanation: a player on the offense moved, even slightly, before the snap of the ball

penalty yardage: 5 yards

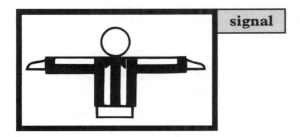

signal

penalty: unsportsmanlike conduct

explanation: a player or a member of the coaching staff behaved in an unsportsmanlike manner—for example, by arguing with an official excessively, using obscene language or gestures, throwing equipment (especially a helmet), or fighting with another player; if the penalty is called against a coach, the penalty is enforced against whatever unit (offense, defense, or special team) of the coach's team is on the field for the next play

penalty yardage: 15 yards; if the infraction is **flagrant** in the judgment of the officials, the player may be **ejected** or **disqualified**.

TIME·OUT

In any case where the yardage marked off for a penalty would move the ball over a goal line (for example, if a 15-yard penalty were called against one team when the ball is on its own 10-yard line), the penalty yardage assessed is half the distance to the goal, meaning that the ball is spotted on the yard line that is the number of the yard line the ball is currently on divided by 2. Thus, in the example in the first sentence the ball would be placed on the 5-yard line in front of the goal line.

After giving any of the penalty signals above, the referee points with an outstretched arm to the offense or defense to show which unit the player who committed the infraction belongs to and therefore which team will be penalized if the infraction is enforced. For example, if the offense is on the left side of the line of scrimmage when viewed from the press box and an infraction was committed by an offensive player, after giving the signal for the specific penalty the referee stretches out his right arm and points to the offense.

If the penalty were against the defense, he would point to the right toward the defense with his left arm. The above actions by the referee, indicating just the penalty and the team to be called for it without announcing specifically which player was called for the infraction and what the exact results of the enforcement will be, is called the **preliminary indication** of the penalty. After the preliminary indication, the referee explains to either the quarterback (if the penalty is called against a defensive player) or the captain of the defense (if the penalty is against a player on the offense) how many yards will be **marked off** and which down the next play will be.

After hearing this, the quarterback or captain can **accept** the penalty or **refuse** (or **decline**) it. Teams usually accept penalties called against the other team, because they result in the ball being moved farther toward their opponent's goal line— at least by the five yards of most minor penalties. But in some cases it is better for a team to refuse a penalty against the other team. One obvious example is when a team scores a touchdown even though a player on the other team committed a penalty. If the penalty were accepted, the yardage would be marked forward from the previous line of scrimmage and the team that scored would have the ball again but the touchdown would not count. In this case, the offense would almost certainly refuse the penalty so that they would get the 6 points of the touchdown.

In other cases, the decision to accept or refuse the penalty may not be so easy. For example, some penalties against the offense do not result in a loss of down, so if such a penalty is called, a defense must decide whether or not the field position the offense would be left in if the penalty yardage were marked off is more of a disadvantage to the offense than if the defense refused the penalty and accepted the result of the play with the accompanying loss of down (unless, of course, the play resulted in a first down, in which case the defense would surely accept the penalty). Another example is when the team on defense is trailing late in the game and needs to get possession of the ball as quickly as possible so that its offense can try to score. If a penalty is called against the offense on a third-down play that doesn't result in a first down, the defense will likely refuse the penalty in order to bring about a fourth down—on which the offense will probably have to punt the ball and thereby give possession of the ball to the other team. Accepting the penalty would have given the offense another third down and therefore another chance to get a first down and keep possession of the ball.

T I M E · O U T

There is a general principle in football that a team never wants to take points off the board—that is, accept a penalty that would result in nullifying a score the team made on a previous play. The reasoning behind this principle is obvious in examples like the first one above, where accepting the penalty would result in a 6-point touchdown not counting, but it may be less clear-cut in other cases. For example, if a team kicks a field goal from a relatively short distance (about 30 yards or fewer) from the other team's goal line and a penalty is called against the defense on the field goal attempt, this team may want to consider accepting the penalty because (since the field goal attempt was most likely attempted on a fourth down) the penalty could give the offense a first down deep within its opponent's territory and therefore a good chance of scoring a touchdown within one or a few offensive series.

Thus, in some cases the choice to accept or refuse a penalty is obvious and can easily be made by the quarterback or the defensive captain. In some of the more difficult cases, as described above, a quarterback or captain may have to consult with teammates or with the coaching staff, usually by shouting and signaling since the coaching staff can't come onto the field during a game (unless a time-out is used, which is unusual for merely deciding on the acceptance of a penalty). Once a decision is reached, it is told to the referee by the quarterback or captain. If the penalty is accepted, the referee walks off the penalty and sets the ball down on the new line of scrimmage. He once again walks a few steps toward the sideline with the press box. If equipped with a microphone that is linked to the stadium's public-address system (see "Officials" in chapter 2), he turns it on at this point. Then, whether he is speaking over the public-address system or not, the referee announces the specific penalty called while again making the signal for the penalty, as described above. After giving the signal, he again points to the team whose player committed the penalty, and this time he also announces the number of the player. Then, if the penalty is accepted by the other team, he announces the yardage of the penalty and the down the next play will be. If the penalty is refused, he will announce this decision, giving the signal at right for a refused penalty.

Similar to the way public-address announcers speak in announcing a game (see "Football Fields and Stadiums" in chapter 2), the speech of referees in announcing penalties is clipped and formulaic—for example, "Holding, number seventy-two on the offense, five-yard penalty, still second down" or "Defensive pass interference, number twenty-four, penalty is declined, first down." When the referee has finished with his announcement, the game and play clocks are restarted on the signal of the officials and the game resumes.

Occasionally, more than one penalty may be called on a single play, though only one can be enforced. If the penalties are committed by one team, the other team usually chooses the more or most severe penalty to be enforced. If both teams are guilty of an infraction, the penalties are **offsetting**; the next play will be whatever down it was on the previous play and will begin at that play's line of scrimmage, but the time on the game clock that went by on the previous play is not put back.

Even though they are well trained and have very good judgment, football officials, like all human beings, are not perfect and sometimes **blow the call**. The most common mistake is not to notice an infraction being committed, which is understandable since on any play so many players are moving over a large portion of the field and, especially at the college and professional levels, at great speed. Players against whom a missed penalty was committed often complain to officials after the play, but almost never do officials call a penalty for something that happened during a play once the play is over. (At most, such complaining by players may make officials watch the player against whom the complaints were leveled more closely during the rest of the game.)

Sometimes officials throw a flag when they think they see an infraction being committed even though there is no actual infraction. Despite the inevitable protests of the player and the team against whom the erroneous penalty is called, decisions by officials are rarely reversed. When a reversal does occur, it usually happens only after a conference of the officials on the field with the referee, who has the final say on whether or not a penalty stands as called.

T I M E · O U T

The NFL tried out a system called "instant replay" to correct mistakes made by officials, using videotape made of the game as it was happening, often taken from a television network's broadcast of the game. When the officials called a penalty or made some other call (such as a ruling on a fumble) with which one team strongly disagreed and requested a review, the game was stopped and an official in the press box rewound the videotape to view the play, stopping the tape or playing it at slow speed to determine whether or not the officials' call was correct. Then this replay official would contact the referee on the field by telephone and inform him of his interpretation of what he saw in the tape. From that, the referee could rule that the call made on the play was correct or incorrect and he would change the outcome of the play as he saw necessary. For example, if the officials ruled that one team fumbled and the other recovered, but the replay showed either that there was no actual fumble or that the other team did not recover the ball legally, possession would be given back to the team that was on offense on the previous play.

Instant replay was last used during the 1991 NFL season. It was taken out of the game because many teams felt that the number of reviews during games (there were usually at least a few during every game played) slowed the games down. It was also argued that the fact that instant replay could overrule the decisions of officials made the officials less comfortable in their duties and less likely to call penalties. There have been some calls to go back to instant replay in the NFL—and even to institute it for the first time at other levels of football—but so far it has not been reinstated.

Finally, in addition to the signals for penalties listed above here are some other signals commonly used by officials and what they mean:

Signal	Meaning(s):
	a touchdown has been scored *or* the field goal is good *or* the extra point is good
	the field goal is no good *or* the extra point is no good *or* the pass attempt is incomplete *or* the penalty is refused (see above)
	a safety has occurred
	it's a first down (a new offensive series has started) *or* the team advancing in this direction now has possession of the ball (e.g., after a fumble or interception)

it's fourth down *or*

the neutral zone has been established (i.e., the offensive linemen are in position)

a time-out has been called

followed by the referee putting his hand on top of his cap

a referee's time-out has been called

followed by the official swinging his arm at his side

the kick or punt is a touchback

the game clock should be started or kept moving

followed by blowing his whistle

the game clock should be started when the official blows his whistle

Some Fundamentals of Playing Football

Tackling

Tackling has been referred to many times so far in this book; this section will discuss in more detail the fundamentals of this important action in football. A player with the football is considered tackled or **down** if at least one of the player's knees touches the ground as the result of contact with a player from the other team. When this happens, an official blows his whistle to declare the play over and the ball dead. If a player falls to the ground without any contact from an opposing player, the player can get up and keep running until tackled. If a player is on the ground but has not been tackled or forced down by another player, a player on the other team only has to touch the player on the ground for the latter to be called down. Every now and then, a ballcarrier will be held on to by one or more defenders so that the ballcarrier is unable to move forward but the defender(s) are still unable to bring him or her down. In this case, the official will whistle the play over on the grounds that the player's forward progress has been stopped.

One way of tackling a player running with the ball is to grab one—and preferably both—of the player's legs. Stopping the ballcarrier's legs from moving in this way, combined with stopping the ballcarrier's motion forward, is enough to bring a player down in most cases. But a better method of tackling, especially if the ballcarrier is not running forward at full speed, is for defenders to wrap their arms around the ballcarrier's legs or midsection while driving a shoulder into the runner's lower body. If possible, the tackler should also try to lift the ballcarrier slightly off the ground so the ballcarrier won't be able to keep running and will be easier to force to the ground. Using the whole body in tackling like this is the classic method; it is emphasized by football coaches instead of the less effective method of arm tackling—defenders simply reaching out for any part of the ballcarrier—which often does not stop the runner at all. If a defender does get a grip on the ballcarrier and is strong enough, the defender might actually throw the ballcarrier to the ground for a legal tackle, but the defender must be careful not to do it with too much force, lest he or she get a penalty for **unnecessary roughness**.

The above methods of tackling all involve the tackler's holding on to the ballcarrier, but a tackle can be made without having to grab the other player. If a defensive player runs into a ballcarrier with such force that the ballcarrier falls to the ground or is pushed out of bounds, this is also a legal tackle. This method of tackling is one of the reasons football is often criticized for having too much violence; considerable force is usually needed to bring down a ballcarrier in this way, and defenders have to be running hard to do it. Also, it is common for defensive backs, in order to break up a pass, to run into pass receivers at the precise moment the receivers are catching the ball; receivers often have to jump off the ground to catch passes, and being in this vulnerable position when hit by defensive backs often causes serious injuries to the receivers. Nevertheless, this is a legal method for backs to bring down a receiver with the ball (as long as the hit doesn't occur *before* the pass is actually caught; if it does, this is a pass-interference penalty).

Even though legal tackles can be as violent as two players running into each other at full speed, there are some methods of tackling that are prohibited. For example, a defensive player cannot grab the face mask of a ballcarrier. Sometimes this is accidental in the fast and furious action of football, but it is still a penalty. If the officials determine that the grabbing of the face mask was not intentional, the penalty is only a minor one (5 yards). But if the officials think the defender grabbed the face mask deliberately, it is a 15-yard penalty because if a player's face mask is grabbed, the player's head can be twisted backward as the rest of the body moves forward, and a severe neck injury could result.

Another method of tackling that is prohibited is **spearing**, which results in a 15-yard personal-foul penalty. The penalty for spearing is so severe because the helmet is the hardest piece of equipment players wear (as it must be to protect players' heads). In fact, tackling in this way can result in a serious neck injury, even partial or total paralysis, to the tackler. And even though players' heads are fairly well protected by helmets, players are prohibited from intentionally hitting other players in the head. A blow to the head by another player's helmet, arm, or leg can still give a helmeted player a concussion.

More than one player is allowed to try to tackle a ballcarrier as long as the ballcarrier is not yet down, and sometimes more than one tackler is needed if the ballcarrier is very large, heavy, and/or strong. In that case, a good strategy for defenders is for one tackler to hit the ballcarrier's upper body while another goes for the legs. Sometimes, especially in short-yardage situations where many players line up around the line of scrimmage, there will be several players on the ground shortly after the play begins and it may not be clear that the player with the ball is down. In these situations one defensive player after another may jump on the ballcarrier until the sound of an official's whistle indicates the ballcarrier has been stopped; this tackling by several players, called **piling on**, is legal as long as the contact is made before the play is over. But if a defensive player makes contact with a ballcarrier after the whistle, that is a personal-foul infraction called a **late hit**.

Blocking

Football is a game of force with a lot of physical contact—and not just between a ballcarrier and a tackler. On every play most of the players on the offense are involved in blocking defensive players. **Blocking** is using one's body and physical actions to keep a defender from moving toward a ballcarrier so that the ballcarrier won't be tackled and can advance the ball. A lot of blocking is accomplished by an offensive player standing straight up in front of a defensive player and pushing the defender backward with arms that are bent over the blocker's chest. In another method, the blocker drives forward with one shoulder into the defender's midsection; this is the method linemen often use to block pass rushers or defensive players trying to block kicks, since the latter are usually in an upright position and may have their arms raised.

These two methods are the ways that linemen usually block, but a more effective means of taking defenders out of the play is for the blockers to run right into them and knock them down; usually only backs or ends have the time or space to block in this manner. If a lineman knocks a defender down through straight-up blocking, that is legal—and perhaps more desirable since the defender has to spend a second or two to

get up and back into the play (blockers cannot keep blocking defenders while they are on the ground, nor can a blocker hold a player down).

Another method of blocking is a **body block,** in which a player turns sideways and throws one whole side of his or her body into the midsection or thighs of the defender. And blocking can also be accomplished with no physical contact at all— by means of a **screen** or **pick.**

T I M E · O U T

Some players use a variation of the body block called a **chop block,** in which the blocker throws his or her body toward the defender's legs. This kind of block is dangerous to defenders because it can easily result in a knee or other leg injury, since defenders are usually moving forward when they receive this block. Knee and leg injuries are among the most serious injuries football players can suffer since they are often **career ending.** Therefore, defensive players often react with anger when they think an offensive player has tried to chop-block them.

Every offensive play has a plan for not only what the quarterback, running backs, and ends will do with the ball but also which players on the defense are going to be blocked by each player on the offense. These are called **blocking assignments,** and they are very precise in terms of which defenders are to be blocked by whom and in what direction they are to be blocked. On some running plays, for example, one offensive player is designated as the **lead blocker** and has the assignment of running ahead of the ballcarrier, either through a hole or around an end of the line, to block the first defenders who get in a position to tackle the runner. Sometimes this lead blocker is a guard or a tackle who **pulls.**

On some plays, the blocking assignments call for **double-teaming** one defensive player. This kind of blocking is normally used only against an exceptionally good defensive player, since putting two players on one defender leaves another defender unblocked. But if the player who is the object of this double-teaming, or **combination blocking**, is good enough and enough of a threat to their offensive plans, a team may feel it is worth the risk.

There are some things blockers cannot do. For example, blockers cannot hold on to any part of a defender's body with their hands. Doing so results in a penalty called **holding** (see "Officials and Penalties," above). This is one of the most commonly called penalties in football, since in the action of a play it is rather easy for a blocker to grab a defensive player accidentally. Sometimes, however, defensive players, who have no such restrictions against using their hands to ward off blockers, start to get past their blockers so fast that out of desperation blockers grab the defenders to keep them from getting all the way around. Offensive players and blockers on kick returns must also be sure to block only defenders who are facing them; blocking a player from behind is an infraction called **clipping** (see "Officials and Penalties," above).

Player Conduct

The previous sections have discussed what football players do in the course of playing the game. In this section, some of the things players do during a game that have no real part in the game itself will be considered.

Players on the same team talk to each other frequently on and off the field during a game, but players don't converse with members of the other team very often, even when they are in contact on the field. When conversations do take place, they are usually short, owing to the fast pace of the game. The talking may be friendly, but more often than not if there is talking at all it is unfriendly due to the intense competition and physical nature of the game. There may be "jawing," which is when a player complains about illegal play or unnecessary roughness on the part of another and the other player argues right back. Sometimes this complaining is directed at officials whom the players think should have called a penalty, but players must be careful not to complain too much or too forcefully or they may receive an unsportsmanlike conduct penalty (see "Officials and Penalties," above). As in other sports, like basketball, **trash talking** has also become a part of football, especially at the professional levels, but it has also recently filtered down as far as the high school and youth levels (largely as a result of the influence of television). Excessive taunting, however, especially if it is accompanied by physical gestures, can result in an unsportsmanlike conduct penalty.

Just as there may be congenial conversation between teams in football, there is sometimes friendly physical contact like handshakes, pats, or backslaps; but more often than not, contact outside of the play will be the result of anger. A player hit too hard or hit after the whistle may respond with a shove to another player, and if this continues and intensifies it can

TIME·OUT

Too much taunting can lead to a penalty, but so can excessive celebrating. Players usually celebrate when a member of their team scores a touchdown by raising both of their arms in the same signal officials use to indicate the score (see "Officials and Penalties," above) and by running up to and hugging the scoring player. The player who scores the touchdown often **spikes** the ball, and sometimes does a dance joined by his or her teammates. If these celebrations go on too long in the judgment of the officials, the team that scored can be penalized for delaying the game.

result in a fistfight between these players and may spread to their teammates. But unlike fights in sports like baseball or basketball or even ice hockey, fights between football players rarely amount to anything serious, like a player getting injured, because football players already wear so much protective equipment. However, players can be ejected for fighting, and penalties (usually offsetting ones) are routinely called when fights break out.

Football players usually do not interact much with members of the crowd. An obvious reason for this is that in most football stadiums the seating areas for the crowd are separated from the field by fences or walls. Players may occasionally go up to the fence or the wall to greet or talk to spectators, especially if they are people they know personally. In professional and major college football, players may also sign autographs for fans. Any of this direct contact with spectators almost always takes place only during the pregame warm-ups or after the game; players, even nonstarters, are expected to focus only on what's happening on the field while a game is in progress and ignore the crowd in the stands as much as possible.

But players of the home team may try to use the crowd to their advantage during a game. Since most of the spectators at a game favor the home team, players often swing their arms in an upward motion to get the crowd to cheer loudly at critical points in the game when the home team is on defense. The noise of the crowd, it is hoped, will keep the players on the offense from hearing the quarterback's signals or will just rattle them. In the same way, when the home team is on offense, a quarterback and members of the offense may wave their arms in a downward motion; this is a signal for the crowd to be quiet so that the offensive players can concentrate and hear the quarterback's signals.

Whatever arguments and fights may break out during a football game, at the end of a game there is usually much sportsmanship and friendliness (although fights may still break out at the end of very competitive games, especially ones where there were several fights during the game). When the time on the game clock expires (or sometimes during the time when the final seconds of a game whose outcome has already been decided are ticking down), the players, coaches, and other team personnel come onto the field from their team areas to talk and shake hands with their counterparts on the other team. In shows of sportsmanship, the coaches and members of the losing team congratulate the winners, and the winners usually praise the losers' efforts. This can last for several minutes before all the members of both teams go back to their locker rooms.

If the game was a postseason game (see chapter 4), if it was won in a dramatic fashion (e.g., if the winning team won the game after being far behind, or if the winning score was on or almost on the last play of the game), or if the victory was against a team that is a traditional rival, the members of the winning team also celebrate as they come onto the field and as they leave it. This celebrating can take the form of jumping up and down, shouting, raising arms into the air, and backslapping. Another way teams celebrate a big win is by lifting the head coach over two or more players and carrying him off the field while he sits on their shoulders.

T I M E · O U T

Prayer is part of American football. During a team's meetings in the locker room before and after games, all the players may join in a prayer, which may be led by a clergyman or sometimes a coach or a player. When some players score a touchdown, they immediately kneel and bow their heads in a short prayer of thanks, even before they celebrate the score with their teammates. And at the end of many games, some of the players from both teams kneel in a circle somewhere on the field and pray together in a show of religious faith and sportsmanship.

General Offensive Strategies

Earlier in this chapter, the two basic ways of advancing the ball on offense—running and passing—were discussed. This section will examine the factors a team considers in deciding whether to run or pass on each down. It will also discuss running and passing plays as part of the overall offensive strategies that teams use during a game.

The basic difference between **running the football** and **going to the pass** is that running plays tend to be less risky than passing, but a successful passing play usually picks up more yards than a rush. On the great majority of rushing plays, the runner will gain at least a few yards and will not fumble. A series of downs featuring only rushes will thus probably keep possession of the ball for the offense but may not earn a first down. It is true that a runner getting a handoff may break free for a **long gainer** or even a touchdown, but most rushing attempts are stopped not far from the line of scrimmage.

Passing plays gain on average several more yards than rushing plays. Indeed, a receiver can run downfield as far as is needed to get a first down, and if the pass to the receiver is complete the offense gets not only the first down but maybe more yardage if the receiver can keep running. And, of course, bombs can gain 30, 40, or 50 more yards and often result in touchdowns. The risk, of course, is that every time quarterbacks pass they are giving up possession of the ball for at least those few seconds between the time the ball leaves the quarterback's hands and gets into the receiver's hands. While in the air, the ball can easily be intercepted by any of the players on the defense. Also, if the quarterback either doesn't get the pass off in time or doesn't have an **open** receiver to throw to and is sacked, the loss of yardage is usually more than five yards, which is more than the average for a loss on a running play. And a pass that falls incomplete gains no yardage at all and loses a down, whereas on most running plays the rusher will gain at least a few yards.

These basic facts about running and passing plays determine which type of play is attempted in different game situations. On first down the chances an offense will try a run or
a pass play are roughly equal, though running plays are slightly
more common on this down. If it is second or third down and
a team needs only a few yards to get a first down (this is called
a **short-yardage situation**), a running play will probably be
attempted, since the odds are very good that this kind of play
will pick up the yards needed without turning the ball over.
On the other hand, if it is second or especially third down (the
last real chance before having to punt on fourth down)—or a
first down after a penalty against the offense—**and long**, a
passing play is more likely, because in spite of the risks of passing the offense needs to try to gain several yards in a single
play. These are called **passing situations**.

Thus, short-yardage situations usually result in a rush and
passing situations require a pass, but occasionally offenses go
against these tendencies in order to surprise the defense.
Defenses are aware of what offenses will probably do in the
above situations and will prepare accordingly. For example, in
a short-yardage situation the defense will put more players
than usual up at the line of scrimmage in anticipation of a run.
More important, the individual players on the defense will be
expecting a running play and therefore will **key on** the running backs, because they think one of them will be getting a
handoff. But if in such a short-yardage situation the offense
tries a pass, the play has a fairly good chance of succeeding,
since by keying on the running backs the defense may not cover
receivers as closely as on other plays, especially if, as is normal
in these situations, the offense lines up in a running formation
with two or more running backs in the backfield and maybe
two tight ends. Similarly, in a passing situation offenses will
sometimes try a draw play, as this play is often effective against
a defense that is expecting a pass (see "Running Plays," above).

Weather also sometimes plays a factor in a choice between
running and passing plays. In games played outdoors in windy

conditions, teams are much less likely to try a passing play on any down, since a thrown ball will be blown around by the wind, probably won't get to the intended receiver, and could be intercepted. And if the weather is cold, passes are not attempted as frequently as in normal conditions, since footballs become harder and more slick in cold weather, making them difficult both to throw and to catch.

Particular game conditions and situations are not the only factors that may determine a team's choice of plays. Most teams—or, more accurately, their coaching staffs—have a special overall approach to running their offenses throughout a game. Some teams favor a **ball-control** type of offense, which uses mostly rushing plays, throwing passes only when necessary (e.g., when behind late in the game or when needing 10 or more yards for a first down). The offenses of such teams are specially designed for such an offensive philosophy, having large linemen and running backs who can endure the physical demands of so many running plays. Ball-control or **conservative** offenses are often used by teams who play many of their home games in cold weather, owing to the problems with passing a football in the cold, as described above.

Some teams, on the other hand, prefer an offensive style featuring a lot of passing. One of these styles is called the **run-and-shoot** offense. This offense features formations with as many as four wide receivers, no tight ends, and only one running back in the backfield, whose primary function is not to receive handoffs but to block for the quarterback. Having so many receivers ensures that at least one of them will probably get open for the quarterback to throw to, and this offense often scores a lot of points, but it largely lacks a **running game**, which the team may want to use in short-yardage situations.

Another type of predominantly passing offense is called the **no huddle** or **hurry up**. In this style, the members of the offensive team do not go into a huddle after the conclusion of a play but instead immediately line up in their positions. The quarterback usually lines up in the shotgun and then uses an audible (see "The Down Position, the Quarterback Count, and the Snap of the Ball," above) to call the next play for the members of the offense. Since the quarterback is in the shotgun, he or she usually calls a passing play, but running plays, particularly draw plays, are still possible in this offense. The no-huddle offense actually had its origins in the two-minute drill (see "Late-Game Strategies," below), a style of offense used by teams late in a game in which they're behind; not going into a huddle saves time when the game clock keeps running after the end of a play, and if a team needs to score quickly it usually tries to pass. When this style is used throughout a game, and even when the team that uses it is ahead in the score, its purpose is to keep the defense from bringing in new players in situation substitution (see "General Defensive Strategies," below); lining up almost immediately after a play gives the defense little time to bring in new players before the offense snaps the ball again.

Most teams, however, prefer a balanced offensive strategy in which both running and passing plays are used with roughly the same frequency and the choice of plays depends largely on the particular game situations. One example of a balanced offensive attack is what is called the **West Coast offense**, so named because it was featured by the NFL's San Francisco 49ers, based in California on the West Coast of the United States, who won several Super Bowls during the 1980s and 1990s. The West Coast offense relies on both running and passing plays, and the passing plays are designed not to be long passes that have little chance of being completed but short passes that are **underneath** and are more likely to be completed, even though they may gain only a few yards each time.

Whichever offensive strategy a team prefers, before every game the coaching staff of a team always makes a **game plan** based on their analysis of the strengths and weaknesses of both their own offense and their next opponent's defense. For example, if the coaches feel the opponent has a weak **secondary**, they will likely plan to attempt more passes than normal. Or if a team's starting quarterback is injured and cannot play in the next game, the team will probably rely more on running plays than normal, instead of trusting the relatively inexperienced **backup** quarterback to be able to execute the team's passing plays successfully.

TIME·OUT

Some coaches are so insistent on having a precise game plan that they **script** the plays they will have their offense run during the first part of the game. The offense then runs these plays in the exact order they were scripted, no matter what the specific game situation is before each play. Only later in the game, based on how the game is going, is the offense given some flexibility in play calling.

One of the biggest differences between Canadian football and football as played in the United States is that in the former the offense has only three downs to make a first down; hence, Canadian offenses tend to pass much more than U.S. football teams do. This and the fact that the Canadian football field is both longer and wider than a U.S. field (see "Football Fields and Stadiums" in chapter 2) tend to make the Canadian game more wide open, with more passing and more space for players to move around. Especially conducive to pass plays are the 20-yard-deep end zones, with so much room for receivers to run around and get open for a touchdown pass.

General Defensive Strategies

It is a fact of football that the offense has control of the ball and thus has a large say in what will happen on every play, whereas the defense can do little more than react to what the offense does and just try to stop the offense's play from being successful. Nevertheless, defenses usually prepare in different ways for what they think the offense might do, and there are even ways a defense can take the initiative and force the offense into doing certain things that are not to its advantage.

One of the most important things a defense can do is have on the field the appropriate players for the particular situation of the down. This is accomplished through **situation substitution**. For instance, if it is a short-yardage situation and the defense therefore believes that the offense is going to try a running play, extra linebackers and linemen, players who are better at stopping the run, will be sent into the game and a few of the defensive backs will be taken out. Similarly, if it is thought the next play is going to be a pass, extra defensive backs will be put into the game to substitute for linemen and linebackers; one such substitution is called a **nickel defense**.

In defending against a running play, a defense must make sure to **shoot the gaps,** that is defensive players must be able to ward off the blocks of offensive linemen or running backs who try to push them back from or to one side of the holes. Defenses must also guard against running plays that go around the end of the line, and the best way to do this is to have linebackers who have good lateral movement, meaning that they can quickly run from their positions behind the line of scrimmage to catch up with a ballcarrier coming around the end.

Pass defenses tend to be more complex than rush defenses, since on passing plays one or more receivers will be running past the line of scrimmage, and each, as a potential receiver of a pass, must be covered. On running plays, by contrast, once a running back receives a handoff and gets near to crossing the line of scrimmage, the defense can pretty much key on just this player. Pass defenses use various **coverage schemes**, but there are two basic types: **man-to-man** and **zone** coverage. In man-to-man coverage, one or two defensive players are assigned to watch each wide receiver, running back, or tight end who could go out for a pass. When these offensive players cross the line of scrimmage and run their patterns, the defensive players assigned to them must stay as close as possible to them at all times so that not only will the defenders be able to break up any pass to these receivers, but as a result of this tight coverage the quarterback won't even try to throw a pass and will be forced to scramble, possibly leading to a sack.

In a man-to-man coverage system, cornerbacks are generally assigned to cover wide receivers, usually the ones they line up against before the play starts. Linebackers are assigned to cover tight ends or fullbacks but usually not running backs, who are generally faster runners than linebackers. Speedy running backs are usually watched by the safeties.

Man-to-man coverage generally provides tighter coverage than a zone defense, but the main disadvantage of the man-to-man coverage scheme is that if a defender covering a receiver is beaten, the pass will probably be completed to that receiver, since in man-to-man coverage usually only one defender is assigned to each receiver. This flaw is the primary argument in favor of the zone coverage scheme, which divides the territory on the defense's side of the line of scrimmage into zones that are patrolled by one defender so that receivers running their routes through more than one zone will be guarded by more than one defender. Thus, if a receiver running a route gets by a defender covering a zone close to the line of scrimmage, the receiver going deeper will enter a zone guarded by one of the safeties and still be covered. Another advantage of zone defense over man-to-man coverage is that it positions players in specific parts of the field instead of having them run all over the field chasing receivers. This often has the effect of taking away the **passing lanes** or **seams**, since it is more likely that a defender will be in a position between the quarterback and a receiver.

As mentioned above, defenses can do little but prepare—through formations and personnel changes—for what they think the offense will do, but there are some other things defensive units can do to take a more active role in the game. For example, defensive backs are allowed to **bump** receivers as they go out for passes, but only once and only within five yards of the line of scrimmage. Bumping can be very effective in disrupting the precise timing of the pass patterns that quarterbacks and receivers work on in practice, making it more difficult for the passes to be completed (see "Passing Plays," above).

A more dramatic way defenses can take the game into their own hands is by blitzing. A **blitz** occurs when a defensive player charges through the line of scrimmage as quickly as possible at the snap of the ball, so that he or she cannot be blocked, then tries to tackle the quarterback before either a hand-off or a pass. Blitzes are usually attempted by linebackers or defensive backs since these players have enough quickness to make the play work. Because these players don't cross the line of scrimmage on most plays, a blitz usually surprises the offense. More than one player may blitz on a single play.

Usually, blitzing players come from one end of the line instead of trying to run through the line where one of the offensive linemen can block them. Cornerbacks may also blitz from their positions on each side of the line (this is called a **corner blitz**). This type of blitz can be very effective if the cornerback approaches from the quarterback's blind side—when quarterbacks drop back to pass they usually stand sideways with their backs to one of the sidelines, and if a cornerback blitzes from the side toward which the quarterback's back is turned, the quarterback will probably not see the cornerback coming, or at least not until it's too late to avoid getting sacked.

Offenses are not helpless against blitzes, however. Often a defense will **show blitz**, usually when one or more players creep up to the line of scrimmage during the quarterback's signals. If quarterbacks notice this, they may change the play through an audible to a play that's more likely to succeed in the face of a blitz. One play that is effective in beating a blitz is a screen pass, since in this pass play the quarterback does not need to drop back far and the pass usually goes to a running back who is already in the backfield, blocking for the quarterback. The running back may also see a blitzing defensive player coming and block that player.

Late-Game Strategies

During the first two quarters of a football game, both teams try to execute the game plan they prepared before the game. By the end of the first half, both teams have a pretty good idea of how their plans are working. At halftime the score may be tied, one team may have a small lead, or the lead may be very large. During their meetings in their locker rooms at the end of the first half, both teams make **adjustments** and plan their strategies for the rest of the game based on the current score and the success of their game plans in the first half. This section will discuss the strategies that football teams use toward the end of games.

The score of the game as the second half begins is probably the most important factor in determining what a team will try to do for the rest of the game. If one team is leading the other by a big margin (14 or more points—i.e., at least two touchdowns), the team that is ahead will most likely try to protect its lead. It will do so by employing a ball-control offense that is less likely to lead to turnovers and, more important, will **eat up the clock** (or **kill the clock**) so that the game will finish more quickly with the team maintaining its lead and winning the game. On defense, the team with the lead will employ a **prevent** defense in which the defensive backs and linebackers will be positioned deeper than normal to try to prevent the other team's offense from getting **big plays**. A team using this prevent defense is willing to give up the short pass—that is, by positioning its pass defenders deep it allows the other team to complete short passing plays that gain only a few yards at a time and have little chance of resulting in a score. Prevent defenses are used when the other team is in a position where it has to throw the ball on almost every down, and these defenses may use just three defensive linemen in the down position to rush the quarterback, since there is little need to put several defenders around the line of scrimmage. Defensive pass rushers like this situation because they can run full speed at the quarterback and not worry about having to watch for a run.

The team that is behind in the third and fourth quarters must use the opposite strategies on offense and defense. On offense, the team must risk passing the ball for long completions in order to gain yardage quickly and possibly get a score. The defense will be expecting the other team, which is ahead, mostly to run the football; one thing the defenders on this team must do is try to get a turnover by forcing a fumble or **stripping the ball**.

If a team has a very large lead (about 21 points or more) going into the third or fourth quarter, it is highly unlikely that the other team will come from behind and win. In this situation, both teams make certain adjustments. The team with the big lead will probably try to control the ball and run out the clock as described above, but occasionally a team with a lead will try to **run up the score**. A team might try to run up the score for a number of reasons. One is that playoff positions in football leagues are occasionally determined in part by the number of points a team scores during a season, so it would be to a team's advantage to try to score as many points as possible in all of its games. Another reason a team might try to run up the score might have to do with a rivalry between the teams; if the team with the lead in one game had been beaten badly by the other in a previous game, this team might now try to get some revenge by also trying to win by a large margin. Personal rivalries may play a part, too: a coach could have his team try to run up a score because he is angry with the other team for previously firing him; because that team's players, coaching staff, or ownership made derogatory comments about him and/or his team; or perhaps because the other team has **played dirty** in the game.

The team that is far behind may try desperation measures to score, perhaps not so much to win the game but at least to make the final score a little less one-sided for the sake of pride. This team might do things like try a fairly long pass on every play, even on fourth-down plays and even when the line of scrimmage is in its own territory.

When a game is out of hand and neither team is making a serious effort to change the game's outcome, both teams tend to take their starters out and bring in their **second-string** and **third-string** players—that is, the players who **back up** the starters. Backup players are brought into the game for two main reasons: one is to keep the starters, who as mentioned above are the best players on a team, from being injured and therefore becoming unavailable to play in the next game(s); and the other reason is to give these second- and third-string players some playing time so that they get more game experience.

T I M E · O U T

A less important—but not insignificant—reason for occasionally letting substitute players play is for their morale. All football players go through the drills and calisthenics of practice sessions, but usually only a few get to play during actual games. Players don't like to **warm the bench** throughout the whole game, especially at the high school and Division II or III levels of college football, where many players join a football team primarily to play for fun. Even at the major college level, where almost all players on a team have scholarships (see chapter 4), and at the professional level, where all players are paid good salaries, players want to be in games and not just **ride the bench**.

Close Games

If a football game is near its end and the score is tied, or if one team has a lead of only 10 points or fewer, the action of the game tends to be more exciting than in games where one team has a big lead. When the team that is behind has possession of the ball—or when one team has possession of the ball with only a few minutes left on the game clock—it will use a strategy called the **two-minute drill**, which is similar to the no-huddle offense discussed above. The offense tries to get as much yardage in as little time as possible, mostly by using passing plays in which the receiver runs out of bounds, thereby stopping the game clock until the start of the next play. Even incomplete passes will stop the clock, which is another reason offenses usually only pass in the two-minute offense. Sometimes, though, a receiver will be unable to get out of bounds after catching the ball or the quarterback will get sacked, and in both of these cases the game clock will not be stopped. Therefore, a team will be forced to call a time-out to stop the clock, if it has any remaining (teams must be careful to reserve as many of the three time-outs they get per half until as late in the game as possible, so that they can use them when they're really needed).

TIME·OUT

Another way the offense can stop the clock is by having the quarterback spike the ball down on the ground immediately after getting the snap. This counts as an incomplete pass and stops the clock, although the offense does lose a down.

If the two-minute drill is successful and the team advances deep into its opponent's territory, the team has to decide whether to try for a field goal or a touchdown. Much of this decision is based on the score of the game at the time; obviously, a team that is trailing by more than 3 points has little choice but to go for a touchdown. If there are only a few seconds left in a game in which a team that is trailing its opponent by more than 3 points has the ball, the team will often try what is called a **Hail Mary pass**. In this play, as many eligible receivers as possible run toward or into the other team's end zone, and the quarterback throws a very long pass downfield. Even though the defense expects this play and puts as many defensive backs as it can deep downfield to cover the receivers, the hope is that the pass will be caught by at least one of the receivers in or near the end zone for a final touchdown (possibly after being batted around by the many hands of the offensive and defensive players who will be reaching for the ball). If the touchdown is scored, the extra-point attempt must be allowed even if there is no time left on the game clock, so even if the Hail Mary pass doesn't give the team that scored the touchdown the lead, the extra-point attempt, whether it is for one or two points (see above), could still win the game.

If the team with the ball is trailing by 2 points or 1 point, it will try in the last minutes of the game to get into **field goal range**. Exactly how close a team needs to get depends on how far its field goal kicker can kick and on the weather, but generally a team must get inside its opponent's 40-yard line to have any realistic chance of a field goal attempt being good. The team will try to advance the ball as close as possible to the goal line until there are just a few seconds left on the game clock or until it is fourth down. Then the team brings in its field goal unit to attempt a field goal that may give the team the lead and, with a just a few seconds left, most probably win the game.

TIME·OUT

There are some rituals involved in the kicking of these last-second field goals. If it has any left, the defense usually calls a time-out when it sees the kicker and the field goal unit coming onto the field. The reason for doing this is to rattle the kicker; defenses hope that during time-outs kickers will make themselves nervous thinking about the upcoming field goal attempt and how by kicking it they could win the game single-handedly and be the hero—or how they could miss it and be the **goat**. By making the kicker think too much about the kick, the defense hopes the kicker will be affected emotionally and miss the actual attempt. On the offensive side, there is a tradition for the players on the kicking team to avoid talking to the kicker before the field goal attempt in the belief that doing so would distract the kicker or even jinx the attempt.

If the trailing team has the ball in the last minutes and is behind by exactly 3 points, the team may try for a field goal to tie the game, but sometimes it will try to score a touchdown to win the game even though a touchdown is more difficult to score. The basis for this decision often is the level of football being played. In the NFL, every game that ends in a tie in regulation is followed by an overtime period (see "Length of the Game," above), so a team that kicks a field goal to tie the game at the end of regulation can still win the game in overtime. But in college and high school football, there usually is no overtime period except in championship games, so the team that has the ball often has to decide between trying to kick a field goal—and at best end up with a tie—or going for the win by trying to score a touchdown at the risk of failing and losing the game.

If a team's two-minute drill fails because the team does not score and possession of the ball reverts to the team that has the lead, that team will do certain things to run out the remaining time on the clock. The offense will line up in an extremely tight formation, with no wide receivers and everyone on the line of scrimmage except for the quarterback and one or two running backs, who line up very close behind the quarterback. At the snap of the ball the quarterback will simply kneel to the ground, which is equivalent to downing the ball, and the play will be whistled dead even before any defensive players have time to get past the line of scrimmage and touch the quarter-back. Unless the team on defense has time-outs left and calls them, the clock will continue to run. The quarterback lets as much time on the play clock expire as he or she can without getting a penalty, then does the same on the next snap, and this continues until there are fewer than 40 seconds on the game clock. At this point, the offense does not need to run another play because the game clock will run out before the play clock does, and the rest of the players on both teams start to come onto the field for the postgame handshakes (see "Player Conduct," above).

Sometimes the two-minute drill is successful, and the team that is trailing in the game scores. If there is still time left on the game clock, this team must now kick off. If the kicking team now has the lead, the team will probably not risk kicking the ball all the way to the regular kick returner, the best runner on the receiving team, who is standing at the goal line, but will try a **squib kick**. A kicker produces a squib kick by making contact not with the lower part of the ball on the tee, as on most kickoffs, but near the top of it. **Up men** are usually not skilled players like backs and receivers and are not used to handling and running with the ball, so the hope is that one of them will catch the squib kick and fumble the ball. Even if the player does not fumble, the chances are the player will not be able to run very far and give the receiving team good field position to score in the final seconds of the game.

If the team that scored in the final minutes still does not have the lead, the team will most probably try an **onside kick(off)**. An onside kick is one meant to be recovered by the kicking team, and this is legal as long as the ball goes at least 10 yards and is touched by a member of the receiving team first (in professional football, the ball needs only to go 10 yards before it can be recovered by the kicking team). On most onside kickoff attempts, all the members of the kicking team line up on one side of the kicker, often in a down position similar to that of runners in a footrace. This formation is an obvious sign that an onside kick is being attempted, but onside kicks are almost always attempted only late in games with the kicking team behind, so there is little point in trying to fake a normal kickoff. Occasionally, though, teams may try an onside kickoff during other points in the game when it is not expected by the receiving team, and in these cases the kicking team lines up as normal, with half the members on each side of the kicker.

At a signal from the kicker or another player, all the players on the kicking team start running forward and the kicker, standing in the normal position in the middle of the field, kicks the ball lightly in a diagonal direction along the ground so that it will be bouncing directly in front of the onrushing members of the kicking team. The kicker also tries to make the ball bounce high, which makes it harder for members of the receiving team to handle it. As mentioned above, the ball must travel at least 10 yards, so the receiving team positions almost all of its players exactly 10 yards from the line the kicker kicks off from. Moreover, when an onside kick is expected the players on the receiving team are usually the "hands" team, composed of receivers and backs who are used to catching and handling the ball. It is hoped that one of them will catch and fall on the kicked ball before any member of the kicking team has a chance to get it, thereby giving the receiving team possession of the ball in fairly good field position and effectively ending any hopes the other team has of winning the game.

Sometimes, though, onside kicks are successful and a member of the kicking team will recover the ball, especially as a result of the ball bouncing up and touching a member of the other team who isn't able to grab it in time. In this way, the kicking team gets possession of the ball and another opportunity to score, which is certainly possible given that recovery of an onside kick usually results in possession of the ball close to or maybe even inside of an opponent's territory.

Chapter 4

The Organization of Football

There is much more to American football than the play of the game on the field. Football is an integral part of American culture as well as an important North American industry, and this chapter will examine these aspects of the game. It will discuss the different levels of organized football played in the United States and Canada, including high school football, college football, and professional football as played in the National Football League, the Canadian Football League, and NFL Europe. (Other levels and variants of football, such as youth football and arena football, will be discussed in the next chapter.)

Organizational Aspects Common to All Types of Football

Team Names, Leagues, and Schedules

There are some things that all levels of organized football have in common. One is that all football teams have names. A football team's name usually has two parts. For professional teams, the first part of the name is the name of the city, state, or province in which the team is based and plays its home games. For college and high school teams, the name of the school is the first part.

The second part of a team's name is its nickname. The nickname is usually a plural noun and can be anything from wild animals (usually ones that suggest speed or power, like *Bulls* or *Tigers*) to names taken from the history or culture of the school or local area. Examples of the latter are the NFL's New England Patriots, whose nickname is the name of a group of important figures in the American Revolution who were active in the region of the eastern United States called New England, and the Texas Longhorns of the University of Texas (the names of high school, college, and university teams usually don't include the words *high school, college,* or *university*), who are named for a breed of cattle raised in Texas and important in the history of the state. The nicknames of some football teams are singular nouns—for example, the Calgary Stampede of the CFL or the Stanford Cardinal (of Stanford University)—and sometimes simply the name of one of the team's colors, like the Harvard Crimson (Harvard University).

T I M E · O U T

Like teams in other sports, many U.S. football teams have nicknames representing Native Americans—for example, the NFL's Washington Redskins and the Florida State (University) Seminoles. However, many Native Americans and other people object to naming teams in this manner (even though the practice has been common throughout the history of football), believing that such nicknames make fun of or otherwise degrade Native Americans. As a result, many football teams with such nicknames have adopted other nicknames and logos, but some of the teams' longtime fans don't like to see their team's traditional nickname changed.

All football teams also belong to organizations called **leagues** (or sometimes **conferences**). Each league may be further divided into smaller units called **divisions**. The main purpose of football leagues is to provide for organized competition in the form of a **schedule** of games for each **season**. Every team in a league is usually scheduled to play the same number of games in a season, and depending on the number of games scheduled and the number of teams in the league, the schedule makers try to have each team play against all the other teams in the league at least once. Normally, a team is scheduled to play half of its games **at home** and the other half **on the road** (the latter games are called **road games** or **away games**). Sometimes, though, a team may be scheduled to play an uneven number of games, resulting in one more home than road games or vice versa.

T I M E · O U T

For practical and psychological reasons players on football teams prefer to play their games on their home field. The home team does not have to go through the not-inexpensive and often tiring journey to another town or city to play a game, and the players are already familiar with their home field or stadium and its surroundings. Furthermore, home teams play in front of crowds that support them vocally and cheer when they do well. In contrast, visiting teams receive few if any cheers (usually just from a few fans of theirs who have traveled to their team's road game) and often get booed, and it is an unfortunate fact that some fans verbally harass members of visiting teams and sometimes even throw objects at them (though this last action is illegal and any fan caught doing it will be forced to leave the stands by stadium security). Though many football players deny it, these things have subtle effects on the visiting team players that impair their performance during the game.

During the same period every year (from the late summer to early winter in most football leagues), a new football season with a new schedule is played. The schedule is almost never identical to what it was the previous season. Though a team's opponents may be exactly the same as the previous season (though this is unusual also), the order of games and their location are usually different; in leagues where teams play other members only once, if a team is home against a certain team one season it will most likely be scheduled to travel to that team's home field for their game the next year.

Practices and Training

Football schedules typically require teams to play one game per week, usually on the same day of the week (see below for the normal days that high school, college, and professional teams play their games). Because most football players are usually exhausted and sore for a day or so after playing a full game, a team is never scheduled to play more than one game on a certain day or even in a period of at least four days. Football players usually get the day after a game off, but for most of the rest of the days between one game and another they must attend practice sessions (also called practices). At football practices, the whole team or smaller groups of players (e.g., all the offensive linemen) meet with the coaching staffs to discuss past performance and future strategy, there are drills and calisthenics to improve the players' stamina and agility, and the team rehearses offensive and defensive plays that are cataloged and diagrammed in detail in a team's **playbook**. During practices, a team's starting offense may **scrimmage** against the starting defense or, commonly at the higher levels of football, the first-team offense and defense may practice against the team's second- or third-string defensive and offensive players. Occasionally, teams may also arrange **scrimmages** against other teams that serve as practice sessions for both.

TIME·OUT

A playbook can list a great number of plays, and generally the higher the level of football the more complex a team's playbook may be. A typical playbook of an NFL team, for example, may have 500 different plays, but only a fraction of these are used in any one game.

Practices customarily do not take place on the actual fields where teams play their home games. Instead, most teams practice on fields that are adjacent to their home fields or stadiums or, especially at the major college and professional levels, that are located at special practice facilities that may be miles away from their home stadiums. Wherever teams practice, they do so on fields that are laid out with the lines of standard-size fields and usually have goalposts. Near the field there may also be equipment for training players, such as **tackling dummies** and **blocking sleds**.

During practices, teams not only rehearse plays from their own playbook but also prepare for what their next opponent might do in the game. This information on the tendencies of opponents may come from various sources. If a game has already been played against this opponent, the team not only has the experience of what happened in the game but can also study film that was taken of the game to examine what plays the other team ran and also how the opponent reacted to the plays the team itself attempted. If the opponent has not been played recently, the team can obtain film of games that the opponent has played or can rely on the reports of **scouts** who have gone to the opponent's games and made observations.

However the information about opponents is obtained, it is often used by a **scout team** during practices, especially at the college and professional levels. While a team's **first-string** units focus on learning and practicing their own plays during scrimmages, the scout team lines up in the opponent's formations, runs the same plays, and generally does the kinds of things the other team is expected to do.

During the practices in the week before a game, teams generally engage in full contact, meaning that they wear all their equipment and block and tackle one another about as hard as they would hit their opponents in an actual game. But on the day before a game, teams generally do not practice as vigorously so that the players will be well rested for the game. These practices are short, involving few calisthenics or drills and mostly **walk-throughs** of plays, and there is so little contact that most players don't even wear their pads.

Besides practice sessions, between games players also engage in other activities that help their development. Because being big and strong is so important in modern football, most players engage in weight training, which is a program of weight lifting, exercise, and diet designed to increase players' bulk and strength. Most major college and professional teams employ coaches, trainers, or even physicians who specialize in improving the strength and conditioning of players. Unfortunately, in some instances players illegally take strength- or performance-enhancing drugs like steroids, occasionally with the knowledge and even help of team personnel. For this reason, some football leagues have a policy that their players must be tested for the use of such drugs, and if players are found to have used them they may be **suspended**.

Because of the frequency of injuries in football, many players also must participate in physical rehabilitation under the guidance of their team's medical staff. The treatment is meant to help the players recover from their injuries so that they can play again in games, and especially so they can play at their full ability. Out of concern for the player's overall health, team medical staffs do not want to rush players back into action before they have completely healed, but since football seasons last only a few months there is some pressure to get injured players back into action as soon as possible, especially if they are star players.

Game Statistics

Once football games have been played, the results of the game—which team won, which team lost, and the final score of the game—are recorded, and also the statistics, or "stats," detailing what went on in the game (particularly how individual players performed) are registered. In all football leagues, there is an official record, called the **standings**, that indicates how many games have been won, lost, or tied by each team in the league. However these weekly standings are made available—whether posted in a league office or at the headquarters of teams, published in newspapers or magazines, or shown on television or computer sites—they are arranged with the name of the team with the best **record**—that is, the team with the most wins and fewest losses—at the top of the standings, followed by the number of games it has won and lost. The team's record may also be given in the form of a percentage (to three places) showing

```
┌─────────────────────────────────────────────────┐
│  ┌─────────────────┐                             │
│  │ T I M E · O U T │                             │
│  └─────────────────┘                             │
│                                                   │
│  The following abbreviations are often used when  │
│  giving football standings in print: W = wins,    │
│  L = losses, T = ties, GB = games behind,         │
│  PCT (or Pct.) = winning percentage, PF = points  │
│  for (total points scored), PA = points against   │
│  (total points scored by opponents in games       │
│  against this team). As an example, here are the   │
│  final standings of the NFL's AFC Central          │
│  Division after the 1996 season:                  │
```

	W	L	T	GB	PCT	PF	PA
Pittsburgh Steelers	10	6	0	–	.625	344	257
Jacksonville Jaguars	9	7	0	1	.562	325	355
Cincinnati Bengals	8	8	0	2	.500	372	369
Houston Oilers	8	8	0	2	.500	345	319
Baltimore Ravens	4	12	0	6	.250	371	441

what percent of its games it has won. The rest of the teams in the league or division and the number of games they've won and lost are listed below the team in first place in order of their own records, the teams with better records listed after the team in first place, and so on down to the team with the worst record. The records of all the teams that are not in first place may be followed by a number indicating how many **games behind** they are. And following all the above information, the standings could show how many points each team has scored in all its games and also how many points in total have been scored against it.

Football Championships

At the end of a football league's season, when all the scheduled games have been played, the standings are often important in determining the champion of the league. In the simplest system, used most often at the high school and Division II and III levels of college football, the team at the top of the standings at the end of the season is declared the champion of that league, conference, or division. Sometimes a team has such a good record that it **clinches** first place even before all its games have been played.

In some leagues, especially at the major college and professional levels, being in first place at the end of a season is not enough to guarantee a championship. There may be a **playoff** (**game**) between the teams in first or second place in a league or division or between the first-place teams of a league's divisions. Sometimes more than one playoff game may be held; **semifinal games** (or **semifinals**) may be played by the four or more best teams in a league, with the winners of these games advancing to a **final** or **championship game**. The winner of this game is declared the champion of the league even if, as often happens, the team that wins this game actually did not have the best record during the season (often referred to as the **regular season** to distinguish it from the round of **postseason** games). But finishing the regular season with the best record is still an asset because a team that does this usually gets **home-field advantage** in all its playoff games. In addition, some leagues allow the one or two teams with the best regular-season records to have a first-round **bye**.

T I M E · O U T

In some leagues that normally have no postseason play, when two or more teams are tied at the top of the standings after the regular season each team is declared a cochampion. In other leagues, teams tied for first place may play a special playoff game to determine the champion.

The reward for being a champion of a football league is often no more than the pride team members may feel for this accomplishment. In most leagues, however, teams who win a championship are rewarded with something more tangible, often a trophy inscribed with the team name and the year it won the championship. Especially if the championship is won in a playoff game, the trophy may be awarded by league officials to the winning team in a brief ceremony immediately after the game—in the locker room of the victorious team or perhaps even on the field at the end of the game so that the home crowd (if the home team wins the game) can share in the celebration of its team's victory.

Team and Individual Player Statistics

Statistics kept during a game can give an indication of how well a team performed no matter what the final score was. Some of the records kept for both teams during a game are the total yardage gained by each team's offense (which can be broken down into yards gained through rushing and through passing), the total number of first downs earned, the number of turnovers and takeaways, the total number of penalties called against each team, and the amount of yards each team was penalized.

Statistics on the performance of individual players are also kept. These include pass attempts and completions, yards passing, and interceptions by quarterbacks; rushing attempts and yards gained by running backs; numbers of passes received by receivers and how many yards they gained; field goal attempts and field goals kicked by placekickers; and punt attempts and punt yardage by punters. These individual statistics are published in newspaper reports of games, and they may also be given on radio or television reports or broadcasts of the game as it is happening. They are also kept by each team (and often other teams in the league keep statistics on players on other teams) and are important for the purpose of evaluating players; players' statistics not only help in decisions about which players get to be starters but also are used in determining which players are allowed to remain on the team and which players get **cut**. Leagues also keep track of the performance statistics of players over a season, since these help in determining the best players in the league overall or at individual positions, and often help in the presentation of awards after the season is over.

T I M E · O U T

Passing and receiving yardage is calculated from the line of scrimmage to the yard at which the receiver catches the ball, plus any yardage the receiver picks up by running with the ball. Thus, both a completed pass from the quarterback to a receiver 10 yards away, who then runs 40 yards for a touchdown, and a bomb that goes 50 yards downfield to a receiver who is in the end zone or who gets tackled at the spot of the reception would both be counted as 50 yards in the quarterback's passing yards and the receiver's receiving yardage.

Exhibition Games

There are some games on a football team's schedule that are not considered official games—that is, they are not counted in the standings and the players' performances in the games are not included in individual or team statistics for the season. These are called **exhibition games**, and they are usually played before the regular season starts against opponents that the team doesn't play during the regular season. The purpose of exhibition games is primarily to give teams some practice before the regular-season games start, but they may have some other public-relations purposes, such as to demonstrate the game of football in new markets (see "National Football League" under "Professional Football," below). Exhibition games are typically played only by professional teams, but high school and college teams also play games similar to exhibition games, often called nonleague or interleague games. The difference between these and exhibition games is that the former do count in the standings, even though the teams may be from different leagues or divisions. A similarity between these games and exhibitions is that they are normally scheduled to be played at the beginning of the season since in order to increase the competitive value of their games, teams from the same league play each other toward the end of the season, when victories or losses in single games could decide league championships. Also, games between **traditional rivals** tend to be the last or nearly the last games of the year, especially at the college and high school levels.

Another kind of exhibition game is an **all-star game**. This game is between two teams made up of players chosen from all of the teams in a league. The players selected for all-star games are ones who have played exceptionally well during the season, and the selection is usually made through a vote of the head coaches in the league (in professional football, players also have a vote). All-star games are usually held only after the conclusion of a league's regular season and postseason, so that if players get hurt in the all-star game—not an unlikely possibility given the risks of football, even in a game like this in which players usually don't play as hard as in games that count—their teams won't miss their services during the regular season or playoffs. The players are divided into two teams, usually based on the divisions of the league (i.e., all the players from teams in one division or conference form one team, and those from teams in the other make up the opposing team). As mentioned above, the competition in all-star games is not very intense. One reason for this is that the players are not used to playing with each other, and another is that the players do not have as much motivation to win, since all-star games are held mainly to honor the outstanding players of a league; there is usually no incentive for a team to win except pride, though occasionally a trophy or money prize may be given to the winning team (as in the NFL; see "National Football League" under "Professional Football," below).

Media Coverage of Football

The popularity of football in North America leads to—and many people would say is in large part caused by—the great attention the game gets in the various popular media. Football at all levels (like most major North American sports, it must be conceded) gets extensive coverage in the sports sections of newspapers and magazines and on television and radio sports reports. There are also print publications and television and radio shows devoted exclusively to football, usually concerned with a specific level of football or even just one team. The publications that focus on a single level of football often include ratings of the best players at that level, and coaches and scouts often consult these (as when colleges look for high school players to recruit; see "College Football," below). And football is well covered in new media; there are numerous sites on the World Wide Web devoted to football, many dedicated to a single team or star player. Some professional and major college teams also display signs with the address of their official World Wide Web sites inside their stadiums, making sure the address is visible to viewers of the television broadcasts of their games.

Almost all high school, college, and professional football games are broadcast live either on the radio or on television (and often both), and most people in the United States and Canada are exposed to football in this way instead of playing in or attending games themselves. Indeed, broadcasts of college and professional football games are among the most popular sports programs on television, and it can be argued that the prevalence of football on television is the major reason for the popularity of the sport. (See especially "National Football League" under "Professional Football," below, for a discussion of how major television network coverage of NFL games, particularly on ABC's *Monday Night Football,* helped make the NFL the dominant sports league in the United States.) TV and radio broadcasts of football games usually feature one announcer who does the **play-by-play** and at least one other announcer who provides the **color** or commentary on the action of the game, talking (usually only between plays) about the strategy of the teams, the current and past performance of the players, or background on the game, teams, or players. On television, commentators can use video replays of previous plays to talk about them, and they often use a device called a Telestrator to make marks—pointing to such things as the ball or specific players and their movements—that appear on viewers' screens and help them understand details of the action.

Fan Attendance at Football Games

Football games at all levels are attended by spectators, who are also often called **fans**. These spectators pay fees to be allowed into a football field (which is usually fenced off) or into a stadium to watch a football game. The fees range from a few dollars to see some high school games to 50 dollars or more for a good seat at a regular-season professional game (prices for postseason games are even higher). In stadiums or fields where individual seats in the stands are numbered, a spectator buys a printed ticket with the number of a seat on it and thus reserves the seat to watch one game. Tickets may be bought at a ticket window or booth right outside the stadium on the day of the game or during the week before it, or the tickets may be ordered in advance from the home team or through a ticket-selling service. Generally, the closer the seat is to the field the more expensive the price of the ticket will be, and seats that face one of the sidelines are more expensive than end-zone seats, which are seats in a section of the stands opposite one of the end zones. Also, some stadiums have an upper deck, and these higher seats are less expensive than ones that are lower and closer to the field.

T I M E · O U T

Often tickets can also be bought from people who purchased them previously and sell them outside of stadiums just before a game because for some reason they can't or don't want to use their ticket. These people usually sell the tickets for the same price they bought them or for a lower price, but occasionally they will try to get more for the tickets than they paid for them, especially if it's an important game. This is called **scalping**, and in many places it is illegal. Buying tickets from private individuals is also risky, because there is the chance that the tickets may be counterfeit. Many people who buy such tickets end up going into the stadium, finding the holders of the real tickets in the same seats, and being told to leave the stadium by the authorities. If they're lucky, they will find the person who sold them the phony tickets, but this is difficult with the huge crowds milling around stadiums before games.

Fans can also purchase **season tickets** for the home games of most major college and professional football teams. People who buy season tickets usually get the best seats in a stadium, as well as other benefits, such as membership in certain clubs for fans of the team and a good choice of seats at the stadiums where the team plays its road games during a season. (Some fans of teams are willing to travel—sometimes thousands of miles—to other sites to watch their team play.)

A newer type of seating at football games is luxury boxes or luxury suites (or skyboxes, which are high up in the stadium). Found mostly in professional football stadiums, these are areas at the press-box level that are set off from the rest of the seating areas in the stadium and provide services like catering and communications to one group of fans. These luxury boxes are expensive, costing several thousand dollars, and they are usually rented not by individuals but by corporations or other organizations that can afford the high fees. This kind of seating has become such an important source of revenue for professional football teams (and for other major sports teams as well) that most modern stadiums have been specifically designed to include them, and many teams have moved out of cities because their stadiums, which the teams may have played in for years before, had few or no luxury suites.

Even though ticket prices may be high and going to a football game often requires an investment of several hours of a person's time (spent not just watching the game but in traveling to and from the stadium, which is often time-consuming because of the large crowds and resulting traffic jams), people who attend football games are not necessarily rabid football fans. For some Americans, going to a football game may be just something to do with other people, like going to a movie or some other sporting event. Other people may actually be interested in football but are casual fans; if their home team has a good record going into the game or if it is playing against another good team or in an important game, they may decide to go to the game and the game may become a **sellout**, meaning that the tickets for all the seats have been sold. If the team is not doing well or the game does not promise to be competitive (or if the weather is bad), a smaller crowd may attend and there may be many **no-shows**. The number of spectators who attend football games may range from a few hundred at a high school game to a crowd of more than 100,000 at some of the larger stadiums. (Interestingly, the football stadiums in the United States with the biggest seating capacity are not stadiums for professional teams but ones used primarily for college football; two of the largest are the Rose Bowl in Pasadena, California, and Michigan Stadium in Ann Arbor, Michigan.)

The behavior of spectators at football games varies with each individual's personality, but fans at all football games can be expected to act in certain ways. They cheer, applaud, or whistle when the home team makes a good play or scores, and some fans boo when the home team plays poorly or something good happens for the visiting team. Boos are also heard when the officials penalize the home team or when they don't penalize the visiting team for commiting what the fans think is an infraction. If a penalty is called against the visiting team, the home fans usually cheer.

Fans may do more than just react to what's happening in the game; sometimes they may try to affect it. As mentioned in the last chapter, when the visiting team is on offense, the home crowd often cheers loudly as the quarterback is calling signals, especially on crucial plays in the game, in order to distract the offensive players and make their hearing the signals difficult. When the home team is on offense, fans may cheer loudly to spur their team on, but they always quiet down as the quarterback calls signals. If the team has a fourth down and short yardage, members of the crowd will often shout "Go!" to encourage the team to go for the first down instead of punting, and they may boo loudly if the team decides not to try for the first down (even if the team's coach has sound strategic reasons for not trying for a first down in the situation). Fans also often boo play calling that they think is too conservative—for example, running the ball when the fans think the team ought to pass, such as when the team is behind in the game. And when the visiting team attempts a field goal or an extra point, the fans who are sitting in the end zone seats directly behind the goalpost toward which the kick will be attempted make noise and wave their arms, hoping that this will distract the placekicker.

To show support for their team, fans often come to games wearing replica team jerseys or other apparel with the colors, name, or insignia of their team, or sometimes they just wear clothing that is the same color as one of their team's primary colors. Fans may also bring signs or posters expressing support for the team or one of its players, and some of the larger posters made from cloth may be hung on walls inside the stadium. At major college or professional games that are going to be televised, fans may also bring signs with the name or logo of the television network broadcasting the game in the hope that the network's cameras will focus on them during breaks in the action. If they do get on camera, the fans often mug for TV by waving, gesturing or shouting things in support of their team (which the TV audience may not always be able to hear). As mentioned above, a football game often has a festive atmosphere and some fans can display exuberant or even bizarre behavior (especially if they've had too much beer; see below). Spectators may come dressed in costumes that have nothing to do with the game or the teams playing in it (for example, they may come dressed as gorillas, Elvis Presley, etc.), and some male fans might undress completely above the waist even in freezing weather. Another tradition among crowds at football games and other American sporting events is to do the **wave**. And sometimes a fan will toss a large inflated ball, such as a beach ball, up in the air and members of the crowd will amuse themselves by hitting it and keeping it bouncing in the air as long as possible.

At almost every football game, spectators can purchase food or drinks from booths, called concession stands or concessions, located outside the field or stadium or in the inner parts of stadiums away from the main seating areas. The choice of food at concessions is usually not very great—really just snacks—though a few of the newer stadiums feature built-in restaurants. Occasionally alcoholic drinks like beer are sold at football games, but the sales are usually restricted to the game's first half to prevent spectators from getting drunk and causing trouble. At many games, fans can also purchase souvenirs or merchandise relating to the home team or to other football or sports teams. The concessions and merchandise stands do most of their business during halftimes and before games as spectators are entering the stadium. Some sales may take place when games are over and the fans are leaving (though many fans leave games before they are officially over, especially if the games are one-sided), but usually the crush of people filing out of a stadium makes transacting business difficult, especially for the customers.

T I M E · O U T

Another tradition is **tailgating** or holding **tailgate parties**. These are gatherings of fans in the parking lots near football fields or stadiums in the hours before the start of a game. Because most games are attended by large crowds, fans going to the game in their own cars must arrive early both to get a parking space close to the stadium and to avoid the congestion that occurs in the hour or so immediately preceding the start of the game. The fans who arrive early often stay in or near their cars, since spectators are generally not allowed inside stadiums earlier than about an hour and a half before kickoff time. These fans often bring food and drinks, and may even bring portable grills for cooking the food, and they pass the time before going into the stadium by eating and socializing. The name of these parties comes from the word *tailgate*, which is a name for the door at the rear of some cars and trucks that opens downward; fans often put food or even sit on these open doors during tailgate parties.

Cheerleaders and Mascots

Last but certainly not least, another aspect of football that doesn't involve the game itself but is an integral part of the culture of football at all levels is **cheerleaders**. These are people dressed in special uniforms who, during games, remain outside of the limit or restraining lines on one side of the field near or behind an end zone and interact with fans, especially those closest to the field. As their name implies, cheerleaders lead the crowd in ritualized cheers in support of one team, often through the use of an instrument called a megaphone that amplifies the cheerleaders' voices. These cheers are usually accompanied by stylized movements of the cheerleaders' bodies, made more noticeable when they are holding **pom-poms**. Sometimes cheerleaders may do more than these simple routines to entertain and stimulate the crowd; they may attempt acrobatic maneuvers such as a "pyramid," in which a group of cheerleaders will stand or kneel on the ground, a smaller group will stand on the first group's shoulders or kneel

on their backs, a smaller group will get on top of the second group, and so on until one cheerleader is at the top of the formation. Especially at the professional football level, cheerleaders may be highly trained dance and musical performers who go through sophisticated routines for the audience during time-outs or other breaks in the action of the game. Cheerleaders can even become celebrities in their own right; probably the best example is the Dallas Cowboy Cheerleaders, who are also popular and sought-after entertainers outside of Cowboys football games.

Most cheerleaders are female, but, particularly at the high school and college levels, some cheerleaders may be male. Like players, cheerleaders have to try out and be selected to get on a team's cheerleading squad; the criterion for selection is usually the person's ability to perform cheerleading routines, but physical attractiveness does play an important role, especially for professional football cheerleaders. Cheerleaders practice their routines as much as players practice their plays, and being a good cheerleader often requires learning the fundamentals early in life (indeed, alongside many Pop Warner football programs for boys there are cheerleading programs for girls; see "Youth Football" in chapter 5).

Cheerleaders often work in conjunction with personnel called **mascots**. These are persons who dress in costumes that have something to do with a team, especially its nickname (for example, the mascot for a team called the Hawks might wear a hawk costume). Mascots function like cheerleaders—that is, they interact with and excite the team's fans, and they may even participate in the cheerleaders' routines—but more often mascots just roam the areas near the stands independently. The costumes mascots wear are often comical, and mascots may perform funny routines, clowning around with fans and with people on the sidelines (but usually not with players, coaches, or other team staff or officials, who are expected to be paying serious attention to the game in progress).

TIME·OUT

The term *mascot* used to apply to live animals that were brought onto the field and kept on the sidelines, either in cages or on leashes. These animals were often the same as the nicknames of the teams—for example, a team nicknamed the Panthers might have an actual panther in a cage as its mascot.

High School Football

The first organizational level of football to be examined for its special characteristics is high school football. As the name indicates, this is football played by players who are students at U.S. and Canadian secondary schools, usually lumped together under the term *high schools*. Thus, the general age range of the players is from 14 to 18, though most high school football players are 16 or 17 years of age. Most players at the high school level are male, but there are some female players. All students who want to play high school football (or any other competitive sport) must pass a physical examination by a medical doctor (this is also called a physical) before they even start to practice, since a player with an undiagnosed medical condition like a heart problem could have a serious health risk in playing a strenuous game like football.

When a high school football team has many members and a wide age range, the team may be divided into **varsity** and **junior varsity** squads. The varsity consists of the oldest and the best players and is the unit that competes during the team's regularly scheduled games. Some exceptionally good-sized or talented sophomores or freshmen may also be allowed to compete on the varsity level. The junior varsity consists of the younger players who are not yet starters (but many of them will be when they are juniors and seniors), and occasionally the junior varsity may scrimmage or play some games on its own against the junior varsity units of other schools so that the players get some game experience and improve their playing skills.

High school teams do not have as large a coaching staff as college or professional teams do. At most, there may be a head coach and a few assistants; some smaller schools may have only one coach who handles all the coaching duties. Also unlike their college and professional counterparts, high school coaches usually have few team-related duties in the **off-season**. The main reason for this is that high school coaches, unlike the coaches at higher levels, do not have to **recruit** players, since the players available to play for a high school team are taken from that school's population of students, which is usually determined by the students' residence in the boundaries of the school district. (Even private high schools, which accept students in most cases irrespective of where they live, usually do not spend a lot of money or effort recruiting football players.) And few school districts are willing to spend the money needed to maintain a football organization in the off-season, since high school football competition doesn't offer schools the kind of monetary and publicity value that college football does. As a result, high school football coaches normally hold other jobs in their school districts; often they coach other sports when these are in season, or they may be full-time teachers of physical education or other subjects.

The leagues into which high school football competition is organized are based on geography and the size of school districts. Every U.S. state sets up leagues and levels of competition for its schools—not just for football but for all sports. The state is divided into several regions, and within each region or section schools are classified based on the number of students in each district, which can vary from several thousand to only a few hundred students. Football leagues are then set up in each region that consist of schools in the same class, meaning they have roughly the same enrollments. The reason that leagues are set up this way is to ensure that competition between the schools will be balanced; a school district with a large number of students has a much larger talent pool, and the chances of finding more big and talented athletes are greater in this district.

Schedules are made for each of the teams in the leagues or conferences into which they are placed. These schedules may include a few games against nonleague opponents, but high school teams are rarely scheduled to play more than eight regular-season games. Games are played either on Friday nights at fields that have artificial lighting or on Saturday afternoons. Teams generally travel to road games in school buses, sometimes fully dressed in their uniforms and equipment if there are no locker rooms available at the facility where they'll be playing. Practices are held on weekday afternoons after the students' school day is over (i.e., after around 3 o'clock in the afternoon).

At the end of the regular season, most states have a playoff system to determine the state champion in each class. The class champions from each section (who are often determined by a playoff game or games between the best teams within the region) play each other in a series of **single-elimination** games until there is one team that has won all its games; this team is declared the state champion for its class. Because there would be a competitive disadvantage, teams from different classes do not play each other to determine an overall state champion.

As in college football (see below), high school football has ways to honor its best players. Many leagues and most sections select **all-stars,** and in some cases there may be a special game between groups of these all-stars (college scouts may attend these games looking for outstanding high school players to recruit). Most states also honor their best high school football players by naming them as all-state players. These all-star and all-state players are usually selected through the votes of coaches and sometimes sportswriters.

Many players, coaches, and parents of players take high school football very seriously, seeing it especially as a means for obtaining a college scholarship. But for the most part, high school football lacks the competitiveness and businesslike aspects that characterize higher levels of the game. In high school football in particular, other participants besides the players play conspicuous roles at a game, partly due to the intimacy that results from the fact that a high school team represents a relatively small community (a school district). Cheerleaders, for example, are noticeable at a game, especially since they can be easily heard in the small confines of most high school fields. Similarly, the school marching bands that are present at almost every high school football game are hard to ignore, especially since they make music almost continually between plays, both to entertain the crowd and to encourage their team. (School bands often sit in a section of the stands during each half, coming onto the field only during the pregame and during halftime.) And on the day or night before a big game (or sometimes in the afternoon before a game to be played later that night), a **pep rally** may be held.

Finally, it should be noted that high school football does not get as much exposure in the media, especially the broadcast media, as college and professional football do. Some high school games are broadcast on local radio stations and occasionally games are seen on television, especially playoff or championship games or important games between large schools. High school football does get fairly good coverage in local newspapers, however. An important aspect of newspaper coverage of high school football is the weekly rankings of the best teams by class in each state, based on polls of sportswriters and coaches.

College Football

Who Plays College Football

As the name indicates, college football is played by teams made up of students from U.S. and Canadian post-secondary institutions, which are colleges, universities, and other schools students attend after finishing high school. There is a great variety of post-secondary institutions that may field football teams, from two-year community colleges (often referred to as junior colleges) with a few thousand students and even smaller technical or specialized schools to larger four-year public or private colleges or major universities with thousands of students. In the rest of this section, these various post-secondary institutions will all be referred to with the term *college*.

To play football for a college team, a player must have been admitted to the college under normal admissions procedures. This means that the student must be a graduate of an accredited secondary school and to play at four-year institutions, he or she must have achieved an acceptable score on standardized academic achievement tests such as the SAT (Scholastic Aptitude Test) or the ACT (American College Test). If a high school student doesn't have a high enough score to be admitted to a four-year college or just is not academically prepared for post-secondary education, the student may spend a year or so at a preparatory (or "prep") school, which is a private secondary school that specializes in preparing students for college. At such a school, the student may also keep playing football, playing for the prep school's team if it has one.

Only undergraduates (students in their first four years of college) can join college football teams. After entering college, a student can play no more than four years of college football. However, NCAA rules permit players to **redshirt** for one football season, usually during their first or freshman year. Redshirt freshmen can participate in team practices but cannot play in games; in this way players are able to retain their eligibility to play for the next four seasons. During their redshirt year they get valuable exposure to the world of college football and they also receive extra time to adjust to college academics. They may also use the time to get bigger and stronger through weight training and conditioning and through the natural development that comes from being a year older. If a player does play during his or her first year in college, the player is called a **true freshman.**

U.S. college football teams belonging to the NCAA are organized into three major divisions based primarily on their level of competitiveness, which derives from factors such as the school's student population and athletic budget. These divisions are referred to as Division I (the most competitive level), Division II, and Division III (the least competitive). Furthermore, Division I is split into two subdivisions: Division I-A, the more competitive, and Division I-AA. A major difference that separates Division I teams from Division II and III and also junior college programs is that most Division I schools offer **scholarships** to their players.

Because Division I colleges offer scholarships that are worth thousands of dollars, these schools attempt to recruit the best high school players. The recruiting of most Division I players usually begins before these players' senior years in high school, and sometimes even before they are in high school. Through a network of scouts who work for the colleges directly or offer their services independently, Division I colleges try to identify **prospects** while they are in high school or in some cases as early as when they are playing youth football (see chapter 5). National sports magazines that include rankings of top high school players can also be consulted. And sometimes high school players—or their parents or high school coaches—will contact colleges themselves to let them know of their interest in playing for these schools, sometimes including in their correspondence videotape of the players in action in games.

From their knowledge of the high school players available every year, Division I colleges make decisions about which players they want to recruit. Most colleges try to recruit players from all over the United States and Canada (and sometimes from other countries as well), but recruiting usually emphasizes regional players. For example, recruiters from a college located in the state of Georgia might focus on trying to attract players from schools in the southern region of the

United States, knowing that their chances of successfully recruiting players from this region are better—these players will more likely be familiar with this college's and other regional football programs, and they will probably be more comfortable attending a college closer to home. In general, colleges try to recruit the most talented players, but sometimes particular players are targeted to fill certain needs on the team; for example, if a college team's starting quarterback is going to be lost to graduation—that is, unable to play the next season because the current season is the player's fourth and final year of eligibility—and the current backup quarterback will take over the starting role next season, the team will want to find a high school quarterback to become the backup or perhaps even be the starter the next season.

The responsibility for recruiting players falls the heaviest on the coaching staffs of college teams. Head coaches, in particular, are usually too busy during the season to scout prospective players, so occasionally assistant coaches may travel to watch high school players in person (though usually assistant coaches are also too busy during the regular season). But in the off-season, coaches—including head coaches—spend most of their time contacting recruits and traveling to the recruits' hometowns to meet them and their families. The recruiting process usually starts with a letter sent by the team's coaching staff to the recruit, indicating the college's interest in the player. The letter usually invites the player to make a visit to the college and usually makes an informal offer of a scholarship. If the recruit is especially desirable, the player may be contacted by phone and/or asked to allow a visit by a member of the coaching staff. If the coach does get to visit the player, the coach will try to convince the player—by appealing to the player's family, if necessary—to attend and play football for the college. Sometimes a member of the college's alumni association who lives in the player's city or area will also contact the player on behalf of the college.

TIME·OUT

The NCAA has very strict rules against any form of payment or giving of gifts to recruits as either an inducement for them to play for a certain team or as an incentive at any time while they are in college playing for the team. College football players are supposed to be amateurs, and any violation of the rule that players are not to be paid are punished with sanctions against the college and/or the declaration that the player is ineligible to continue playing college football.

Most players who are contacted by one college are recruited by at least a few others (some highly prized recruits may hear from as many as a hundred college football programs). Recruits who return the interest of a college may make an official visit to the college's campus. In some ways these are similar to the visits any prospective student may make to a college campus, but for football recruits they are much more structured, including meetings with some of the team's coaches and players and tours of the college's football and other facilities. An official visit by a football recruit is reported to the NCAA and is seen as one of the clearest signs that a player is seriously considering attending that particular college.

The final step in the recruiting process is the signing of a **letter of intent**. This is done after the high school player makes a decision about which college to play for, the decision often being based on how much playing time the player can expect to get (i.e., whether the player can expect to be a starter in a reasonable amount of time—say, by the player's junior year). Every year the NCAA establishes a date in early February on or before which all senior high school players must sign a letter of intent that locks the players into attending a certain college for at least their freshman years. Students can also make a decision on which college to attend well before the national letter of intent day. Some players may decide even before their senior year in high school which college they plan to attend and may make a verbal commitment to sign a letter of intent at the appropriate time; this leads other colleges to stop trying to recruit that player.

Players also occasionally transfer from one college to another. This is permitted as long as players do not exhaust their overall NCAA eligibility. For example, if a player plays two full seasons at one school and transfers to another, the player will have only two more years of eligibility at the new school. If a scholarship player transfers to another college, the player will usually be awarded a scholarship at the new school, though this is not guaranteed (and thus there is some risk for scholarship players who want to transfer out of one program because they are unhappy about a lack of playing time, because they don't like the coaching staff, etc.). It is also common for junior college players to transfer to a four-year college, where, depending on how long they played at the junior college, they may have two or three years of eligibility left.

Even at Division I-A colleges, not all the players on football teams receive scholarships. Under NCAA rules, each college can offer only a limited number of scholarships to players, and the number of scholarship players admitted under these rules would not be enough to field a complete team. Therefore, most teams have several **walk-ons**, who end up as third-string players or even lower on the **depth chart** and rarely get to play in games. However, a few of these players improve their skills so much—or get a chance to show their ability, which was somehow overlooked when colleges were recruiting and offering scholarships to other players—that they become regular players and might even receive scholarships for their final year(s) on the team. Some walk-ons even become star players and get drafted into professional football.

Division II and III college football teams also recruit players, but since they cannot offer scholarships, the best high school players invariably go on to attend Division I colleges.

Therefore, Division II and III teams focus their recruiting efforts on players who are not likely to be sought by Division I colleges—that is, players who are smaller and/or less athletically talented. Particularly in Division III, many college students try out for and make football teams without having been recruited while they were in high school.

T I M E · O U T

Some special cases regarding football scholarships and Division I football should be mentioned. First, colleges belonging to the Division I-AA conference known as the Ivy League (see below) are unusual among Division I colleges in that they do not offer scholarships to their football players or to any members of their other sports teams. Part of the reason has to do with the high academic reputation of the Ivy League colleges, which are considered to be among the best post-secondary institutions in the United States; the emphasis on athletics that many people think would be shown if scholarships were given at these schools is avoided by not offering scholarships. This means that students who play football for Ivy League schools must find other ways to meet the costs of tuition and room and board, like all other students at these colleges (and tuition at Ivy League colleges is among the highest of any U.S. colleges). Nevertheless, Ivy League teams still attract some very good players who may pass up full scholarship offers at other colleges but who think getting an Ivy League education while also playing Division I football is worth the cost.

The second special case is that of the institutions for training officers for the U.S. armed services, namely the U.S. Military Academy at West Point, New York (whose team is usually referred to as just "Army"), the U.S. Naval Academy in Annapolis, Maryland (called "Navy"), and the U.S. Air Force Academy in Colorado Springs, Colorado ("Air Force"). These are accredited institutions of higher education just like other U.S. colleges, but students are admitted to these academies through a special procedure starting with nomination by their local congressional representative. Candidates for admission to these military academies must be highly qualified both academically and athletically.

At the academies, students are trained to become officers in the respective branches of the U.S. military, but each academy has a variety of sports teams that compete with other NCAA colleges. Since the education and training the football players receive at these academies is free, they can in a sense be considered scholarships; but the experience of players at the academies, enduring the rigors of military training and academy life, is considerably different from that of players at other colleges. Another difference between football players at the U.S. military academies and other college players is that immediately after the former graduate, they must serve five years in their respective branches of the U.S. armed forces. Thus, the few military players who are good enough to be drafted by the NFL must wait these five years before playing professional football, though in some cases a special waiver may be made so that players can fulfill their military duty at a later time and play professional football immediately after graduation, while they are younger and their football skills are fresh.

In discussing college football and its relation to high school football, it should be emphasized that only a small percentage of high school players get the opportunity to play football in college, and fewer still get a college football scholarship. (And among all college football players including scholarship players, very, very few get the chance to play professional football.) Nevertheless, recent high school players remain the primary source of college players, and thus the general age range of college football players is from 18 to 21.

There are many college players older than 21 due to military service, serious injury, or some other reason that kept them from entering college immediately after high school or temporarily interrupted their college careers. It is even not unknown for some players in their 30s and 40s to be playing college football, especially at the Division III and junior college levels; these older players may have entered college much later in their lives than most college students do and just wanted to exercise their right to try to play college football, with little illusion that at their ages they would have any shot at playing professional ball.

The College Football Season

College football teams play 10 or a few more regularly scheduled games. The first games are played in early September, often during the weekend preceding the American Labor Day holiday (which falls on the first Monday in September), and sometimes the first games are played in late August. Games are scheduled for every week that follows; there may be some **open** or **bye weeks**, but a team usually has no more than one open week in a row. Most of the last regularly scheduled games take place in November before the holiday known as Thanksgiving (the fourth Thursday in November), though games may be played into the first week of December. Then comes the college postseason, which consists of bowl games (see below); these begin in mid-December, though most, especially the most important ones such as the Orange, Fiesta, Sugar, and Rose Bowls (see below), are played around the beginning of the New Year, either on New Year's Eve (the day before the New Year), New Year's Day, or the day after the beginning of the New Year (January 2). Thus, teams playing in bowl games have a break of two or more weeks between their last regularly scheduled game and the bowl game. And a few college all-star games (see below) are played in early January.

T I M E · O U T

A few college teams play their first games of the season at **neutral sites**, some of which may be outside the United States. There is also a special game, called the Kickoff Classic, played at the beginning of every college football season at Giants Stadium in East Rutherford, New Jersey, which is traditionally the first Division I-A game of the year.

Most of the games college teams play are against teams from their own conference or league; college teams usually play each team in their league once. Most teams also play a few games against opponents from other conferences but usually at the same competitive level—that is, Division I-A teams play only other Division I-A teams and so on, though games between teams at different levels (particularly between Division I-A and I-AA teams) are not unheard of. These nonleague or nonconference games do not count in determining the championship of the league, but they are part of a team's overall record, which is what often determines the team's chances for postseason play. Thus, even though these games may lack the intensity and rivalry of games against teams from the same conference, they are still important. And some nonleague games may in fact be very highly contested, especially if they are between teams that have been traditional rivals even though they are not in the same conference (or most games any team plays against Notre Dame, which is the team with the richest tradition in college football) or between teams from different leagues that are nonetheless close to each other geographically (a game between Florida and Florida State, for example). Nonconference games are usually arranged between colleges several years before the seasons in which the games are actually played, though the specific dates usually are scheduled only about a year in advance and the specific times of the games may not even be set until the week before the game, based on the programming needs of the networks broadcasting the games on television (see below).

Almost all teams at the Division I, II, and III levels belong to a conference, though there are some **independents**. More and more independent teams are joining established conferences or forming new ones with other independents, however. One reason for this is that it is becoming increasingly difficult for independent teams to schedule games against teams that belong to conferences, since, as mentioned above, the latter teams are obligated to play most of their games against teams from the same conference. Another important reason for a team to be a member of a conference is that the regular-season champions of most Division I-A conferences get automatic **bowl bids**; very good independents may still get invitations to a bowl game, but this is not guaranteed. Belonging to an established conference is also seen as an advantage in recruiting new players, since prospective players will most likely want to play for a team that has a good chance to get a bowl bid by winning a conference championship.

Below is a list of the conferences of both Division I-A and Division I-AA college football and the names of the colleges that belong to them. The words *College* and *University* have been omitted from these names, and the teams' nicknames are also not given here. Some conferences and colleges are better known by acronyms of their names; these are given in parentheses after the full names.

Division I-A Conferences

Atlantic Coast Conference (ACC)

Clemson
Duke
Florida State

Georgia Tech
Maryland
North Carolina
North Carolina State
Virginia
Wake Forest

Big East Conference

Boston College
Miami [of Florida]
Pittsburgh
Rutgers
Syracuse
Temple
Virginia Tech
West Virginia

Big Ten Conference

Illinois
Indiana
Iowa
Michigan
Michigan State
Minnesota
Northwestern
Ohio State
Penn State
Purdue
Wisconsin

Big 12 Conference

North
Colorado
Iowa State
Kansas
Kansas State
Missouri
Nebraska

South
Baylor
Oklahoma
Oklahoma State
Texas
Texas A & M
Texas Tech University

Big West Conference

Boise State

Idaho
Nevada
New Mexico State
North Texas
Utah State

Conference USA

Cincinnati
Houston
Louisville
Memphis
Southern Mississippi
Tulane

**Mid-American
Conference (MAC)**

Akron
Ball State
Bowling Green
Central Michigan
Eastern Michigan
Kent
Miami [of Ohio]
Ohio
Toledo
Western Michigan

**Pacific Ten Conference
(Pac 10)**

Arizona
Arizona State
California
Oregon
Oregon State
Stanford
University of California at Los
    Angeles (UCLA)
University of Southern
    California (USC)
Washington
Washington State

Southeastern Conference

East
Florida
Georgia
Kentucky
South Carolina
Vanderbilt
Tennessee

West
Alabama
Arkansas
Auburn
Louisiana State University (LSU)
Mississippi
Mississippi State

Western Athletic Conference (WAC)

Pacific
Air Force
Colorado State
Fresno State
Hawaii
University of Nevada at Las
   Vegas (UNLV)
San Diego State

San Jose State
Wyoming

Mountain
Brigham Young University
New Mexico
Rice
Southern Methodist University
   (SMU)
Texas Christian University
   (TCU)
Tulsa
Utah
University of Texas at El Paso
   (UTEP)

Independents

Alabama Birmingham
Arkansas State
Army
Central Florida
East Carolina
Louisiana Tech
Navy
Northeast Louisiana
Northern Illinois
Notre Dame
Southwest Louisiana

Division I-AA Conferences

Big Sky Conference

California State Northridge
California State Sacramento
Eastern Washington
Idaho State
Montana
Montana State
Northern Arizona
Portland State
Weber State

Gateway Conference

Illinois State
Indiana State
Northern Iowa
Southern Illinois
Southwest Missouri State
Western Illinois

Ivy League

Brown

Columbia
Cornell
Dartmouth
Harvard
Pennsylvania
Princeton
Yale

Metro Atlantic Athletic Conference (MAAC)

Canisius
Duquesne
Fairfield
Georgetown
Iona
Marist
Siena
St. John's
St. Peter's

Mid-Eastern Athletic Conference (MEAC)

Bethune Cookman
Delaware State
Florida A&M
Hampton
Howard
Morgan State
North Carolina A&T
South Carolina State

Northeast Conference

Central Connecticut
Monmouth [of New Jersey]
Robert Morris
St. Francis [of Pennsylvania]
Wagner

Ohio Valley Conference

Austin Peay
Eastern Illinois

Eastern Kentucky
Middle Tennessee State
Murray State
Southeast Missouri State
Tennessee Martin
Tennessee State
Tennessee Tech

Patriot League

Bucknell
Colgate
Fordham
Holy Cross
Lafayette
Lehigh

Pioneer Conference

Butler
Dayton
Drake
Evansville
San Diego
Valparaiso

Southern Conference

Appalachian State
The Citadel
East Tennessee State
Furman
Georgia Southern
Marshall
Tennessee Chattanooga
Virginia Military Institute
Western Carolina

Southland Conference

Jacksonville State
McNeese State
Nicholls State
Northwestern State
Sam Houston State

Southwest Texas State
Stephen Austin
Troy State

Southwestern Athletic Conference (SWAC)

Alcorn State
Alabama State
Grambling
Jackson State
Mississippi Valley State
Prairie View
Southern
Texas Southern

Yankee Conference

New England Division
Boston University
Connecticut
Maine
Massachusetts
New Hampshire
Rhode Island

Middle Atlantic Division
Delaware
James Madison
Northeastern
Richmond
Villanova
William and Mary

Independents

Buffalo
California Polytechnic San
　Luis Obispo
Charleston Southern
Davidson
Hofstra
Liberty
Morehead State
Samford
Southern Utah
St. Mary's [of California]
Towson State
Western Kentucky
Wofford
Youngstown State

Most nonconference games are scheduled for early in the season, leaving the conference games—which are generally more important to teams' postseason hopes—for the middle and end of the season. And usually teams play the last game of the regular season against teams that are their traditional rivals; examples of such rivalries in college football are Harvard versus Yale, Ohio State versus Michigan, and Army versus Navy.

Almost all college football games are played on Saturdays during the regular season. A few games might be played on Sundays or other days of the week in the early days of the season (especially if the NFL season has not started yet) or during the bowl season, and most weeks there is one game played on Thursday nights that is broadcast on national television by the cable network ESPN. The starting times of games on Saturdays may vary. If the game is not going to be televised (as is the case for most games at the Division I-AA, Division II, Division III, and junior college levels), a college game usually starts early in the afternoon (1:00 and 1:30 P.M. are typical starting times). If the game will be televised, its starting time is often determined by the network broadcasting the game. These networks often broadcast more than one game on a Saturday and thus would like one game to end just as another one begins. Therefore, some games may start at noon (Eastern time) and others may be scheduled to start at 3:00 or 3:30 P.M. (or at the equivalent times in other time zones—for example, noon or 12:30 Pacific time). Other games may be scheduled to start in the early evening, provided, of course, that the stadiums where the games will be played have lights (see "Football Fields and Stadiums" in chapter 2).

With most games being played on Saturdays, college football teams practice from Monday to Friday (the players usually have Sundays off, though the coaching staffs and some players may spend Sundays analyzing the films from the game played the previous day). Since the college football season coincides with most of the colleges' fall semesters (or quarters, for those that are on this system), practices are usually held in the late afternoons after all the players have finished with their classes during the day. It cannot be emphasized too strongly that college football players are first and foremost *students*, in spite of claims that, especially at the Division I level, players are little more than preprofessionals in a kind of farm system for the NFL and are in college only to play football and not to study for degrees. It is true that because of the travel demands of college football (most opponents a team plays during road games are a considerable distance away, often requiring the teams to travel to the destination the day before the game), players have to miss many classes on Fridays and other days, but the players may also receive special academic support services such as tutoring. Football players must also maintain satisfactory academic performance throughout their years in college or they will not be allowed to play for the team.

TIME·OUT

Players may be kicked off college football teams for other reasons besides poor academic performance. Many kinds of misconduct, such as excessive alcohol consumption and participation in unruly behavior, can result in players being suspended or permanently barred from the team. And it is an unfortunate fact that many (but still a very small minority of) college football players have committed minor and serious criminal offenses, including sexual and other kinds of assault, and this has resulted in some damage to the image of college football.

In addition to the practices and games during the regular season, most Division I-A college football programs also have a short period of practices and training during the springtime that usually culminates in an intrasquad game, in which the team divides into two halves that play each other in a full game or sometimes just a scrimmage. Furthermore, most college football players try to stay in shape during the off-season either by keeping to approximately the same regimen of weight training and conditioning as they go through during the regular season or by working out in other ways.

Like high school games, college football games are attended by spectators who pay admission. These spectators may be students or employees of the colleges—who generally pay lower admission prices than the general public—alumni of the colleges, or just members of the local community who, even though they may have no official connection to the college, may be as devoted to the team as they would be to a professional team in their community (in fact, in some smaller communities that have no professional teams in any sport, college football or other sports teams often serve as a substitute and even a source of pride for the local residents). The price of admission to college games, however, is generally higher than that of high school games, and for college games fans generally must purchase tickets in advance or at the gate to be admitted. Season tickets to the home games of most Division I teams may be purchased, and major college football programs offer such amenities as luxury boxes at their home stadiums, just as professional football teams do.

The revenue generated by charging relatively high admission to games is important to college football programs and to the colleges in general. It is expensive to field a team in any organized tackle football league, mainly because of the cost of equipment, but college football programs, especially at the highest levels, have many more expenses. Even though the players in these programs are not paid like professional players, there are high costs associated with paying the professional coaching staff, scouting, and support personnel, and high expenditures are involved with travel to road games; besides the cost of transporting the whole team to the game site itself, the personnel must be housed in a hotel or motel and fed the night before and the morning of the game.

Another important source of revenue for college football programs is selling the rights to broadcast the team's games on radio or television. College football games receive considerable attention in the newspaper, television, and radio sports media, and almost all college games are broadcast live by either a radio or television station or network. Often, the two colleges' own student-run radio stations will cover the games, and they may also be carried by local or regional radio stations. Junior college and Division III games are usually not televised live, and the telecasts of games at the higher levels are usually handled not by individual TV stations but by networks. Moreover, networks usually negotiate not with an individual team to broadcast its games but with the conference of which the team is a part, obligating the network to show the games of more than one team during the season. (An exception is the deal that the independent Notre Dame has with the major U.S. television network NBC, the National Broadcasting Company, to show its games, which, as mentioned above, usually attract a lot of viewers just because of the football tradition of this university.) In return for the rights to broadcast the games, the network pays the conference a substantial sum of money, which the networks usually get back from the fees they charge advertisers to show commercials during the broadcasts of games. The money the networks pay for broadcast rights is usually divided equally among the teams in the conference. In addition, three major U.S. networks—ABC, CBS, and ESPN—have arrangements with the NCAA to show important games featuring teams from all conferences, including interconference games. As a result of this exposure, top players on Division I-A teams often attain a celebrity status like that of professional athletes, and it should be pointed out that the players on Division I teams often make public appearances and perform community service (e.g., visiting children's hospitals) in their local areas, especially if the colleges are located in smaller cities and towns where the team's status as a major athletic program makes it and its players all the more important in the community.

Having a very good team and getting its games covered on major television networks is thus another important source of income for a college. But if a team is good enough to get into a **bowl game** (or a **bowl**), its status is increased even more, because not only are bowls broadcast on national television but both teams in a bowl game receive a substantial amount of money just for participating.

As mentioned above, many of the participants in bowl games are the champions of individual conferences, but some bowls may extend an invitation to the second- or third-place teams in one of the six traditionally strongest conferences (the ACC, the Big East, the Big Ten, the Big 12, the Pac 10, and the Southeastern Conference). Also, as mentioned above, college bowl games take place from late December to the New Year's holiday. The sites for bowls are in locations in the United States where the weather is likely to be warm even during December and January, such as in the states of California,

Texas, and Florida. A warm-weather location for a bowl game is desirable whether or not the game is played outside or in an indoor stadium, since the atmosphere around bowls is often festive (for example, on the day of one bowl game, the Rose Bowl in Pasadena, California, there is a famous parade) and the comfort of the people in town to watch the game is almost as important as that of the players. Both teams in a bowl game usually arrive at the site at least a week before the game—not only to prepare for the game but also for public appearances and perhaps some sight-seeing of the local area. In addition, many students and fans of both colleges travel to the games, and they, too, often arrive as early as a week before the game is played. Since these fans spend a lot of money on things like accommodations, meals, and shopping at the site of the game, bowl games provide valuable boosts to the economies of the games' sites.

Below is a list of the Division I-A college bowl games. These are given in roughly the order in which they are played, though each year may bring some variations. The four games at the end of the list, however, are the ones that are most likely to be played New Year's Eve, New Year's Day, or January 2, since they are considered the most important bowls.

Major College Bowl Games

Name	Location
Las Vegas Bowl	Las Vegas, Nevada
Aloha Bowl	Honolulu, Hawaii
Liberty Bowl	Memphis, Tennessee
Carquest Bowl	Miami, Florida
Copper Bowl	Tucson, Arizona
Peach Bowl	Atlanta, Georgia
Alamo Bowl	San Antonio, Texas
Holiday Bowl	San Diego, California
Heritage Bowl	Atlanta, Georgia
Sun Bowl	El Paso, Texas

Independence Bowl	Shreveport, Louisiana
Outback Bowl	Tampa, Florida
Gator Bowl	Jacksonville, Florida
Citrus Bowl	Orlando, Florida
Cotton Bowl	Dallas, Texas
Orange Bowl	Miami, Florida
Rose Bowl	Pasadena, California
Fiesta Bowl	Tempe, Arizona
Sugar Bowl	New Orleans, Louisiana

T I M E · O U T

Most bowl games have major corporate sponsors who contribute to the **payout**. These sponsors are actively involved in promoting their bowl games, because they view the games as a way to advertise themselves and their products.

Besides their importance in their own right, the results of each season's bowl games are used in determining the national champion of college football for that season. The three most prestigious bowls—the Fiesta, Orange, and Sugar (and, after the 1998 season, the Rose Bowl as well)—are in an alliance in which one of them hosts the teams that are at the top or near the top of the national college football **polls** at the conclusion of the regular season. There are two main college football polls. One is the Associated Press (AP) poll, which is a national survey of sportswriters who cast votes for the best teams in the country. The other is the Cable News Network (CNN)/*USA Today* poll, which surveys the coaches of college teams for their votes for the best teams. The team with the most votes is given the rank of number 1, meaning that it's the best major college team in the country, and the next 24 teams are ranked in order of how many votes they received. Teams that are undefeated generally get the highest rankings, followed by teams with only one or two losses. The AP and CNN/*USA Today* rankings of the top 25 teams generally agree, though there may be differences in the order of a few teams, which could have important ramifications in the final poll of the season (see below) to declare the national champion.

The two polls are released every week during the college football regular season. The polls are conducted when all the college games are over on Saturdays, and the polls are released early on Mondays to be published in newspapers and reported in television and radio sports news broadcasts. The rankings released the previous Monday are also used in talking about the matchups for each Saturday's games; for example, if Washington is ranked first in the poll and Arizona State is ranked third and the teams are scheduled to play against each other, the game may be described as "Number 1 Washington visits number 3 Arizona State," or immediately after the game the score may be given as "It was number 1 Washington over number 3 Arizona State, 17 to 10" or "Number 1 Washington 17, number 3 Arizona State 10."

Generally, teams that won on the previous Saturday rise in the polls—that is, they get more votes and therefore have a higher ranking than in the previous week's polls—and teams that lose fall in the rankings. Occasionally teams may stay in the same position as the previous week even if they won their games, especially when the two or three teams ahead of them in the previous week's poll also won. Conversely, a loss may not cause a team to fall in the rankings if the teams below them also lost. Teams generally do not fall more than a few places from week to week unless they lose badly to a team that was a considerable **underdog**. However, the teams and their rankings in the preseason polls may be very different than the final polls taken at the end of the year (see below); for example, a team that was expected to do very well at the beginning of the year and was ranked very high even before playing a game may lose several games during the season and thus may not even be among the top 25 teams at season's end. And the opposite may happen as well; a team that was unranked may win all or most of its games, including several against highly ranked teams, and may end up as one of the most highly ranked teams in the final polls.

When all the bowl games have been played, a final poll is taken by both the AP and CNN/USA *Today* and on the basis of these results the team that is number 1 is declared the national champion. Sometimes the choice is clear—for example, when a team that was number 1 before its bowl game wins the game. In other cases, the ranking of a team as number 1 in the final poll is disputed, especially since under the current bowl system a number 1 team often does not play the team ranked number 2. For this reason, many people are dissatisfied with the current system of "crowning" or selecting a national college football champion. These people stress that the top-ranked team in the final polls is the "mythical" national champion, insisting that only a series of **head-to-head**, single-elimination playoff and championship games can decide the issue of which team is the champion. However, with so many major college teams such a playoff process would take several weeks to complete, so it would probably never be practical to adopt.

It should be mentioned that there are weekly polls for the best Division I-AA, Division II, and Division III teams as well. These polls may be both national and regional—for example, there may be a poll ranking the Division III teams in just the Northeast region of the United States. In addition, these levels of college football do have a playoff system designed to produce a national champion at each level. After winning regional playoff games, the finalists at each level meet each other in semifinal and championship games played at neutral sites.

Besides honors for the best team, college football also honors its best players every year. At the end of the season, the AP also polls its respondents for their votes on the best players at each position at each level of college football. Those who get the most votes are first-team **All-Americans,** the players who get the next-most votes are second-team All-Americans, and the next are third-team All-Americans, players who also get many votes are called honorable mentions. There is also an award given for best player in college football, which is called the Heisman Trophy. This award is normally given only to a player in Division I-A, though in the past some players at lower-level programs have been candidates for the Heisman. In the weeks or even months before the Heisman Trophy winner is named, potential candidates for the award—the most outstanding players in college football—are identified and sports information directors or other officials at the players' colleges may even try to lobby in favor of their players by sending game reports, videos, and other material detailing the players' accomplishments to the college football writers who will vote on which player will receive the trophy. The award is presented at a ceremony at the Downtown Athletic Club in New York City shortly after the college football regular season. The leading candidates for the Heisman Trophy are present at the ceremony, which is also broadcast on national television, and the winner is announced and presented with the official trophy.

The winner of the Heisman Trophy is usually an offensive player like a quarterback or a running back, but players from other offensive positions and even defensive players have won it in the past. The Heisman Trophy winner, recognized as the best player in college football, often—but not automatically—becomes the first pick in the NFL **draft** (see below). One reason a Heisman Trophy winner may not be the first pick—or may not even be selected in the first round—of the NFL draft is that the professional game still has slightly different requirements than those of college football; for example, a quarterback who performs well in college may not be desirable in the NFL because he's not tall enough to perform quarterback duties in the professional game with defensive players who are bigger and taller than those in college. (In cases like these, sometimes the player may be drafted by an NFL team but converted to a different position than the one he played in college—for example, a relatively short but fast college quarterback may be made into a wide receiver or a defensive back in the NFL.)

```
┌─────────────────────────────────────────────────┐
│  ┌───────────────────────────┐                  │
│  │  T I M E · O U T          │                  │
│  └───────────────────────────┘                  │
│                                                  │
│  Another award given in college football is the  │
│  Outland Trophy, which is presented to the best  │
│  offensive lineman. The award recognizes the     │
│  importance of offensive linemen, whose          │
│  contribution to the success of other offensive  │
│  players is often overlooked.                    │
│                                                  │
└─────────────────────────────────────────────────┘
```

As in other levels of football (see "Exhibition Games" under "Organizational Aspects Common to All Types of Football," above), college football also puts on all-star games featuring its best players. Unlike other football all-star games, however, the players take these games seriously, since they know many NFL scouts will be watching these games. Players play hard and try to perform well in order to impress the scouts, who might then recommend to the teams they work for that they draft these players (most players in college all-star games are seniors and therefore eligible for the next NFL draft; see "National Football League" under "Professional Football," below). Another difference between college football and other levels of football is that there are actually more than one college all-star game. One game is the Blue-Gray Classic, held every year in Montgomery, Alabama. In this game, players representing teams from colleges located in the southern part of the United States form the "Gray" team, which plays against a team composed of players from northern U.S. colleges (the "Blue" team). (Blue and gray were the respective colors of the Northern and Southern armies, or the Union and the Confederacy, in the American Civil War.) The Blue-Gray Classic is played *before* the major bowl games, and as a result players from teams that will play in bowls do not play in this all-star game, as they must keep practicing with their own teams right up until their bowl game. In spite of this, the Blue-Gray Classic features some of the finest players in college football, even if they are not members of the best teams in the country, most of whom play in bowl games (see above).

Another college football all-star game is the East-West Shrine Classic, played in Stanford, California. In this game, players from colleges in the eastern part of the United States play against a team of players from western U.S. colleges. Since this game is played after the major bowl games, players from bowl teams may participate; thus, it is more truly a college all-star game. Similarly, the Hula Bowl, held every January in Honolulu, Hawaii, features the best college players, and in this game also there is an East team and a West team. The Senior Bowl, played in Mobile, Alabama, after the major bowl games, features some of the best graduating players and is also played between North and South all-star teams.

Finally, there is a hall of fame that pays tribute to the best players who have ever played college football in its long history (which is actually longer than that of professional football in the United States). The College Football Hall of Fame is located in South Bend, Indiana, which is fitting, since this is the location of the University of Notre Dame, which over the years has had some of the finest players in the college game.

Professional Football

By definition, the difference between high school football, college football, and all other types of amateur football on the one hand and professional football on the other is that players in the latter receive money or other compensation. This first fact leads to another difference between professional and amateur football—namely, that the quality of play in professional football is much higher, since payment is an inducement to get the best players to play for a team.

In the United States, professional football (or pro football) is virtually synonymous with the NFL, but American football is played professionally in other organizations in North America and the world. The following sections discuss the NFL and two other types of pro football—the CFL and NFL Europe—and chapter 5 discusses a few other types of professional football.

National Football League (NFL)

The Teams and Organization of the NFL

The National Football League is an organization of professional football teams that are based in cities all across the United States. These teams (which are also called clubs or franchises) are first and foremost private businesses in operation to provide entertainment in the form of football games to the public. Like other privately owned enterprises, NFL teams can be bought and sold, and if the teams are losing money in their business operations, could fold. Though no teams have folded in the recent history of the NFL, it happens frequently to teams in other professional leagues.

T I M E · O U T

The Green Bay Packers are unique in the NFL in being community-owned, which means that citizens of Green Bay, Wisconsin, where the team is located, or people anywhere else can buy shares in the team.

Every NFL team has an owner, who may be a single individual or a group. The owners of NFL teams need to be wealthy, since the costs of operating an NFL team are enormous; the players' salaries alone amount to several million dollars. In spite of this, it may be less expensive to be an owner of an existing team than to own an **expansion team**. Occasionally, the NFL expands by creating a few new clubs, but the

NFL requires owners of expansion teams to pay very large fees to be admitted into the league. Certain other conditions are imposed as well, such as the construction of a new, modern stadium for the team.

NFL teams are based in the largest cities in the United States. The obvious reason for this is that in these locations the teams have the best chance of attracting fans to their games and receiving coverage in major media markets. These things result in greater income for the teams, which is sorely needed in the present state of the game, with the operating costs for teams being so high. In fact, some clubs may find that they cannot support their operations in the cities where they currently play, either because not enough fans attend their games (often because the team loses many of its games) or because the team plays in an older stadium that does not have luxury boxes and other special facilities that bring in a considerable amount of revenue (see "Fan Attendance at Football Games," under "Organizational Aspects Common to All Types of Football," above). As a result, the club may decide to move to another, larger city that may have tried to attract the team beforehand by doing things like building a new stadium. If a team moves to a new city, it may adopt a new nickname, with new colors and uniforms, while keeping the same ownership, organization, and players. But it is not guaranteed that the largest U.S. cities will be able to attract and/or keep NFL teams; just a few years ago, for example, the second-largest metropolitan area in the United States—Los Angeles, California—had two NFL teams, but both have since moved away (the Raiders back to their original home in Oakland, California, and the Rams to St. Louis, Missouri).

The teams of the NFL are organized into two main conferences: the American Football Conference (AFC) and the National Football Conference (NFC). The American Football Conference actually was once a separate professional league called the American Football League; it merged with the NFL in 1970. The teams of the original NFL became the National

Football Conference, but three teams—the Pittsburgh Steelers, the Cleveland Browns (now the Baltimore Ravens), and the Baltimore (now Indianapolis) Colts—transferred from the NFC to the AFC so that both conferences would have the same number of teams. As in all forms of organized football, each NFL team has a nickname (see "Leagues and Schedules" under "Organizational Aspects Common to All Types of Football," above) and a place-name. The place-names of most NFL teams are the cities they play in, but some (for example, the Minnesota Vikings and the Arizona Cardinals) are named after the states they are located in. One reason for this naming practice is that with the general shift of the U.S. population from urban areas to the suburbs and rural areas, teams need to develop a fan base that is concentrated not just in a city but in the larger area surrounding it (this is also called the team's market).

Here are the teams in the three divisions of both of the NFL's conferences:

American Football Conference (AFC)

Eastern Division	Central Division	Western Division
Buffalo Bills	Baltimore Ravens	Denver Broncos
Indianapolis Colts	Cincinnati Bengals	Kansas City Chiefs
Miami Dolphins	Jacksonville Jaguars	Oakland Raiders
New England Patriots	Pittsburgh Steelers	San Diego Chargers
New York Jets	Tennessee Oilers	Seattle Seahawks

National Football Conference (NFC)

Eastern Division	Central Division	Western Division
Arizona Cardinals	Chicago Bears	Atlanta Falcons
Dallas Cowboys	Detroit Lions	Carolina Panthers
New York Giants	Green Bay Packers	New Orleans Saints
Philadelphia Eagles	Minnesota Vikings	San Francisco 49ers
Washington Redskins	Tampa Bay Buccaneers	St. Louis Rams

NFL clubs are complex entities, needing much organization to handle the various tasks necessary to keep the team operating—including scouting, marketing, ticket sales, and public/media relations—in addition to the management of players. Most team owners do not involve themselves much in the day-to-day operations of their clubs, often because they are businesspeople who have many other enterprises to occupy their attention. Perhaps the most important person in the **front office** of an NFL team is the **general manager** (or **GM**). This person, who has a large role in deciding what players will be on the team, evaluates scouting reports of college and other professional players, deciding which college players to draft, making trades for other players, and signing free agents (see "NFL Players," below). The team's head coach and other coaches are involved to some extent in these player-personnel matters as well, but less so than coaches at other levels of football, the main reason being that coaching in the NFL is a difficult and complex job that keeps coaches busy pretty much all year. The coaching staff, in fact, is answerable to the GM, who often has the duty of firing a head coach and hiring another when the team doesn't win many games (even though a team's misfortune is often not directly the head coach's fault).

The NFL has an organizational structure as well. At the head of the league is the **commissioner**, who is chosen by the owners and retains the post until resigning or being forced to leave for poor performance. The commissioner of the NFL generally acts as a liaison between the players and the owners, and among different owners or groups of owners, and makes rulings affecting players and clubs (including suspending players for misconduct, on and off the field, such as for the use of illegal drugs, especially performance-enhancing drugs like steroids). The NFL also has a Competition Committee, composed of head coaches from teams in the league, which each year considers changes to the rules of NFL football for various reasons—for example, to make the game more competitive (and therefore more interesting to the public) or to protect players against injuries. For example, if complaints arise during one season that the NFL rules favor the defense and there is thus not enough scoring, the committee may make changes that allow offensive players greater freedom in using their hands when blocking in order to make it less difficult for offenses to advance the ball and score.

NFL *Players*

By far, the greatest source of players for the NFL is college football. Almost every NFL player played college football, and most were starters for two or more years. A very few NFL players may not have played any college football; these are usually specialty players like kickers, many of whom are originally from countries where American football is not played. Most NFL players who have played college football moved directly from the college into the NFL, but some take a more indirect route; before joining the NFL, many players first play in other professional leagues—for example, the CFL, NFL Europe, the Arena Football League (see chapter 5), or a semiprofessional league—where they improve their skills or showcase their abilities to such an extent that they are given an opportunity to play in the NFL.

Since the vast majority of NFL players are products of college football, the youngest NFL players are in their early 20s. A few may be as young as 20 or 21; most of these players did not complete their college eligibility but **came out** for the NFL draft in their junior years and were selected and offered a contract by an NFL team. Usually only exceptionally talented college players come out early, because they must be fairly certain that they will be drafted and signed to a lucrative contract that will compensate for ending their college careers without getting a college degree. The NFL itself discourages college players from entering the draft before senior year and advocates that students complete their college educations (of course, college teams don't want players leaving early, since they would like to have these outstanding players' services for the full period of their NCAA eligibility).

How long a player plays in the NFL depends on several factors. Perhaps the most important one is how long the player's body—or his spirit—can take the physical strain of playing in the NFL. Indeed, the careers of most NFL players last only a few years, with those of many players cut short by career-ending injuries. This varies by position: Players like running backs and linemen are most susceptible because they engage in the most punishing physical contact in a game, whereas the careers of players who don't get as much physical contact, like kickers and quarterbacks, tend to be longer. Occasionally, some players may receive an injury that does not directly affect their performance but may lead to a crippling physical condition if the players receive further injury, and thus on the advice of doctors the players retire instead of risking a condition like lifelong paralysis. And even if not forced to stop playing because of injuries, many players complain that long after their careers are over they continue to suffer constant pain from playing in the NFL. (Many players take painkilling drugs, sometimes excessively, to help them overcome the pain of their injuries enough to keep playing, and this often makes their injuries worse.)

Since the NFL is the highest level of competitive football, only the best players get to play in the league, and a player must perform to the absolute best of his ability at all times or he will quickly be replaced. As players get older, they naturally become slightly less quick and strong, and even this slight diminishment of their ability might be enough to cost them a place on a team in the highly competitive NFL. Players realize this will happen to them eventually, and some retire voluntarily after they have played for several years to avoid the humiliation of being demoted to a second- or third-string role or being cut from the team. Other older players try but fail to stay on the team during training camp (see below), or are cut during the season because it becomes apparent that they simply can't compete with younger players. Speaking very generally, an NFL player over the age of 30 is considered old or past his prime, and this has a lot to do with the way the demands of playing in the NFL prematurely age players. However, there are certainly very many NFL players older than 30 who continue to play and perform well, and even many who are the best at their positions. In fact, some NFL players (usually quarterbacks) have played into their early 40s.

Each team in the NFL is allowed to keep 45 players on its **roster** plus a reserve called a **practice squad**. If a player on the regular roster is injured, a player may be brought in from the practice squad to take his place, which is advantageous since the practice squad player will have already been practicing with the team and will be familiar with its plays and regular players. Furthermore, if a player on the 45-man roster gets injured and will not be able to play for one or more of the team's future games, the player may be put on **injured reserve**. After putting a player on injured reserve, the team can bring in a player from the practice squad, as described above, or can sign a new player to play for the team temporarily.

In April of every year, the NFL holds a **draft** of college players. Once drafted by an NFL team, the player can sign a contract (see below) only with that team, at least for the player's first year in the NFL or for as many years as specified in the contract the team makes with him, unless the team trades the player to another team (see below). The purpose of the draft is to provide a fair distribution of the best college players to all the teams in the league. Also for the purpose of fairness, there is a specific order in which teams may draft players. The team that had the worst record in the previous season gets the first (**draft**) **pick** in the NFL draft and thus usually selects the best college player available (who is often but not always the Heisman Trophy winner; see "College Football," above). The second pick in the draft goes to the team that had the second worst record in the league, and the draft order continues in this way until the team that won the Super Bowl (i.e., was the best team in the NFL the previous season) makes its selection. When all 30 NFL teams have thus made their selections of one player each, it is said that the first **round** of the draft is complete. Then the first team to select in the previous round, which will again be the team with the worst record, makes another selection, and each team selects players in the same order as in the first round. This continues until seven rounds have taken place, and the draft for the current year is then complete. After the draft, all the teams are free to contact any undrafted college players and invite them to their training camps. Most of the players who get selected in the NFL draft are from Division I-A programs, but many players from Division I-AA colleges and occasionally a few from Divsion II or even Division III colleges may be drafted.

T I M E · O U T

The draft order in each round is not always exactly the same as it was in previous rounds. Sometimes when teams make trades (see below), part of the deal may involve trading a draft pick in a certain round. For example, a team may trade one player for another's first-round pick in the next year's draft or the draft in any year in the near future. This kind of trade is beneficial to the team that traded for the pick only if the other team has a relatively bad year in the season before the draft so that this team's selection will be relatively high (one of the earliest picks in the round).

The NFL draft is more than just teams announcing their choices. It is now a major event, given live coverage on ESPN even though the entire draft may last for several hours. Several representatives from each team, including coaches and general managers and often owners, gather in one location for the announcements of each team's selections. Most of the top college prospects are also present at the draft, and as each is selected he comes up to the podium from which his selection was announced and usually receives a ceremonial jersey from the team that selected him.

The team officials who come to the draft are well prepared. They are thoroughly familiar with all the players who are likely to be drafted and have definite plans about which players to select, who may not be the most talented players available at each opportunity but may be intended to fill specific needs the team has; for example, a team whose defense performed poorly during the previous season may focus on drafting good defensive players, or if a team's starting quarterback is injured, retired, aging, or has become a free agent (see below), the team may look especially for a talented quarterback who could be ready to start in the NFL soon, if not right away. In fact, many team officials and many of the journalists covering the draft can predict with some accuracy which players will be selected by all the teams in each of at least the first few rounds.

Much of the information teams use to decide which players to draft comes from an event known as the Combination Workouts, or Combine, held before the draft. At this event, the top college players are invited to workouts where they are observed by NFL coaches and team officials in order for the NFL teams to evaluate in person how skilled each player is. Also included in these sessions are psychological tests to see if the players have the right "stuff," or mental toughness and tenacity, to play in the NFL.

Once a player is drafted by an NFL team, he needs to sign a **contract**. Some NFL contracts can be for just one season, but most are for at least a few years. Older players (see above) usually receive short contracts, since they are less likely to be playing in the NFL more than a few years into the future. All players in the NFL, including **rookies**, must be paid a minimum salary, but the best players have yearly salaries that are in the millions of dollars. There are few standards for how much players must be paid, however, and almost all players have to negotiate their contracts—that is, try to get their teams to pay them as much as possible, depending on how much the team is willing to pay them, which in turn depends on how well they performed the previous season. In these negotiations, each player is represented by an agent who is a professional negotiator for athletes and usually has more than one athlete client. Most negotiations between clubs and players and/or their agents result in an agreement on a contract, but often the player will be dissatisfied with the team's offer and **hold out** for a better contract (refuse to report to training camp, to practice, or to play in any games for the team until it agrees to his contract demands). Most players end their holdouts before the beginning of the season by accepting their team's offer, but some players don't return to the team until well into the regular season. It is usually the best players on a team, or high draft picks, who hold out for more money believing that the team will want their services so badly that it will be willing to pay them the high salaries they demand.

Likewise, players whose contracts have expired also need to sign new contracts to keep playing. In most cases, if a player has performed very well during the length of his contract, he will renegotiate his contract and ask for a higher salary, and this is usually granted. If a player is not satisfied with his team's contract offer or if he just does not want to play for the team anymore, he can become a **free agent**. A free agent may sign a contract with any other team in the league and usually signs with the team that offers him the most money; if the player is one of the better players in the league, teams may offer to pay him several million dollars for his services. The team the player played for the previous season always has the right to match any offer made by another team, but because teams are limited under the salary cap (see below), many find they are unable to make equivalent contract offers, and therefore have to let these players go.

As mentioned at the beginning of this chapter, NFL clubs are privately owned businesses, and like other business arenas there are considerable differences in the financial

T I M E · O U T

If a team loses more players as free agents than it is able to sign from other teams, it is awarded one to four compensatory picks in the NFL draft.

resources of each team. Some teams, especially ones in the largest American cities with their (usually) great number of fans who attend games and with all the media coverage their games get, resulting in millions of dollars in broadcast fees and advertising revenues, are quite wealthy, while other clubs located in smaller cities and markets do not have as many resources. Consequently, if free agency were really free and unrestricted, it would not take long for the wealthiest teams to attract the best football players and thus dominate the league and destroy its competitive balance. For this reason, the NFL requires that the combined total of the salaries of all the players on a team be less than the **salary cap**. Accordingly, under this rule the maximum a team could spend on paying its players would be the same as any other team, no matter how rich the club is, though of course players' individual salaries can and do vary widely. One effect of the salary cap is that teams often are forced to make a choice between keeping one highly paid but very good player and letting other players who are not paid as much become free agents. In some cases, teams may request to renegotiate the contracts of current players in order to pay them less so that they can offer large contracts to other players or free agents. Often these players agree to be paid less money because they understand how valuable it would be to the team to acquire or hold on to the services of the other players.

Because a player signs a contract doesn't mean the player is guaranteed long-term employment with the team. All NFL players must perform well or they will be cut from the team so that a better player can be brought in. Many players are cut during training camp (see below), at which teams begin with all their returning players, draft picks and free agents—which can total some 80 players—but by the end of which teams have decided on the 45 best players to keep. Some players may be released during the regular season for failing to live up to expectations of the team or suffering a career-ending or other serious injury. These released players must be **waived**, and even if no team selects a released player right away, NFL teams keep track of these available players in order to call on them to fill any future vacancies in their own rosters.

Teams may also get rid of players they no longer want by trading them to other teams in return for players on those teams whom they do want. Teams make trades or deals in order to eliminate weaknesses on their team by giving up players in areas where they think they are strong; players who play the same positions are usually not traded for each other. Some trades may involve just one player on each team going to the other, others may have one player being traded for two or more, or there may be multiplayer deals in which several players on both teams are exchanged. As mentioned above, teams may trade players for draft picks and also may include cash as part of their trades—for example, if both teams agree that one team gets slightly better players as part of the deal and the other team should receive more compensation. There may even be three-way trades in which one team sends a player or players to a second team and as a result this team sends a player or players to a third team, which completes the trade by sending a player or players to the first; thus, each team gives up players but gets some in return. Whatever trades are made, they must be completed before a certain deadline which usually falls late in the regular season. This trading deadline is established in order to prevent teams who are clearly not going to be in the playoffs from making special deals with playoff teams to trade their best players to these teams just to help them advance in the playoff rounds (see below).

TIME·OUT

All players in the NFL, like high school and college players, are required to undergo physical examinations at least once a year. After a player is traded to a new team, this team usually requires the player to have a physical almost immediately since it is possible that the player will have a serious physical injury or medical condition his old team didn't mention when the deal was made (and may have been a reason that the team wanted to trade him). If the player doesn't pass the physical, the new team can cancel the trade.

Like many employees of businesses, all NFL players are represented by a labor union, the NFL Players' Association. This organization works for the players' interests on various issues such as free agency. Occasionally, the players' union may be so dissatisfied with the progress of negotiations with team owners and/or the NFL administration that it may organize a job action or a strike in which the players refuse to play in regularly scheduled games. When this rare event occurs, the league may either postpone or cancel these games or may bring in replacement players to play the games.

Because of the great exposure the NFL gets in the United States (and in many other parts of the world), NFL players, and particularly its stars, are true celebrities in American popular culture. Even some head coaches, especially successful ones, are celebrities. Many of the most well-known players make millions of dollars through **endorsements**, in addition to their multimillion-dollar playing contracts. And in the local areas where their teams play, NFL players and head coaches, even the ones who are not well known nationally but are popular just for being members of the local club, often make public appearances such as autograph signings, are involved in community service, and frequently have their own television or radio talk shows (usually concerned with their team and perhaps sports in general). Some players, either while they are still playing or, more often, after they have stopped playing football, get into acting in television and movies, where their fame as football players often helps them get started (and often makes up for their lack of training or talent in acting). When they quit playing the game, many NFL players go into football broadcasting, others stay involved with football by becoming coaches or working in the front office of NFL clubs or college teams, and a few may even coach at the high school or youth levels.

The NFL Season

Like other kinds of football, NFL games are played during only a portion of the year. But the business of the NFL, being a professional football league, really has no beginning or end, as activity and development take place throughout the year. To describe the NFL's season, though, one might begin with the combined workouts and the NFL draft, which take place early every spring (see "NFL Players," above). As mentioned previously, a short while after the draft each team holds one or more minicamps lasting for a few days in which all the team's returning players, draft choices, and free agents get together for a team orientation and go through some limited drills so that the coaching staff can do a preliminary evaluation of the players. A team may also have a short camp just for its rookies.

The next major event in the NFL year is **training camp**. Beginning in mid-July, all the players and coaches of a team gather at a location (often a small college) that is usually near the team's home field or city. Some training camps may be a considerable distance from the team's home, however; the New Orleans Saints, for example, have their training camp not in Louisiana but in Wisconsin, as the summer in this northern state is normally mild and thus more bearable for the players as they go through the rigors of training camp. For the next several weeks, the players and coaches live at the facility and almost every day have at least two full sessions of drills, practices, and calisthenics to make sure the players are in good physical shape. (Knowing how difficult it is to get and keep a position on an NFL team and how important training camp is for doing so, many players come to camp already in good shape from physical training during the off-season.) During this period, the coaches carefully observe all the players, who include all the team's draft picks, and must decide which players will best help the team win. Those who are not the best are cut, though only some of these players are sent home during the first few weeks of camp.

A few weeks after the NFL training camps have opened, the NFL's exhibition season or preseason begins. All NFL teams play at least four exhibition games from late July into August, with some teams playing five. Most of the exhibition games are played on Friday or Saturday evenings at the home stadiums of one of the teams, but several games are played at neutral sites. In fact, in recent years many exhibition games have been played in stadiums outside the United States, in countries such as Canada and Mexico, in European nations like the United Kingdom and Germany, and also in Japan. The first exhibition game is always the annual Hall of Fame Game held at the Pro Football Hall of Fame at Canton, Ohio. This game, held on the same weekend as the ceremonies to honor the newest inductees into the Hall, always features one team from the AFC playing against one team from the NFC. In the other exhibition games, any NFL team may play against any other from either conference, but often teams are matched on a regional basis—that is, teams close to each other geographically play against each other. For example, in most exhibition seasons the two teams from the New York City metropolitan area, the NFC's New York Giants and the AFC's New York Jets, meet in an exhibition game.

Exhibition games give teams practice against other opponents before the real season starts, and they also enable coaches to evaluate how their players perform in actual competition. Unlike in regular-season games, almost all the players on the team get to see some action during exhibition games through constant substitution; the regular starters usually play only during the first quarter or sometimes for only a few offensive or defensive series. Early in the week following each exhibition game, the NFL requires that each team reduce its roster to a certain number, and coaching staffs, based largely on their observations of how well players performed in the exhibition games, are able to decide which players they want to keep and which to cut.

When the exhibition season ends and each team has made its final cuts to reduce its roster to the 45-man limit, the regular season begins, usually just one week after the last exhibition game. In fact, most teams are down to their limit *before* their last exhibition, so this game, with all the players who will start the season playing with the team, serves as a final tune-up for the regular season. The NFL regular season begins in early September or sometimes late August, usually the weekend before Labor Day, and lasts until late December and occasionally into the first few days of January. Each NFL team plays a 16-game regular-season schedule. The teams in each division in both conferences play each other twice, once in each team's home stadium. Each team plays four other games within its conference: two games against two teams in one of the other divisions and two games against two other teams in the other division of the conference (usually the team will play one home game and one away game against opponents from each division). The final component of the NFL schedule is the interconference games, which are games featuring an AFC and an NFC team. Every team in the NFL plays four interconference games per year. To simplify the schedulemaking, all of a team's interconference opponents in one season come from just one division of the opposite conference, and all of the other teams in that team's division play opponents from the same division of the opposite conference. The division against which a team plays its interconference games will not be the same from one season to the next; there is a rotating schedule under which every third season a team again plays teams from the same division of the other conference.

A team's opponents outside of its division are not selected randomly. The NFL has a scheduling policy whereby it tries to maintain competitive balance in its matchups as much as possible. This means it tries to schedule games between teams that are at roughly the same level of competitiveness—that is, the better teams play against each other, as do the weaker teams. This is done both to be fair to the weaker teams in the league and also to increase the interest of fans in the games; games in which a very strong team is scheduled to play against a weak one do not promise to be very competitive and probably will not draw as many fans to the stadium or viewers to the television broadcast of the game. The schedule is made well in advance of the season, however, so there is really no way to be certain which teams in the upcoming season will be good and which will play poorly; the pairings of the teams are based solely on the teams' records during the preceding season. Very often a team will do much worse or much better than its record the previous year, yet it must play out the schedule that was set for it. And, as mentioned above, every team must play all the other teams in its division twice a season no matter what their records were the previous year.

In addition, during the NFL regular season each team is given one **bye week**. As a result, the NFL regular season actually lasts 17 weeks even though all the teams play no more than 16 games. Teams have the same bye week as at least one other team (so that all the other teams will be in action against each other), and as many as four teams are idle during the same week. No team's bye week is scheduled during the first or last four weeks of the season. An advantage of the bye-week system is that it gives the players on a team a chance to rest or recover from injuries in the middle of the season. However, teams that are performing well and on a **winning streak** don't like to have their season interrupted by a bye week, the reason being that not having played a real game in two weeks will make them less prepared for their next game (teams practice during their bye weeks, but practices are seldom good substitutes for playing an actual game). And teams that are not performing well or are on a **losing streak** are afraid that during the bye week they will think too much about their team's lack of success and not be **up for** their next game.

Most NFL games are played on Sunday afternoons. Games start at either 1:00 P.M. or 4:15 P.M. Eastern time so that TV networks can show two games, or a "football doubleheader," on each Sunday. Any Sunday games that take place in cities in the Rocky Mountain or Pacific time zones of the U.S. always start at 4:15 P.M. Eastern time (this is 2:15 and 1:15 in these zones, respectively). Every week, one game is also played on Sunday evenings starting at 8:00 P.M. Eastern time (except on Sunday nights in October, when a baseball playoff or World Series game is scheduled). And one game per week is played on Monday nights starting at 8:15 P.M. Eastern time.

During the last three weeks of the season, when the college and high school football seasons have ended, two games are also played on Saturdays, one game starting at 12:30 P.M. Eastern time and the other at 4:15. And every year on the Thanksgiving Day holiday two games are played, starting at 12:30 and at 4:15. Each game is hosted either by the NFC's Dallas Cowboys or the Detroit Lions, and one of the games must involve an AFC team (so that one game can be shown on the CBS television network; see below).

Every NFL regular-season and playoff game (and many exhibition games as well) is shown live on television and is broadcast by at least two radio stations (one from the city of each team), and a national radio network may also cover the game. Major American television networks pay millions of dollars to the NFL for the rights to broadcast NFL games, and the money is well spent, since NFL regular-season and championship games are often among the highest-rated programs on American television. Currently, the Fox television network has the rights to broadcast all NFC conference games on Saturday and Sunday afternoons and any interconference games at these times in which an NFC team is the visiting team. The CBS (Columbia Broadcasting System) network has the rights to all Saturday and Sunday afternoon AFC games and any interconference games with an AFC team as the visitor. Since most games are played on Sunday afternoons and many have the same starting times, it is of course impossible for these networks to broadcast all NFL games nationwide at the same time. Instead, the networks employ regional telecasts in which the game shown in a particular area is the one involving the closest NFL team whether the team is playing at home or on the road. (However, any TV station belonging to these networks that is within 75 miles of the stadium where an NFL game will be played must **black out** the game if the game is not sold out; this is to help the teams make more fans come to the stadium and buy tickets to see the game.) In addition, each week either Fox or CBS has the football doubleheader (see above) and either the 1:00 or 4:15 game will be shown on all the network's affiliates across the country, since it is usually the game featuring the best teams (and is covered by the network's best football broadcasting crew and announcers).

Sunday night games are shown on the ESPN cable network. The games on Monday nights are carried by the ABC (American Broadcasting Company) network. This broadcast, named (ABC's) *Monday Night Football,* has become an institution in American culture. Because the game is scheduled for 8:15 P.M. Eastern time (i.e., during prime time, which is the time when most American families are together after work and school and are thus most available as potential viewers) and is the only game at the time being broadcast nationally, it is a showcase for the NFL. As a result, the NFL tries to schedule its best games every week for Monday nights—or at least what it thinks will be the best games before the season starts. It can be argued that *Monday Night Football* has been a major factor in making the NFL the premier spectator sport in the United States.

TIME·OUT

Every NFL game is caught on camera not only by a television network broadcasting the game live but also by filmmakers from an organization called NFL Films. This organization has put on film—not on tape, which is what the television networks use—all of the action of all NFL games for dozens of years. One use of this film is that it is shown during television programs giving the **highlights** of the previous Sunday's games. But what is special about the films taken by NFL Films is that they are played back in slow motion, helping viewers to appreciate the action of the game, and they are accompanied by special music and a narrator with a distinct, dramatic, even poetic-speaking style. In addition, NFL Films crews often focus on a particular player or coach during a game and put a microphone on him so what he says to other players or coaches during a game can be played back along with the film, again giving a special insight into NFL football for the audience. NFL Films has thus done a lot for the popularity of NFL football.

Like other football teams, NFL teams spend the weeks between games practicing and preparing for the next game. Each NFL team usually has its own practice facility separate, sometimes by several miles, from the stadium where it plays its games. Most teams have one major practice per day and sometimes two—especially if the head coach is unhappy with his team's performance—but teams usually do not practice on the day after a game. Meetings are an especially important part of NFL football practices, and they are more frequent and more detailed than those at other levels of football. On the day before a road game, teams fly to the city where the game will be played. They stay in a hotel and hold meetings most of the evening before the game. In some cases, especially before postseason games, teams may arrive early enough on the day before a game or arrive more than one day early so that they are able to practice in the home team's stadium, thus getting used to the stadium and/or the weather conditions where the game will be played. On game day, the team has a large meal together several hours before the start of the game, then heads for the stadium to get ready for the game. When the game is over, most teams immediately fly home even if the game took place at night, so in some cases the team doesn't arrive home until the early-morning hours of the next day.

When the NFL regular season concludes in late December or early January, the postseason begins. The first step is a series of playoff games that will ultimately determine the champion of each conference. Every team in each conference that is champion of its division gets an automatic **playoff spot**, or **berth**. The three teams in each conference, besides the divisional champions, with the best records make the playoffs as **wild-card** teams. Furthermore, the two teams in each conference that have the best records (these are usually divisional champions) get a bye in the first round of the playoffs. And the team with the best record in the conference gets home-field advantage (see "Football Championships" under "Organizational Aspects Common to All Types of Football," above).

The first playoff games are the wild-card games. In each conference, there are two games featuring the three wild-card teams and the one divisional champion with the worst record (as mentioned above, the other two divisional champions get byes for this round). The two teams in each conference with the best regular-season records among the four teams host the wild-card games. These games are played on the Saturday and Sunday following the end of the regular season. On each day, one AFC and one NFC wild-card game is played, and normally the early game and the late game alternate between conferences; for example, if on Saturday an AFC wild-card game starts at 12:30 and the NFC game is at 4:15, on Sunday the NFC game will be at 12:30 and the AFC at 4:15. Both the Saturday games are telecast by ABC, and the Sunday games are handled by CBS and Fox, covering the AFC and NFC games, respectively.

The weekend after these wild-card games, the divisional playoff games take place. The two teams in each conference that won the wild-card games now face the two teams in their conferences that got first-round byes. Since these last teams had the best records, they host the divisional playoff games. Once again, two games are played on Saturday and two on Sunday, starting at 12:30 and 4:15, and also each day one AFC and one NFC game is played.

The Sunday after the divisional playoff games features the conference championship games. The two teams in each conference that won their games now meet for the championship of their conference and the right to go to the Super Bowl (see below). The games are played at the home field of whichever of the two teams had the better regular-season record; occasionally this will not be one or either of the two teams receiving first-round byes because they were **upset** in the divisional playoff games. Again, one game starts at 12:30 and the other at 4:15. The choice of which championship game, the AFC's or the NFC's, to play first often depends as much on market facts as the team's geographic location. If one game is played in the home stadium of a team in the Pacific or Rocky Mountain time zones, it will usually be the 4:15 game, but if this is not the case, the choice often depends on the size of the markets of the teams playing; games featuring teams from the largest cities will usually start at 4:15 because this is considered the time that will attract more viewers and get higher ratings for the network showing the game (and lead to higher advertising fees for corporations eager to buy time for their commercials during the broadcast).

The two teams that win the conference championships go on to the Super Bowl, which is the championship game of the NFL. The Super Bowl is played two weeks after the conference championships. The game is held at a neutral site that is chosen several years in advance of the game. The site chosen may or may not be the regular home of an NFL team, but it must have a stadium of NFL size (with seating for more than 60,000 fans) and enough hotel rooms to accommodate the teams, their fans and other spectators who will travel to the game, and the great numbers of journalists from the U.S. and world media who will cover the game. Tickets to the Super Bowl are not only expensive ($200 or more) but are hard to obtain, as they sell out very quickly; also, tickets are reserved for fans of both teams, for other NFL teams' players, coaches, and officials, and for other important people and celebrities.

Like college bowl games, since the Super Bowl is played in late January its site is usually in a city in the southern or western part of the United States that is likely to have warm weather even in the middle of winter, though a few Super Bowls have been played in northern cities with domed stadiums (e.g., the Pontiac Silverdome in Pontiac, Michigan, and the Hubert H. Humphrey Metrodome in Minneapolis, Minnesota). Because the Super Bowl is *the* biggest game in the NFL season—and one of the biggest, if not the biggest, annual sports events in the world—American cities are eager to host the Super Bowl and make bids to the NFL to be the site of future games. Cities can host Super Bowls more than once, though usually no more frequently than once every five years or so.

TIME·OUT

Although most Super Bowls are played in cities that already have NFL teams, there has never been a Super Bowl played in the home stadium of one of the two teams. This will surely happen eventually, however.

Though they begin preparing for the game almost as soon as they win their conference championship games, the AFC and NFC champions don't go to the site of the Super Bowl until about one week before the game. Their first full day at the site of the Super Bowl is called Media Day, a day during which all the players and coaches of both teams—the players dressed in their full uniforms except for their shoulder pads and helmets—give interviews to reporters inside the stadium (often in the stands, since no spectators are in the stadium for this event) where the game will be played. The rest of the week both teams engage in practices; team officials try to keep the players focused on preparing for the game and away from the distractions and hype that occur during the week.

In fact, the Super Bowl is more than a football game; it has become an unofficial American holiday. The game is broadcast by CBS or Fox, and the network that carries the game must pay a huge sum of money for the right. The Super Bowl is always one of the highest-rated television programs of the year in the United States, and as a result it commands some of the highest fees for showing commercials of any television program. Advertisers, well aware of the huge television audience for the Super Bowl, usually introduce new commercials and advertising campaigns during the game. In addition, the halftime show at the Super Bowl is always a spectacular production, featuring one or more well-known entertainers as well as hundreds of dancers and other supporting performers, usually accompanied by elaborate special effects.

The Super Bowl is also broadcast all over the world by various international networks. In many countries and even in the United States, the game is watched by people who may be just casual football fans and may not have seen any other NFL games during the season. Many Americans consider the game as just an excuse to have a party, which they do by gathering in their homes or in bars to watch the game while consuming snacks, drinks, and other food. It is a fact that while the Super Bowl is being played and broadcast on television, crime rates in U.S. cities and other areas tend to decrease, since so many people are spending their time indoors watching the game.

The Super Bowl traditionally begins at 6:18 P.M Eastern time, the time of the game's kickoff. Before this, starting at about 6:00 P.M., the players of both teams are introduced and there are other preliminaries, such as the singing of the U.S. national anthem (usually by a popular entertainer).

Every year the AFC and NFC teams alternate as the home and away teams, with the home team having the choice of wearing its dark or white jersey. The crew of officials is an all-star group, each official chosen to honor his service and skill in officiating NFL games during the season and over his career.

After all the pregame hype, the game is finally played. The winner of the game is the champion of the NFL and receives a trophy called the Lombardi Trophy. In addition, each member of the winning team receives a monetary reward (in the 1997 Super Bowl, the amount was $48,000) and a special ring commemorating his team's victory. Each member of the losing team also gets a large sum of money, but not as much as the winners get ($29,000 in 1997); the losers also get commemorative rings, but ones that have fewer diamonds than those given to the winners. One player from the winning team is chosen as the Super Bowl MVP (Most Valuable Player) for being the one player most responsible for his team's victory; the Super Bowl MVP is often an offensive player like a quarterback, running back, or wide receiver, but a defensive player and even a special-teams player may be chosen as MVP if he has done enough in the game to help his team win.

At the end of the regular season, one player is also named the league's MVP. The NFL MVP must be a player who not only has performed exceptionally well throughout the regular season but has done the most to help his team be successful (this does not necessarily mean having the best record of any team in the league, but usually the team must at least make the playoffs). Also, the Associated Press polls sportswriters to select the best NFL players at each position who are then designated as **All-Pro** (like the AP's All-American list, there are first- and second-team All-Pro lists).

T I M E · O U T

Most teams also honor one of their players as the team MVP, and each team's offensive or defensive unit may also name a player as its MVP.

The NFL has other ways to honor its best players each season. One week after the Super Bowl, the league holds its annual all-star game—called the Pro Bowl—in Honolulu, Hawaii (where the weather is warm even though this game is played in early February most years). The all-star players, selected by vote of the rest of the players and coaches in their conference, make up the AFC and NFC Pro Bowl teams. If a player selected for the Pro Bowl has been injured near the end of the regular season or the playoffs and can't play in the game—or, as it is often alleged, the player doesn't want to play in this exhibition game and fakes an injury—the coaches of each of the conference teams that lost each conference championship game select another outstanding player from one of the teams in their conferences. (Unlike the all-star selecting process of Major League Baseball, the AFC and NFC teams don't have to include a player from each of the teams in the conference.) Each team wears a special uniform for the game and each player wears the number of his uniform during the regular season, unless another player from another team has the same number, in which case one of these players chooses another number. The players do wear their helmets from their regular-season teams, however, and any other item of their personal equipment—for example, their shoulder pads—they wish to wear. The Pro Bowl, an exhibition game played at the end of a long season by players who are not used to playing with each other, does not feature quite as much rough physical contact as games during the rest of the season. Therefore, to provide some incentive for the players to make the game somewhat competitive and interesting (it is broadcast on national television), each player on the winning team gets several thousand dollars ($20,000 in the 1997 Pro Bowl), and each player on the losing team gets a smaller sum ($10,000 in 1997).

TIME·OUT

During the regular season, the NFL also recognizes players who have performed exceptionally well in one game or in a series of games by naming a Player of the Week and a Player of the Month.

NFL Europe

NFL Europe, formerly the World League of American Football, is a league of professional football clubs in several countries, at present all located in Europe. As described in chapters 2 and 3, the rules of NFL Europe football are very similar to those of the NFL. Part of the reason for this is the close relationship between the NFL and NFL Europe. Even though the NFL does not have an official minor-league system like that of Major League Baseball, NFL Europe comes closest to being one. Not only does NFL Europe get financial support from the NFL, but all NFL teams send a few players to NFL Europe teams every year. Most of these players are young and inexperienced but have significant potential. Backup quarterbacks on NFL teams are often sent to NFL Europe to give them game experience in NFL-like football to prepare them for when they may have to come into an NFL game suddenly after the starting quarterback is injured. The NFL Europe season begins and ends well before the NFL training camps open, so players can play in both leagues in the same year. Moreover, this nonoverlapping schedule—and the fact that currently both leagues play on different continents—causes very little competition between the two leagues.

Here are the names of the six teams that now make up NFL Europe, followed in parentheses by the city and country in which they are based:

> Amsterdam Admirals (Amsterdam, The Netherlands)
> Barcelona Dragons (Barcelona, Spain)
> Frankfurt Galaxy (Frankfurt, Germany)
> London Monarchs (London, England)
> Rhein Fire (Düsseldorf, Germany)
> Scottish Claymores (Edinburgh, Scotland)

Each NFL Europe team has 42 players, of whom up to 35 may be American and at least 7 must be **national players**. These national players can be from any countries in the world except the United States, and not just from Europe or the countries where NFL Europe teams are based. Moreover, NFL Europe has special rules to ensure that non-American players get to play in games. One national player must be in the game for each team on every other offensive or defensive series. In addition, only a non-American kicker can attempt a field goal or extra point when the ball is snapped closer than 15 yards from the goal line. Nevertheless, most of the players who play NFL Europe games are American, including the players on loan from the NFL, as described above. And NFL Europe also holds a draft of college players, most of whom are from U.S. colleges.

All NFL Europe teams play a 10-game regular season, consisting of one home and one road game against each of the other teams in the league. The regular season starts around mid-April, and each weekend three games are played (thus, all six teams are in action each week). There may be one game played on Saturday evening and two games Sunday afternoon, or two games Saturday evening and one Sunday afternoon. The Saturday evening games begin at 7:00 or 7:30 local time, and the Sunday afternoon games begin at 3:00.

In late June in the week after the regular season ends, NFL Europe's championship game, the World Bowl, is played. The World Bowl takes place in the home stadium of the team that is at the top of the league standings after the fifth week of the NFL Europe regular season, and this team is the home team for the game. The other team that plays in the World Bowl is the one of the five other teams that is highest in NFL Europe standings at the end of the regular season. The winner of the World Bowl game is the champion of NFL Europe, and each of the members of the winning team gets a ring, just as the winners of the NFL's Super Bowl do.

Partly because NFL Europe is supported by the NFL and features NFL and other American players, NFL Europe games are broadcast in the United States as well as in European markets. All NFL Europe games are shown on the American FX cable network, a subsidiary of the Fox network, and the World Bowl is broadcast in the United States on Fox, using many of the facilities and personnel that are utilized in showing NFL games on this network.

Canadian Football League (CFL)

The Canadian Football League is a league of professional football teams that play the type of football known as Canadian football. The basic features of Canadian football and how it differs from the game played in the United States have already been discussed in chapters 2 and 3. This section will focus on the organization of the CFL (which is also known as the LCF, an acronym of the French *Ligue Canadienne de Football*, French and English being the official languages of Canada).

The CFL currently has eight franchises. The CFL's teams are located in the largest Canadian cities, but, as in the NFL and other pro sports leagues, this does not mean they are always financially successful; for example, the Montréal Alouettes, located in Canada's largest city, ceased operations in the 1980s, and Montréal was without a football team until the reestablishment of the franchise a few years ago. And in the early

1990s the CFL expanded, with new franchises created in United States cities such as Sacramento (California), Baltimore (Maryland), Las Vegas (Nevada), and Shreveport (Louisiana). All of these American franchises have since folded, however, and the CFL now consists exclusively of Canadian franchises.

The teams of the CFL are organized into East and West divisions. Here are the teams in each:

East Division	West Division
Hamilton Tiger-Cats	British Columbia Lions
Montréal Alouettes	Calgary Stampede
Toronto Argonauts	Edmonton Eskimos
Winnipeg Blue Bombers	Saskatchewan Roughriders

Like the NFL, the CFL has a commissioner. The CFL's commissioner is chosen by a league organization known as the Board of Governors. The players on CFL teams are a mixture of native Canadians and American players, many of whom come to the CFL after being passed up in the NFL draft or after being released from an NFL team. The American players must learn a slightly different brand of football, but they do so because they want to keep playing professional football (many hope that success in the CFL will eventually lead to a position on an NFL team). To protect the integrity of Canadian football, however, the CFL has rules limiting the number of American players on each team. As in the NFL, the players of the CFL are represented by a union, the Canadian Football League Players Association. And every year the teams of the CFL hold a draft of football players from Canadian colleges and universities.

The CFL season begins in early June of every year with the opening of training camps. Each CFL team also plays two exhibition games in early June. Then, in late June, the CFL regular season begins and it lasts until late October. Each CFL team is scheduled to play 18 regular-season games. During the regular season, each team plays every other team in the CFL at least twice, once at home and once on the road. In addition, each team plays one of the teams in its own division four times (twice at home and twice on the road) and the other two teams in the division three times (once at home and twice on the road against one, twice at home and once on the road against the other). CFL regular-season games are played on Thursday, Friday, and Saturday evenings, with some Saturday and Sunday afternoon games—especially late in the season—and a few games on Mondays and Wednesdays.

The CFL also has a post-season for determining its annual champion. The two teams with the second- and third-best regular-season records in each division play a semi-final game one week after the close of the regular season. The winner of each game plays against the team that finished first in the division in the East or West Final game that is played the following week. The winners go on to the CFL championship game, which is called the Grey Cup (after the name of the trophy given to the winning team). The Grey Cup is played during the third week in November in one of the home stadiums of a CFL team (most of which are not domed stadiums, so unlike the NFL's Super Bowl which is always played either indoors or outside in a warm climate, the Grey Cup is often played in wintry conditions). At the end of the year, the CFL also honors its best overall player with a league MVP (also called Most Outstanding Player) Award. There are other honors for individual CFL players, including an award for the most outstanding native Canadian player.

As in many other cultural and economic matters, the influence of the United States on Canadian football and the CFL is strong, often to the dismay of Canadians. Not only are many CFL players—and many of the best ones—American, but there is some resentment that the NFL, with its huge markets and popularity, is flourishing while many CFL clubs in smaller Canadian cities are struggling financially. However, in 1997 the NFL agreed to provide some financial support to the CFL. The NFL has also talked about expanding into Canada for many years, and NFL exhibition games are played every year at Canadian sites. Thus, the future of the CFL may be uncertain, but it appears that football, though it may never seriously challenge ice hockey as Canada's national game, will still be available to Canadians who are fans of the game.

Chapter 5
Other Kinds of Football

The game of football is played not just at the high school, college, and professional levels in North America or just in organized leagues. Football is played in formal leagues by children and nonprofessional or semiprofessional adult players, and it is played informally by people of all ages. Informal games often do not feature the physical contact that results from tackling—which is so central to organized football, as described in chapters 3 and 4—and instead rely on other, less physical means of legally stopping ballcarriers. There is even a kind of professional football that, though it allows tackling, is quite different from the game played in other professional leagues like the NFL. This chapter will discuss all these variants of American football.

Semiprofessional Football

Professional football is played in North America in leagues other than the NFL and the CFL. There exist several, mostly regional, football leagues whose teams play limited schedules, usually from the late summer into the late fall. Some leagues are part of larger conferences in which playoff and championship games are held between the best teams in each league. These games are generally played under NFL rules, but college rules may occasionally apply and each league may have its own special rule variants. Players also generally wear the same types of equipment as that worn in college or other professional football.

The players who play in these leagues are usually paid much less than their counterparts in the NFL or CFL, often receiving just a small payment for each game they play. As a result, most of the players have to hold other jobs to support themselves, and for this reason this kind of football is often referred to as semiprofessional or semipro football. Because most of the players have to work at other jobs, these teams practice mostly on weeknights and play their games on Saturdays. Semiprofessional games do not draw the large crowds that other professional and even most college games attract, which is one of the reasons semipro players are not paid as much as other professional players. (A team's **gate receipts** are an important factor in determining how much it can pay its players.) One of the reasons semiprofessional football games don't draw big crowds is that the teams are usually based in smaller cities (usually cities that don't already have NFL or CFL teams) and thus simply do not have a large potential fan base. In spite of this, the fans who attend semiprofessional games often support their teams with more passion and loyalty than that shown by most of the fans of NFL teams. One reason for this is that most of the players on these teams are year-round residents of the communities in which they play and are much more involved with the community as part-time players than full-time professional athletes would be; this fosters an intimate relationship between the team and its fans.

Most of the players of semiprofessional football are former high school and college players, though many may not have played football in college and some may not even have played high school football. Most are very good players who are just not skilled enough to play at higher levels like the NFL, NFL Europe, or CFL. Nevertheless, many players play semipro football hoping that they will improve their play to the point where they are noticed by professional scouts and get a tryout and maybe even a contract with a professional team. Although this has happened many times, especially with players who for some reason did not play college football, semiprofessional football does not serve as a baseball-style farm system for the NFL; in other words, NFL teams do not have formal arrangements to promote players from semipro teams the way major-league baseball teams do with the teams of minor-league baseball. Other semiprofessional football players keep playing the game well past their college years not because they have faint hopes of still making it to the NFL, NFL Europe, or CFL, but simply because they enjoy playing the game.

T I M E · O U T

There are also professional football leagues outside of North America, especially in Europe. These leagues have much in common with semiprofessional football in the United States and Canada, not the least of which is the fact that many of the players are North American, though teams in these leagues may also have many players from the countries in which they are based.

Arena Football

Another type of professional football is called **arena football**. The rules of arena football differ considerably from those of regular professional or college football. The most striking characteristic of arena football is where it is played. As the name suggests, this kind of football is played indoors in buildings that are usually too small to be called stadiums (though indoor stadiums that are large enough for regulation football can be modified for arena football). These buildings normally host basketball or ice hockey games, and one step in converting them for arena football is laying down an artificial surface like those used in larger indoor or outdoor stadiums (see "Football Fields and Stadiums," in chapter 1).

Because it is played in smaller venues, arena football has field dimensions that are much smaller than those of outdoor football, and this in turn has an effect on the rules of the game. The field of play is only 50 yards long, half the length of the standard outdoor field, and the field is only 85 feet wide, compared to the 160 feet of the outdoor field. The end zones are also only 8 yards long from goal line to end line, not 10 yards as in outdoor football. The goalposts are only 9 feet wide (compared to the 18 feet 6 inches of NFL goalposts) and the crossbar is 15 feet above the playing surface, 5 feet higher than that in outdoor football. In addition, strung from each side of the goalpost to the sidelines are rebound nets. These nets are hung 32 feet from the roof of the arena and 8 feet above the end lines. Unlike the nets behind the goalpost in outdoor football, which are raised only when a field goal or extra point is to be attempted (see "The Football," in chapter 1), the nets in arena football are kept in place throughout the game, since in some cases a ball that bounces off of them is a live ball (see below). And surrounding the field at a distance of at least 5 feet are foam rubber barriers 48 inches high. These are needed for the players' protection, owing to the limited area of the arena football field and to the fact that the hard boards placed around skating rinks when the arenas are used for ice hockey are often still in place around the arena football field. (In fact, the coaches and substitute players of arena football teams remain outside the boards and enter the field through the same gates in the boards used by hockey players.)

Another consequence of the small field in arena football is that there are only 8 players on offense and defense. In addition, each player on the offense and defense, with the exception of the quarterback, kicker, and designated kick returner, must also be a **two-way** player. Because most players have to play more than one position, arena football teams have only 20 players on their roster, which is considerably fewer than the number of players on outdoor football teams (see chapter 4). In addition, players who are not **specialists** can be substituted for only once in a quarter—that is, a player who comes in for a nonspecialist player must remain in the game for the rest of the quarter.

The offensive line of an arena football team consists of just three players, and there is also a **split end**, who lines up on the line of scrimmage but no closer than five yards to a player on one end of the line. The quarterback, fullback, and two wide receivers make up the rest of the offensive unit. An arena football defensive unit must have three linemen who line up in the down position. The linebacker can blitz, but must start from at least two yards back of the line of scrimmage.

Like an outdoor football game, an arena football game has four 15-minute quarters. Even though there are team time-outs and time-outs for injuries and television commercials, an important difference between arena and other football is that the game clock does *not* stop for incomplete passes and out-of-bounds plays except in the last minute of play. This helps to make arena football games shorter than outdoor games.

Because the field is so small, kickoffs are from the kicking team's own goal line. And also because of the size of the field—and the fact that punting is not allowed in arena football—teams always try a field goal on fourth down if they decide not to try for a first down. As a result, the average scores of arena football games are much higher than those of outdoor football; it is not uncommon for both teams in arena games to score 50 or more points.

T I M E · O U T

In outdoor football, with slight variations depending on the level of play, teams rarely score more than 50 points in a game. The average score of each team is between 10 and 30 points, though one or both teams may score more than 30 points in a game. On the other hand, teams often score fewer than 10 points—even the winning team—and many games end in **shutouts**.

If the ball bounces off of the nets beside the goalposts on a kickoff or field goal attempt (but not on an extra-point attempt), the ball may be caught and returned by a player on the receiving team. On kickoffs, a receiver must return the ball if it is caught in the end zone; there is no downing the ball in arena football. However, all members of the receiving team cannot be any closer than five yards to the goal line or to the receiver before the receiver catches the ball. And if the receiver is tackled in the end zone, the ball is put on the receiving team's 5-yard line.

Just as a kicked ball that bounces off the nets is live and can be returned by a receiver, so also a passed ball that bounces off either the nets or the sideline barriers can be caught by a receiver, as long as it doesn't touch the ground first. Also, a receiver may catch the ball with his or her body against the barrier as long as one foot is touching the ground in bounds.

Another special rule of arena football is that when the score of a game is tied after four quarters, an overtime period is played in which *both* teams must be given an opportunity to score (i.e., it is not a sudden-death overtime; see "Length of Game," in chapter 3). This is accomplished by making sure each team has at least one possession of the ball. If neither team scores during its possession—or if both do—then the overtime is played until one of the teams scores again, and thus wins the game. It should also be noted that anytime a player on a team even touches the ball—for example, if a kick receiver fumbles a kickoff or if a defensive player intercepts a pass but then fumbles it on the return—the receiving or defensive teams are considered to have used their one possession opportunity during the overtime. If the score is still tied at the end of an overtime period during a regular-season game, the game is over and officially ends in a tie, but during a postseason game overtime periods are played until one ends with one team in the lead. Overtime periods in arena football are 7 minutes and 30 seconds long during regular-season games and 15 minutes long in playoff and championship games.

Arena football is played under the auspices of the Arena Football League (AFL), which consists of 14 franchises organized into four divisions, as listed below:

Eastern Division	**Central Division**
Albany Firebirds	Iowa Barnstormers
Nashville Kats	Milwaukee Mustangs
New Jersey Red Dogs	Portland Forest Dragons
New York CityHawks	Texas Terror

Southern Division	**Western Division**
Florida Bobcats	Anaheim Piranhas
Orlando Predators	Arizona Rattlers
Tampa Bay Storm	San Jose SaberCats

The AFL season begins with teams' training camps, lasting a few weeks in April. As in the NFL, the AFL has a Hall of Fame exhibition game held before the start of the regular season. Each AFL team plays 14 games during the regular season, which begins in early May and lasts until early August. Games are played mostly on Friday and Saturday evenings, though some games are scheduled on Thursdays, Sundays, and Mondays. The week following the weekend on which the regular season ends, the eight teams with the best records (including the three divisional champions) play in four quarterfinal games, and the following week the winners of the quarterfinals play in two semifinal playoff games. The two winners of these games play in the AFL championship game, called the Arena Bowl, which is played in the home building of the team that had the better record during the regular season.

Arena football players are on about the same level as American-born CFL and NFL Europe players—that is, they are good ex–college players who just may not be good enough to play in the NFL. Some AFL players do get signed by NFL teams, however, especially since the AFL season ends just before the NFL regular season begins, and many AFL players may play for CFL or even semiprofessional teams.

AFL games are broadcast (not always live) by the U.S. cable television sports networks ESPN and ESPN2. Games may also be broadcast on television or radio by local stations in each team's market.

Youth Football

Though most American schools below the high school level do not sponsor interscholastic football teams, American children can still participate in organized football through an organization called Pop Warner Junior League Football (henceforth Pop Warner football). This organization is named after Pop Warner, a legendary college football player and coach in the early days of the game who introduced many rules and innovations that had a great impact on the development of the game of football. There are several thousand Pop Warner youth football teams in the United States, and almost every American city and town has teams.

Pop Warner football is open to children ages 8 to 15. Most Pop Warner players are boys, but occasionally girls play. In addition to its football programs, Pop Warner also sponsors cheerleading programs for girls that are affiliated with the youth football teams.

The Pop Warner football programs are divided into seven divisions based loosely on the weight and age of players (of course, young players of the same age cannot be guaranteed to have the same weight). The Pop Warner divisions, in order from the one for the lightest players to the one for the heaviest, are tiny tot, junior peewee, peewee, junior midget, midget, junior bantam, and bantam. This organization method is designed to decrease the chances of injury to players and increase fair competition by having youths play only against others of approximately the same weight. Each player's weight is monitored throughout the season (kids sometimes grow very fast) to make sure the players are in the appropriate division.

Though teams play in competitive leagues, the primary purpose of Pop Warner football is to train players in the fundamentals of football while stressing safety and the play of the game for fun. (Nevertheless, some adults and children in the program often lose sight of this ideal and overemphasize winning.) The rules, strategies, and scoring of the Pop Warner variety of football are generally the same as those of high school football. Players wear the same kinds of protective equipment that high school and adult players wear, though of course in smaller sizes for youths. Players' parents are asked to volunteer as coaches, officials, or program administrators.

Children interested in playing Pop Warner football must sign up by the early summer for the upcoming season. The season gets under way in early August, with daily two-hour practices that are reduced to (usually) three times per week in the afternoon after school once the school year starts in early September. Pop Warner teams play a 10-game regular season. If a team makes the local playoffs or goes beyond (see below), its season may extend into November or early December; this sometimes causes problems for players who are forced to give up other after-school activities and sports that may begin in the late fall.

An important aspect of Pop Warner football is that a player's performance in school is considered just as important as his or her play on the football field. This philosophy is meant to keep students from focusing too much on sports and not enough on academics. To qualify for postseason play, players and cheerleaders associated with a team must turn in report cards to verify their satisfactory performance in school. And Pop Warner names a yearly All-American team for players and cheerleaders in all school grade levels, the criteria for selection being not so much the players' accomplishments in football as their grades, honors, and other activities in school. To include as many outstanding players as possible, there are first- and second-team Pop Warner All-American squads.

Pop Warner teams compete in local leagues, and at the end of the season league champions are declared, sometimes through playoff games. The champions of each league play other local champions to determine regional champions within states, and these winners go on to compete for state championships at each level of Pop Warner play. State champions compete in four national regional championships, and the four surviving teams advance to the national championships held in Orlando, Florida, in December. Two semifinal games are played, and the winners play against each other in the Pop Warner Super Bowl (the teams that lost in the semifinals play in a consolation game).

Many young football players attend football camps, which usually have no official connection with Pop Warner football. These camps are brief sessions held on a weekend or for a week in the summer, and usually take place at facilities where the players can live temporarily while they practice and play football. At the camps, players receive coaching in football fundamentals and other skills to make them better players. At most camps, there is a fee that must be paid by the players' families. Many football camps are associated with one or more well-known NFL or college players or coaches, who actually may be affiliated with the camp in name only (as a way to attract players to the camp) and have little to do with the instruction of players that goes on there.

Flag and Touch Football

Up to this point, the types of football described in this chapter and in the rest of the book have had at least one thing in common: tackling as the method for stopping a ballcarrier. This section will describe two other types of football that do not involve tackling and feature other rules for stopping a ballcarrier and ending a play. One of these types of nontackle football is **flag football**, in which all players wear detachable pieces of fabric around their waists and a ballcarrier is ruled down when **deflagged** by a player on the other team. Another type of nontackle football is **touch football**, in which ballcarriers are stopped when defenders **tag** them. Because of the absence of tackling in both flag and touch football, either can be played without a lot of the protective equipment worn by players in organized tackle football—in fact, players rarely wear any equipment while playing flag or touch football. Still, in both touch and flag football body contact through blocking is allowed, and accidental contact from players running into each other is frequent and unavoidable.

The only equipment that is needed to play touch football is a football, which can be smaller than regulation size and can even be a toy, especially in informal games (see below). By definition, flag football requires that players wear detachable flags that are brightly colored thin strips of fabric at least one foot long and an inch wide. The flags are usually red, orange, or yellow, and players on each team wear the same-color flags. Each player wears two flags, one on his or her left side and one on the right, which are attached—usually through a Velcro attachment—to a belt worn around the player's waist. The flags must stay in place when the player runs around on the field, but they should come off easily when grabbed by a player on the other team.

Very often, touch or flag football games—especially informal or **pickup** games—are not played on a regular football field but in a smaller, open area without lines. In games on smaller fields, both sides may agree to play by the rule that in four downs a team has to score a touchdown—not just a first down—or it must punt. Even goalposts are not necessary in informal flag and touch football; the teams can agree on a substitute, such as kicking the ball anywhere over the goal line—which itself may just be an imaginary line between two objects placed on the field—or not even allow field goal or extra-point attempts at all.

Because they require so little equipment and so few players (in informal games, each team can have as few as two or three players, and teams need not have the same number of players), touch and flag football are popular recreational sports in the United States. Games are usually played without coaches, officials, game clocks, or scoreboards, and the game goes on until one team scores a certain number of points or until some or all of the players quit or have to stop playing for some reason. Touch and flag football are often played in gym classes at schools, or as a recreational sport among college students and other young people in a neighborhood. Another reason for the popularity of flag and touch football is that, as indicated above, they are less physical games than tackle football and thus permit players too small and frail to participate in tackle football to enjoy playing the game. In particular, the nature of flag and touch football encourages coed play—games in which teams consist of both male and female players. Since there is no tackling, it is easier for women to compete with men in this kind of football.

T I M E · O U T

It should be noted that not only are flag and touch football often played recreationally, but people sometimes play tackle football in informal pickup games, often without protective equipment like helmets and pads. This is more likely to be done by children and younger people whose bodies are more able to take the physical contact of playing without pads.

Though much of flag and touch football play is informal, these games are often played in organized leagues under established rules. One organization that attempts to be a governing body for these sports is the United States Flag and Touch Football League (USFTL). This entity has established uniform rules for both touch and flag football, and it sponsors clinics and other training for players, coaches, and officials. It also licenses flags and footballs to be used in games played under USFTL rules (men's games must use regulation-size footballs, but smaller balls can be used in games between women's teams or youth teams).

Most of the rules for touch and flag football are like those for tackle football, but there are some differences in games played under USFTL rules. Touch football requires seven players per team, three of whom must be on the line of scrimmage during the snap, and in flag football there are eight players per team, four of whom must be on the line when the ball is snapped. The USFTL also recognizes two other variants of flag football. One, called "ineligible lineman flag football," features nine players per team. Five of these players are linemen who, as the name of the game implies, can't go out for a pass when the team is on offense. Another recognized form of flag football is "4 on 4" featuring four players on each team; in this variant, with its small number of players and more open field, passing attempts are very frequent.

As mentioned above, in touch football a ballcarrier is stopped by touching him or her anywhere above the knees and below the shoulders with both hands at the same time. In flag football, if a ballcarrier's flag has fallen off accidentally before the end of the play, the player can still be stopped by the same kind of two-hand tag as that used in touch football. (At the end of all plays, any flags that were detached from or fell off players must be reattached to the players before the next play can start.) Defensive players are not allowed to hold or otherwise obstruct the ballcarrier to make it easier for them to make a tag or pull the ballcarrier's flag. In addition, a ballcarrier cannot guard his or her flags—for example, by putting one hand over a flag to keep a defender from grabbing it. This infraction receives a 10-yard penalty against the offense and a loss of down. As in tackle football, a ballcarrier in both touch and flag football is down and the play is over if his or her knee touches the ground.

The USFTL also has rules that are designed to minimize physical contact and protect players in touch and flag football. Players are not allowed to dive forward when either carrying the ball, trying to deflag or tag a ballcarrier, or blocking a defender; in other words, they must keep at least one foot on the ground (receivers and pass defenders can dive for a passed ball, however). No double-team blocking is allowed—that is, two players together cannot block one (see chapter 3)—and roughing the passer is called against the defense even when a defensive pass rusher merely touches the passer's arm. A team attempting a punt can request that the receiving team not rush the punter by so informing the referee, and onside kickoffs are not permitted. And when any player fumbles and the ball hits the ground, or when any snap hits the ground, the ball is immediately dead and cannot be recovered by another player. This rule keeps players from both teams from piling on to recover the ball, with all the risk of injury that this kind of frenzied contact usually brings.

The USFTL also administers organized touch and flag football play, both in leagues and in special tournaments. There are local leagues for both men's and women's teams, and there are different levels of competition based on the skill and relative competitiveness of the teams. These levels are usually designated by single letters, with the A level comprising the best teams, B the second best, and so on. Organized touch and flag football teams play under the name of a sponsor (usually a business) or adopt some other distinctive name or nickname, which usually consists of one or a few words and might not give any indication of where the team is from.

USFTL flag and touch football regional championships are held in several locations across the United States in late

November, with the winners advancing to a national championship tournament in Orlando, Florida, in January. The USFTL also has a Hall of Fame, which honors outstanding touch and flag football players, coaches, officials, and team sponsors.

Whether played formally or informally, the widespread popularity of flag and touch football is another testament to the popularity of the game of football in North America. Many touch and flag football players are former tackle football players, but there are many who have never played tackle football or have not played it in an organized league. Especially if they are children or young people, many of these players often wish they could play the tackle game or are inspired by the pro or college football games they watch in person or on television.

Baseball has traditionally been called America's national pastime, and even if this is still true, football is a close runner-up, because in its simplest forms, as described in this section, it can be played by just about anyone.

Glossary

accept a penalty *v.* to agree that a penalty called against the other team should be enforced.

adjustments *n.* changes in the general game plan and other offensive and defensive strategies a team is using based on the observations and opinions of the members of the coaching staff on the field and in the press box (the coaches in the press box usually join the rest of the team in the locker room during halftime).

advance (the football) *v.* to run forward with the football, or pass the ball, in order to give one's team better field position.

ahead *adj.* having more points than the other team.

All-American *n.* a college football player who has been determined by sportswriters to be the best among all college players at his position during a season.

All-Pro *n.* an NFL player who has been determined by sportswriters to be the best among all NFL players at his position during a season.

all-star *n.* a player who has been determined to be the best at his or her position during one season of a league or at a certain level of competition.

all-star game *n.* an exhibition game between two teams consisting of the best players in one or more leagues.

and long *adv.* with several yards to go for a first down.

arena football *n.* a type of football that is played in an indoor stadium on a smaller field than in other kinds of football and has some special rules (one is that most players must play both offensive and defensive positions).

artificial turf *n.* a surface on some football fields that is made from small blades of material like plastic or nylon.

assistant coach *n.* a coach on a football team who assists the head coach and may have various responsibilities—for example, coaching the team's offensive or defensive unit or coaching players in individual positions, such as the linemen or wide receivers.

AstroTurf *n.* a type of artificial turf whose name derives from the Houston Astrodome, the domed stadium where the first of this kind of playing surface was installed.

at home *adv.* on a team's home field.

audible *n.* a play in which the quarterback uses special signals during the count that tell the rest of the offense both that the quarterback is changing the play and what the new play will be.

away game *n.* See **road game**.

back judge *n.* an official who counts the number of players on the defense, who watches for interference infractions and other violations on passes far beyond the line of scrimmage, and who calls penalties like clipping near the spot on the field where punts and kickoffs are caught and returned.

back up *v.* to play in a football game in place of a player higher on the depth chart when that player gets injured or doesn't perform well.

backfield *n.* the area behind the offensive line where offensive backs line up before the start of plays.

backpedal *v.* to run or jog backward.

backup *adj.* describing a second- or third-string player.

ball boys *n.* attendants, usually young persons, who assist football officials in keeping footballs on both sidelines and putting new ones in play when needed.

ballcarrier *n.* a player running with the football.

ball-control *adj.* describing a type of offensive strategy in which mostly rushing plays are attempted, with passes thrown only when necessary. Also called *conservative*.

beat (a defender) *v.* to be able to get far enough away from the defender so that he or she has no chance of breaking up a pass.

behind *adj.* having fewer points than the other team.

big play *n.* a play that results in a long gain and/or a touchdown.

black out *v.* to require that a television station or network not broadcast a certain football game.

blitz *n.* a defensive play in which at the snap of the ball a player charges through the line of scrimmage as quickly as possible so that he or she cannot be blocked and tries to tackle the quarterback before the quarterback can either hand the ball off or pass.

block (a field goal or extra-point attempt) *v.* to make contact with the football as it is being, or has just been, kicked so that the ball does not go forward and the attempt is no good.

block (a player) *v.* to use one's body and physical actions to keep a defender from moving toward a ballcarrier so that the ballcarrier won't be tackled and can advance the ball.

block (a punt) *v.* to make contact with the football as it is being, or has just been, punted so that the ball does not go very far forward or doesn't go forward at all.

blocking assignments *n.* part of offensive play plans indicating which players on the defense are going to be blocked by each player on the offense.

blocking sled *n.* a large platform with one or several large pads against which players, especially linemen, practice blocking. A coach often stands on top of the sled and gives directions, and the sled moves backward on rails when the players hit the pads.

blow the call *v.* to make a mistake in calling—or not calling— a penalty.

body block *n.* a type of blocking in which a player turns sideways and throws one whole side of his or her body into the midsection or thighs of the defender.

bomb *n.* a pass pattern in which the quarterback throws the ball high into the air and far down the field to a receiver; if completed, this pass can result in a long gain and often a touchdown.

bootleg *n.* a running play in which the quarterback, either after dropping back as if to pass or right after getting the snap, runs around one of the ends of the line. Also called (*quarterback*) *keeper.*

bowl bid *n.* an invitation to play against another team in one of the college bowl games.

bowl (game) *n.* a Division I-A college football game played at the end of the season between two of the best college teams.

break up a pass *v.* to touch or bat a passed football so that it hits the ground before the receiver can catch it.

broken play *n.* See **busted play.**

bump *v.* to make contact with.

busted play *n.* a play in which one or more of the players on the offense don't do what they are supposed to according to the plan of the play. Also called *broken play*.

(button)hook *n.* See **come back**.

bye *n.* when the one or two teams with the best regular-season records do not play during the first week, or round, of playoff games but wait to play the teams who do play and win the first playoff games.

bye week *n.* See **open week**.

call a penalty *v.* to throw a penalty flag and signal for a stoppage of the game after the completion of the current play, if the play has already started when a violation is seen.

call a play *v.* to announce to an offensive unit (by a quarterback) or a defensive unit (by a defensive captain) which play the unit is to run on the next down.

captains *n.* a group of players on a football team who may be the best or the most senior players on the team. Each team has at least one captain for its offense and one for its defensive unit, though there may be several captains on a team. The captains have special responsibilities, such as representing their teams during the coin toss and officially accepting or declining penalties for their teams.

career-ending *adj.* describing an injury so severe that it prevents a player from ever playing football again.

center *n.* the player who is in the middle of the offensive line. The center starts every offensive play by hiking the ball to the quarterback at the quarterback's signal.

chains *n.* two poles connected by a chain that is exactly 10 yards long. The chains are used by officials to indicate the distance necessary for the ball to be advanced by the offense to get a first down and also for measurements when it is not certain that the ball has been advanced more than 10 yards. The poles have bright reddish-orange trim (and black and white bars in the NFL), with a circular piece on top, and are at least 5 feet (1.52 meters) tall. The poles are connected to the ends of a small chain that is exactly 10 yards (9.14 meters) long. (In Canadian football, the poles are called *pickets*.)

championship game *n.* a postseason football game, the winner of which is the champion of a league. Also called *final game*.

change of possession *n.* when the team that was on defense goes on offense and vice versa.

cheerleaders *n.* people dressed in special uniforms who, during football games, stand off of the field of play near the stands and perform actions like leading the crowd in cheering for one of the teams.

chop block *n.* a type of blocking in which the blocker throws his or her body toward a defender's legs.

cleats *n.* small stubs on the soles of football shoes that help players keep from slipping as they run on the football field by digging into the ground or artificial turf.

clinch *v.* to be assured of ending the season in first place or with a playoff spot by being more games up over the team in second place (i.e., the second-place team is more games behind) than there are games left in the season.

clipping *n.* a penalty that is called when an offensive player blocks a defensive player from behind.

coaches *n.* personnel on a football team who are responsible for instructing and training players and directing a team's play during a game.

coaching box *n.* See **coaching line**.

coaching line *n.* on college football fields, a 6-foot-wide solid white border just outside of both sidelines that runs between the two 25-yard lines, in which only a team's head coach and game officials or chain crew personnel are allowed during a game. Also called *coaching box*.

coffin corner *n.* a punt that goes out of bounds close to the receiving team's goal line.

coin toss *n.* the procedure at the beginning of a football game in which the referee tosses a coin into the air in the middle of the field, and the captain of one of the teams has to predict which side of the coin (heads or tails) will be facing up when the coin lands on the ground. If the captain is right, his or her team wins the toss and gets the choice of receiving the opening kickoff or deciding which goal to defend.

college football *n.* the variety of football played by teams made up of students from U.S. and Canadian post-secondary institutions, which are colleges, universities, and other schools that students attend after finishing high school.

color *n.* commentary on the action of a football game including the strategy of the teams, the current and past performance of the players, or background on the game, teams or players, which is usually given only between plays.

combination blocking *n.* See **double-teaming**.

come back *n.* a pass pattern in which the receiver runs down the field, stops, then takes a few steps back toward the quarterback. Also called (*button*)*hook*.

come out (for a draft) *v.* to declare that one wishes to give up the remainder of one's eligibility to play college football in order to be drafted by a professional team.

commissioner *n.* the director of the National Football League or the Canadian Football League.

complete pass *n.* a pass that is thrown by the quarterback or another player on the offense to an offensive player who is eligible to receive the pass and who catches the ball before it hits the ground.

conference *n.* See **league**.

conservative *adj.* See **ball-control**.

contract *n.* a legal document indicating a professional football player's agreement to play football for a team for a specific number of seasons in exchange for the team's paying him a certain salary.

convert *v.* to earn a first down.

corner blitz *n.* a type of blitz in which a cornerback rushes in toward the quarterback.

cornerback *n.* a defensive back who lines up close to the line of scrimmage but several yards to one side of the line, directly opposite the wide receivers of the offense.

coverage scheme *n.* a plan that a defense uses to cover the receivers who may go out for a pass.

covered *adj.* closely guarded by a defensive back or another defensive player.

crossbar *n.* the part of the goalpost supported by the base that lies horizontally 10 feet (3.05 m) above the field and supports the two uprights.

crossing pattern *n.* a pass pattern in which one receiver crosses the middle of the field a few yards in front of another receiver.

cut (a player) *v.* to release from a team because the player is not as good as the other players on the team or for other reasons (e.g., the salary cap or disciplinary problems).

dead *adj.* describing a football that cannot be advanced because the play is over or hasn't begun yet.

dead lines *n.* in Canadian football, lines that extend the width of a football field and, along with the sidelines, set off the boundaries of the field.

decline a penalty *v.* See **refuse a penalty**.

deep *adj.* See **long**.

defense *n.* the unit of a football team that tries to prevent the other team's offense from moving the ball forward and scoring and also tries to gain possession of the ball for its own offensive unit.

defensive back *n.* a player on the defense whose main responsibility is to cover a receiver going out for a pass but who may also tackle a ballcarrier and rush the quarterback on blitzes.

defensive coordinator *n.* an assistant coach who is responsible for a football team's defensive unit.

defensive end *n.* a player on the defense who lines up on one end of the defensive line.

defensive lineman *n.* a defensive player who lines up on the line of scrimmage opposite the offensive line.

defensive tackle *n.* in a four-player defensive line, a lineman who lines up between the defensive ends.

deflag *v.* in flag football, to grab and take off a flag worn by a ballcarrier.

delay of game *n.* a penalty that is called when the offense does not start a play before the play clock expires.

depth chart *n.* a ranking of the players on a football team; at the top are the starters or first-string players, followed by the second, third, and perhaps lower strings.

disqualify *n.* See **eject**.

division *n.* a unit of a football league or conference consisting of a small group of its teams.

double-teaming *n.* a style of blocking in which two players are assigned to block one defensive player, each approaching the defender from a different side. Also called *combination blocking*.

down *n.* the opportunity an offense has to run a play that will gain enough yardage for the offense to receive a first down.

down *adj.* tackled.

down (a kickoff) *v.* to not try to return a kickoff by kneeling in the end zone, with one knee touching the ground, after catching the ball.

down indicator *n.* a pole at least 5 feet (1.52 meters) high having a sign on the top that shows the number of the current down; the number signs are flipped over after each play to reveal the next down number.

down position *n.* the position in which offensive linemen must be during the quarterback count before the snap of the ball: bent over in a crouching position with one leg a little in front of the other, supported by one arm with the fingers of the hand or the knuckles touching the ground and the other arm bent over the knee of the leg that's farther back. Also called *three-point stance.*

draft *n.* the selection of college players by professional football teams.

(draft) pick *n.* a selection in a football draft, or the player chosen by a team with this selection.

draw *n.* a type of handoff in which the quarterback drops back as if to pass but hands the ball off to a running back, who doesn't move forward until getting the ball.

dump the ball off *v.* to throw a short pass to a nearby receiver, especially to avoid a sack. Also called *unload the ball.*

eat up the clock *v.* to keep the game clock running by having runners tackled in bounds so that the game will finish quickly with the team maintaining its lead and winning the game. Also called **kill the clock**.

eject *v.* to prohibit a player from playing anymore in a game. Also called *disqualify.*

eligible receiver *n.* a player on the offense who can legally receive a pass; the player must be a back, wide receiver, or a tight end or a lineman who has told an official he or she wants to go out for a pass.

end around *n.* a rushing play in which at the snap of the ball a wide receiver runs backward from the line of scrimmage toward the backfield, receives a handoff from the quarterback, then continues running around the end of the line opposite from where he or she started at the snap.

end lines *n.* two lines that extend the width of a football field and, along with the sidelines, set off the boundaries of the field.

end zone *n.* the section at each end of a football field that extends 10 yards (9.14 meters) out from the end line to the goal line.

endorsement *n.* when a professional football player or coach is paid to appear in a television commercial or other form of advertisement for a commercial product.

equipment *n.* the items football players wear that are designed to protect specific parts of their bodies in collisions with other players, other players' equipment, and the ground.

exhibition games *n.* games on a football team's schedule, usually played before the regular season begins, that are not considered official games—that is, they are not counted in the standings and the players' performances in the games are not included in individual or team statistics for the season.

expansion team *n.* a new team added to a football league.

expire *v.* to run out of time (on a clock).

extra point *n.* a single point that a team scores after a touchdown play by kicking the football through the uprights and over the crossbar of the goalpost. Also called *point after touchdown (PAT)*.

extra-point attempt *n.* the opportunity every team that scores a touchdown is given to try to score one or two more points immediately after the touchdown play.

face guard *n.* See **face mask**.

face mask *n.* metal or hard plastic bars that are joined to the sides of a football helmet and curve around the open front roughly parallel with the player's mouth. Another bar may extend vertically from the forehead part of the helmet down to the horizontal bars. Also called *face guard.*

fair catch *n.* a play in which a punt returner waves one hand in the air as the punt is coming down. This means that the returner will not run with the ball after catching it, and it also means that the members of the punting team must allow the returner to catch the ball (i.e., they cannot be so close to the returner that they interfere with the returner's catching the ball). If the returner catches the ball after signaling for a fair catch, the play is immediately over and the returner's team will take over on offense at the spot the ball is caught.

fake a handoff *v.* to stick the football out to a player who is coming forward as if to receive a regular handoff but not actually give the ball to the player.

fake punt *n.* a play in which an offense lines up on fourth down as though it's going to punt, but after the ball is snapped tries to run or pass the ball for a first down.

fans *n.* spectators who attend football games.

field *n.* the large rectangular space where football is played.

field goal *n.* a kicking play in which the ball is kicked from somewhere on the field so that it travels through the air over the crossbar and between the uprights of a goalpost. A field goal earns the team that kicks it 3 points.

field goal attempt *n.* when a team tries to kick a field goal. Also called *field goal try.*

field goal range *n.* a distance close enough to the goal line of an opponent so that a team has a good chance of kicking a field goal.

field goal try *n.* See **field goal attempt**.

field judge *n.* an official who calls penalties on forward passes and on punts and kickoffs and who, when present among the crew of officials, also indicates when the play clock should be started or stopped.

final game *n.* See **championship game**.

first down *n.* the first in a new series of downs, given to a team when it gains possession of the ball or when its offense advances more than 10 yards on the previous series of downs.

first half *n.* the first and second quarters of a football game.

first-string *adj.* describing players who are highest on a team's depth chart—that is, are the starters.

five-step drop *n.* when a quarterback takes five steps backward after the snap.

flag football *n.* a type of nontackle football in which all players wear detachable pieces of fabric around their waists and a ballcarrier is ruled down when a player on the other team deflags the ballcarrier.

flagrant *adj.* describing an infraction that was clearly and deliberately committed.

flak jacket *n.* See **rib pads**.

flea-flicker *n.* a play that involves unusual actions, such as a running back flipping the ball back to the quarterback after receiving a handoff. Also called *gadget play*.

fly pattern *n.* a pass pattern in which the receiver runs as fast as possible straight down the field. Also called *go pattern*.

football *n.* the ball used in the game of football. It is made from four sections of leather that are sewn together over an inner rubber tube called a bladder. The NFL specifies that the circumference of its footballs be between 21 and 21¼ inches and the CFL specifies a circumference of 20⅞ to 21⅛ inches. Both these professional leagues also require the length of their footballs to be between 11 and 11¼ inches long.

free agent *n.* a player who may sign a contract to play for any professional team.

free kick *n.* a kickoff after a safety in which the team against which the safety was scored sends its special-teams unit onto its own 20-yard line and must then punt the ball to the other team.

free play *n.* a play in which the offense knows that a penalty, usually an offsides penalty, is going to be called against the defense. The offense often tries a daring play like a long pass, with the realization that even if the pass is incomplete or intercepted the penalty against the defense will result in the offense still having the ball and farther upfield from the line of scrimmage.

free safety *n.* the safety next to the strong safety—that is, the safety who does not line up opposite the side of the offense where the tight end is.

front office *n.* the management of a professional team.

fullback *n.* a running back who lines up directly behind the quarterback and usually blocks instead of taking handoffs.

fumble *v.* to drop or lose possession of the football.

gadget play *n.* See **flea-flicker**.

game ball *n.* a football that is traditionally awarded by a team to a player or players who performed especially well during the game or who were especially responsible for the team winning.

game plan *n.* a specific plan for offensive and defensive strategy to be used in a game.

games behind *n.* how many games a team would have to win—and the first-place team would have to lose—for the teams to have the same record and share first place.

gate receipts *n.* the amount of money a football club receives from the sale of tickets or other admissions fees for its games.

general manager *n.* a member of the front office of an NFL team, who has a large role in deciding what players will be on the team by evaluating scouting reports of college and other professional players, deciding which college players to draft, making trades for other players, and signing free agents. Also called *GM*.

giveaway *n.* when a team turns the ball over to the other team.

GM *n.* See **general manager**.

go deep *v.* to go far down the field to receive a pass. Also called *go long*.

go for two *v.* to attempt a two-point conversion.

go long *v.* See **go deep**.

go pattern *n.* See **fly pattern**.

goal area *n.* In Canadian football, the section at each end of the field that extends 20 yards (18.29 meters) out from the dead line to the goal line.

goal line *n.* the lengthwise yard line that marks the inner border of the end zone. Crossing the goal line with the football results in a score.

goal to go *adj.* describing an offensive series in which the offense starts the first down fewer than 10 yards from its opponent's goal line.

goalpost *n.* a structure, usually made from metal, that is located near a football field's end zone. It consists of a base (or pedestal) that supports a horizontal crossbar, and extending vertically from both ends of the crossbar are two poles called the uprights. Points are scored by kicking the ball over the crossbar and through the uprights.

goat *n.* the player who is blamed for a team's loss.

going to the pass *n.* attempting mostly passing plays.

good *adj.* describing a field goal or extra-point attempt that is successful.

good field position *n.* when a team has possession of the football in an area of the field from which they can be expected to score in the next few offensive series.

go-to receiver *n.* See **primary receiver**.

guard *n.* an offensive lineman who lines up on one side of the center.

Hail Mary pass *n.* a passing play in which as many eligible receivers as possible run toward or into the other team's end zone, and the quarterback throws a very long pass downfield in the hope that one of the receivers will catch it. The name of this play comes from the first words of a Catholic prayer, implying that this pass is so desperate that the team has to pray for its success.

halfback *n.* a running back who lines up either in back of but not directly behind the quarterback or behind the fullback and quarterback.

halfback pass *n.* a play in which a running back receives a handoff but throws a pass to a receiver before crossing the line of scrimmage.

halftime *n.* the intermission that occurs at the end of the first half of a football game. During the halftime, both teams go back into their respective locker rooms for a meeting and for some rest, and there is usually some kind of entertainment on the field for the crowd.

hand off *v.* to give the football to another player on the same team, who then tries to advance the ball.

handoff *n.* a play in which a player gives the football to another player on the same team, who then tries to advance the ball.

hang time *n.* the time that a kicked football stays in the air before being caught by a receiver or hitting the ground.

hard count *n.* when a quarterback tries to make the defense jump offside by raising his or her voice at some point in the count but not on the actual snap signal.

hash marks *n.* two rows of yard markers that extend the length of the middle of a football field.

have the lead *v.* to have more points than the other team.

head coach *n.* the leader of a football team's coaching staff. He or she has the final say on all the important decisions the team has to make during a game, such as offensive play selection, defensive and special-teams strategies, and the acceptance of penalties.

head-to-head *adj.* describing an outcome that is decided as a result of a game or games between the two teams involved, such as the competition for a championship or playoff spot.

helmet *n.* an item of football equipment worn on a player's head that is made of hard, unbreakable plastic and has padding on the inside to help cushion blows to the head.

highlights *n.* the scores and most important plays of a game.

hike *v.* to pick up the football from the ground on the line of scrimmage and give it to the quarterback through the legs. Also called *snap*.

hold out *v.* to refuse to report to training camp, to practice, or to play in any games for a professional football team until the team agrees to the player's contract demands.

holder *n.* the player on field goal and extra-point kicking attempts who holds the ball upright on the ground for the kicker.

holding *n.* a penalty in which an offensive player holds on to part of a defensive player's body with the hands while trying to block the defender.

hole *n.* the space between any two of the offensive linemen through which a running back may try to go on a rushing play.

home field *n.* the field or stadium that a team plays about half of its games in.

home team *n.* the team that is playing a football game on its home field.

home-field advantage *n.* when a football team plays a game on its home field, where it usually plays better and thus has a better chance of winning.

huddle *n.* when the whole offensive or defensive unit gathers together behind the line of scrimmage to hear the quarterback (for the offense) or the defensive captain call the unit's next play. In most huddles the players form a circle, but some teams have a huddle formation where the quarterback or captain stands with his or her back to the line of scrimmage and facing the rest of the unit.

hurry up *n.* See **no huddle**.

illegal forward pass *n.* when a player attempts a pass downfield after stepping over the line of scrimmage.

in *n.* a pass pattern in which the receiver runs straight down the field for several yards, turns to the left or the right, then runs toward the middle of the field.

in bounds *adj., adv.* in technical usage, the area of the football field between the hash marks from which the football must be put into play; informally, anywhere on the football field inside of the sidelines and end lines.

in the grasp *n.* a football rule that states that if a defensive player has hold of a quarterback such that, in the opinion of the officials, the quarterback cannot run any farther, the play is immediately whistled over and the quarterback is considered tackled at that spot.

incomplete pass *n.* a pass that hits the ground before reaching the receiver, is dropped by the receiver and hits the ground, is caught out of bounds, or is intercepted.

independent *n.* a football team that does not belong to a league or conference.

ineligible receiver *n.* a player, usually a lineman, who is not allowed to receive a pass and cannot go past the line of scrimmage as if to receive a pass.

infraction *n.* See **penalty**.

injured reserve *n.* a designation of an injured NFL player meaning that although the player is unable to play in the team's games, he is still a member of the team and can play for it again when he has recovered from his injury.

inside linebacker *n.* in a defense with four linebackers, one of the two linebackers who line up between the outside linebackers.

intentional grounding *n.* a penalty that is called when a quarterback or another offensive player throws the football to a place on the field where no receiver could possibly catch it in order to avoid being tacked behind the line of scrimmage.

intercept *v.* to catch a pass that was intended for a receiver on the offense. Also called *pick off*.

interception *n.* when a defensive player catches a pass that was intended for a receiver on the offense, giving the defensive player's team possession of the ball. Also called *pickoff*.

jersey *n.* a pullover shirt that is part of a football player's uniform; it usually has large numerals that identify the player.

junior varsity *n.* the unit of a high school or college football team consisting of younger players who are not yet starters.

key on *v.* to guard or focus on a certain player as a play develops.

kick off *v.* to kick the football from a tee or a holder to the other team at the start of a half or after scoring.

kick returner *n.* a player on a team receiving a kickoff who stands at or near the goal line of the end zone the player's team is defending and who tries to receive the kickoff and return it. Also called *return man.*

kicker *n.* a player who kicks the football during a kickoff or a field goal or extra-point attempt. Also called *placekicker.*

kickoff *n.* the play at the beginning of a half or after one team has scored in which a kicker kicks the football toward the other team and a player on the other team tries to catch the ball and run forward with it.

kill the clock *v.* See **eat up the clock**.

late hit *n.* a personal foul penalty in which a defensive player makes contact with a ballcarrier after an official has blown his whistle indicating the end of the play.

lateral *n.* a pass or toss of the football backward to another player, who then tries to advance the ball.

lateral *v.* to pass or toss the football backward to another player, who then tries to advance the ball.

lead blocker *n.* a player on the offense who has the assignment of running ahead of the ballcarrier, either through a hole or around an end of the line, to block the first defenders who get in a position to tackle the runner.

league *n.* an organization of football teams at roughly the same competitive level. Also called *conference.*

left guard *n.* the guard on the center's left side.

left tackle *n.* the offensive tackle who lines up on the left side of the left guard.

letter of intent *n.* an official letter that indicates which college a high school student plans to attend and play football for.

limit lines *n.* lines outside of the sidelines and end lines that indicate how close persons other than players, coaches, or other team personnel or game officials may be to the playing field during a game. Also called *restraining lines*.

line judge *n.* an official who is positioned on the sideline facing the current line of scrimmage and who calls penalties for illegal formations in the neutral zone.

line of scrimmage *n.* the imaginary line stretching from one sideline to the other that is determined by the spot on the field where the football is set at the beginning of every play.

linebacker *n.* a defensive player who is positioned a few yards behind the defensive linemen.

linesman *n.* an official who stands along the same sideline as the primary chain operators and moves throughout the game so that he is always facing the current line of scrimmage. He calls penalties for any illegal formations in the neutral zone.

line-to-gain indicator *n.* a long, thin strip of brightly colored material that lies on the ground and points to the yard marker needed for a first down.

live *adj.* describing a football that is still in play and able to be recovered by a player on either team.

locker *n.* a cabinet or small open area where football players store their uniforms and equipment and may also keep personal items.

locker room *n.* an indoor area, usually part of a football stadium, where players put on and take off their uniforms and equipment that are stored in their lockers and where teams meet immediately before and after games and during the half-time intermission.

long *adj.* describing a pass that is thrown yards downfield. Also called *deep.*

long gainer *n.* a play that results in a gain of about 10 or more yards for the offense.

long snapper *n.* a player who specializes in hiking the ball several yards through the air to a punter or a holder on a field goal attempt.

losing streak *n.* when a team loses several games in a row.

man in motion *n.* a wide receiver, tight end, or running back who moves out of his or her position in the formation and starts running across the field toward the quarterback before the snap of the ball.

man-in-motion *adj.* describing an offensive play in which a wide receiver, tight end, or running back moves out of his or her position in the formation and starts running across the field toward the quarterback before the snap of the ball.

man-to-man coverage *n.* a coverage scheme in which one or sometimes two defensive players are assigned to cover each wide receiver, running back, or tight end who could go out for a pass.

mark off *v.* to move the football back, for penalties against the offense, or forward, for defensive penalties, from where it ends up at the finish of a play.

mascot *n.* a person who dresses in a costume having something to do with a football team, especially its nickname, and who interacts with fans in ways similar to those of cheerleaders.

measurement *n.* when the chain operators bring the chains onto the field and use them to determine whether the football has been advanced more than 10 yards from the starting point of the current offensive series (i.e., whether a first down should be awarded to the offense).

middle linebacker *n.* in a defense with three linebackers, the linebacker who lines up opposite the center and between the outside linebackers.

mouthguard *n.* an item made from clear or colored plastic that is molded to fit between a player's teeth and that the player keeps in his or her mouth while playing.

MVP *n.* Most Valuable Player.

national player *n.* in NFL Europe, a player who is not from the United States.

neutral site *n.* a field or stadium where a football game is played that is not the home field of either team.

neutral zone *n.* an imaginary zone between the line of scrimmage and the back end of the football on the ground before the start of the play, in which no offensive player besides the center can line up and which no defensive player can enter until the snap of the ball.

nickel defense *n.* a defensive formation with five defensive backs (from the U.S. coin called a *nickel*, which is worth five cents).

no good *adj.* describing a field goal or extra-point attempt that is not successful.

no huddle *n.* a type of offense in which the players do not go into a huddle after the conclusion of the previous play but instead immediately line up in their positions; the quarterback usually lines up in the shotgun and then uses an audible to call the next play. Also called *hurry up*.

nose tackle *n.* on a defense with three linemen, the lineman who lines up between the defensive ends and usually opposite the center.

no-show *n.* a person who bought a ticket to attend a football game but doesn't show up at the game.

off tackle *adv.* around the outside of the offensive line, on one side of a tackle.

offense *n.* the unit of a team that has possession of the football. It tries to advance the ball toward the other team's goal line in order to score points.

offensive back *n.* a player on the offense who lines up in the area behind the offensive linemen.

offensive coordinator *n.* an assistant coach who is responsible for a football team's offensive unit and often calls the offense's plays.

offensive lineman *n.* a player on the offense who lines up near the line of scrimmage.

official *n.* a person in a game of organized football who is responsible for ensuring that the game is played according to the rules of the league.

off-season *n.* the period between the end of one football season and the start of preparation for another, in which there are no games or practices.

offsetting *adj.* describing penalties that are committed by both teams on a play, in which case neither team is penalized.

offsides *n.* a penalty that is called when some part of a player's body was over the line of scrimmage at the moment the ball was snapped.

on the road *adv.* on the home field of an opponent.

onrushing *adj.* describing a defensive player who is running or moving toward the quarterback or the ballcarrier.

onside kick(off) *n.* a short kickoff that is meant to be recovered by the kicking team.

open *adj.* not covered by a defensive player.

open the hole *v.* to block any defensive players who might be in the way of a running back going through a hole.

open week *n.* a week in which a football team does not have a game scheduled to play. Also called *bye week.*

open-field running *n.* when a ballcarrier is past the line of scrimmage and runs in different directions downfield.

opening *n.* an area of the field with no or few defenders, toward which a ballcarrier or a receiver might try to run.

out *n.* a pass pattern in which the receiver runs straight down the field for several yards and then turns to the right or left and runs toward the nearer sideline.

out of bounds *adj., adv.* in technical usage, the area of the football field outside of the hash marks; informally, outside of the sidelines and end lines where, if the ball or a player with the ball goes, the play is over.

outside linebacker *n.* one of the two linebackers who line up on each side of the middle linebacker or the inside linebackers.

overtime *n.* a quarter or quarters played after the regulation four quarters of a football game at the end of which the score is tied.

pass *v.* to throw a football forward to a receiver.

pass *n.* a football that is thrown to a receiver, or a play featuring such an action.

(pass) reception *n.* when a receiver catches a pass.

passing lane *n.* a direct, unobstructed line between a quarterback and a receiver through which a pass can be thrown. Also called *seam.*

passing play *n.* a play in which the offense tries to advance the football by throwing a pass.

passing situation *n.* when the conditions on a certain down require that the offense try to throw a pass to gain several yards.

pass-protect *v.* to block defenders away from a quarterback trying to throw a pass.

pattern *n.* the direction downfield that a receiver runs when going out for a pass. Also called *route*.

payout *n.* the money paid by the organizers of a college bowl game to the two colleges whose teams play in the game.

penalty *n.* a violation of one of the rules of football, or the punishment that a player or team receives for violating the rule. Also called *infraction*.

(penalty) flag *n.* a small yellow piece of cloth that an official tosses into the air to indicate that he has seen a rules violation during a play.

penalty yardage *n.* the number of yards that are marked off against the offense or the defense for a specific penalty.

pep rally *n.* a gathering held in support of a football team in which students, teachers, players, cheerleaders, parents, and other community members make speeches and do other things to show how much they want their team to win.

pep talk *n.* a speech by a coach or other team member that is meant to encourage the team.

pick *n.* See **screen**.

pick off *v.* See **intercept**.

pickoff *n.* See **interception**.

pickup *adj.* describing games in which a number of people who want to play football for fun and exercise simply get together and choose up sides—that is, divide themselves into two teams.

piling on *n.* when several defensive players jump onto a ball-carrier.

placekicker *n.* See **kicker**.

play action pass *n.* a passing play in which the quarterback, after getting the snap, fakes a handoff to a running back, then drops back and tries to throw to a receiver. Also called *play fake*.

play clock *n.* a clock used in football games that is reset to 25 seconds after every play in which the game clock was stopped and that then counts down the time left before the offense must begin its next play. Also called *25-second clock*.

play dirty *v.* to use unnecessary force and even try to injure the other team's players.

play fake *n.* See **play action pass**.

playbook *n.* a list and diagram of a football team's offensive and defensive plays.

play-by-play *n.* a description of the action of a football game as it is happening.

(playoff) berth *n.* See **(playoff) spot**.

playoff (game) *n.* a postseason football game the winning team of which goes on to play in a semifinal or championship game.

(playoff) spot *n.* the right to play in a playoff game. Also called *(playoff) berth*.

pocket *n.* the area of the backfield directly behind the offensive line.

point after touchdown (PAT) *n.* See **extra point**.

poll *n.* a survey of sportswriters or coaches that ranks the best teams in a league or at a certain level of football.

pom-pons *n.* large, round, brightly colored soft objects carried by cheerleaders.

possession *n.* when a team is on offense or returning a kick—that is, when one player on the team is holding the football; the player can try to advance the ball forward toward the other team's goal line in order to score points.

post pattern *n.* a pass pattern in which the receiver runs several yards downfield toward the middle of the field.

postseason *n.* the part of a football league's season that takes place at the end of the regular season and features playoff, championship, or bowl games.

practice squad *n.* players on NFL teams who participate in practices with the team but do not play in games.

pregame warm-up *n.* when players from both teams participate in calisthenics and drills on the field before the start of a football game.

preliminary indication *n.* when after a penalty flag has been thrown, the referee indicates just what the infraction is and the team to be called, without announcing specifically which player was called for the infraction and what the exact results of the enforcement will be.

press box *n.* an area on top or in the middle of the stands of a football field or stadium where members of the media are located while they cover the game and where coaches and officials from both teams may also be during the game.

prevent *n.* a type of defense in which the defensive backs and linebackers will be positioned deeper than normal to try to prevent the other team's offense from getting big plays.

primary receiver *n.* the receiver that the quarterback intends to pass to on a play. Also called *go-to receiver*.

prospect *n.* a talented young football player whom teams want to recruit or draft.

pull *v.* to step backward at the snap and then run around the nearer end of the offensive line to block for a ballcarrier also coming around the end.

pump fake *n.* when the quarterback makes a motion with his or her arm that looks like the start of a pass.

punt *v.* to kick the football by holding the ball with outstretched arms, dropping it, and then kicking it with one foot before it hits the ground.

punter *n.* a player on a football team who specializes in or whose assignment is punting the ball.

pylons *n.* little red or orange tubes made from a soft material that stick up from the eight points on the field where the sidelines intersect both goal lines and end lines.

quarter *n.* one of the four 15- or 12-minute periods into which a football game is divided.

quarterback *n.* an offensive back who calls plays in the huddle and begins every offensive play by getting the ball from the center, having the choice of running with the ball, handing it off to another back, or passing it to a receiver.

(quarterback) count *n.* the signals that a quarterback shouts to the offense before the snap of the ball.

quarterback draw *n.* a running play in which the quarterback drops back as if to pass but then suddenly runs forward with the ball.

(quarterback) keeper *n.* See **bootleg**.

(quarterback) option *n.* a play in which the quarterback runs with the ball around one of the ends of the line with a running back following closely behind; the quarterback can keep running across the line of scrimmage, can toss the ball back to the running back, or can attempt a pass.

quarterback sneak *n.* a running play in which the quarterback takes the snap from the center and immediately moves forward with the ball toward the line of scrimmage.

quick out *n.* a pass pattern in which the receiver runs only a few yards forward and then suddenly turns toward the nearer sideline.

read *n.* an assessment, made before the snap, of the play or strategy the other team will use based on its positioning or movements.

receive a kickoff *v.* to try to catch the football after it has been kicked off.

record *n.* the number of games that a team has won, lost, or tied in a season or at some point in a season.

recover a fumble *v.* to pick up a fumbled ball or lie over it on the ground.

recruit *v.* to try to convince a football player to play for a certain team.

redshirt *v.* to be a member of a college football team but be unable to play in games for the first season.

referee *n.* the chief football official, who announces all penalties and has the final decision on any calls made by the other officials.

refuse a penalty *v.* to not agree to let a penalty called against the other team be enforced (in other words, accepting the result of the previous play even though the other team committed an infraction during it). Also called *decline a penalty*.

regular season *n.* the part of a football season whose games are all scheduled before the start of the season and in which all the teams play the same number of games.

restraining lines *n.* See **limit lines**.

return (a kickoff) *v.* to run with the football toward the other team's goal line after catching the ball on a kickoff.

return man *n.* See **kick returner**.

reverse *n.* a rushing play in which a wide receiver at the snap of the ball runs backward from the line of scrimmage toward the backfield, as on an end around, and receives the ball from a running back who has gotten a handoff from the quarterback. After getting the ball, the receiver runs in the opposite direction from the running back around the end of the line.

rib pads *n.* pads around a player's abdomen that offer protection to parts of the body—the ribs, in particular—that are not protected by the lower shoulder pads. Also called *flak jackets*.

ride the bench *v.* See **warm the bench**.

right guard *n.* the guard on the center's right side.

right tackle *n.* the offensive tackle who lines up on the right side of the right guard.

road game *n.* a game played on the home field of an opponent. Also called *away game*.

roll out *v.* to run to the left or right side of the backfield.

rookie *n.* a player in his or her first year at a certain level of football.

roster *n.* a list of the players on a football team.

roughing the kicker *n.* a penalty called when a defensive player runs into a kicker and, in the judgment of the officials, uses deliberate and excessive force.

round *v.* when all the teams participating in a draft of football players make one selection in the determined order.

route *n.* See **pattern**.

run and shoot *n.* a type of offense with as many as four wide receivers, no tight ends, and only one running back in the backfield, and which usually features passing plays, since at least one of the receivers will probably get open for the quarterback to throw to.

run up the score *v.* to try to score as many points as possible in the remainder of a game even when already having the lead.

runback *n.* the return of a kickoff, punt, or free kick.

running back *n.* an offensive back who may receive a handoff from the quarterback, block for a ballcarrier, or go out to receive a pass.

running game *n.* the ability an offense has to execute running plays.

running into the kicker *n.* a penalty called when a defensive player runs into a kicker on purpose after the ball is kicked.

running play *n.* a play in which a player on the offense tries to advance the football by running forward with it. Also called *rushing play* or *rush*.

running the football *n.* attempting mostly running plays.

rush *n.* See **running play**.

rush *v.* to try to advance the football by running with it, or to run at the quarterback or the ballcarrier in order to make a tackle.

rushing play *n.* See **running play**.

sack *n.* when the quarterback is tackled behind the line of scrimmage before throwing a pass.

sack *v.* to tackle a quarterback behind the line of scrimmage before the quarterback throws a pass.

safety *n.* a defensive back who lines up 10 or more yards behind the line of scrimmage; or a play in which a ballcarrier is tackled within his or her team's own end zone, giving the other team 2 points.

salary cap *n.* the maximum amount of money that an NFL team can spend on the salaries of all its players.

scalping *n.* selling tickets to a football game for a higher price than their original or face value.

schedule *n.* a list of games arranged for the teams of a football league to play on specific dates and at certain locations during a season.

scholarship *n.* the waiver of the full costs of tuition and room and board each year for a college student in return for the student's playing for the college's football team.

scout *n.* a coach, player, or, especially at the professional level, a special employee of a football team who travels to other teams' football games and reports on these teams and/or certain players.

scout team *n.* a unit, typically composed of a football team's second- or third-string players, that plays the role of the next opponent during practices.

scramble *v.* to run, often in more than one direction, to avoid onrushing defensive players.

screen *n.* a type of blocking in which a player simply gets in the way between a ballcarrier or receiver and a defender. Also called *pick*.

screen pass *n.* a passing play in which the pass is usually thrown to a running back who runs just a short distance out of the backfield to the left or right side.

scrimmage *n.* a type of football practice in which actual plays are run but the football is put back to the same spot after every play and no scoring or downs are recorded.

scrimmage *v.* to practice playing football through scrimmages.

script (plays) *v.* to make a list of the plays to be attempted in sequence in a game or part of a game.

seam *n.* See **passing lane**.

season *n.* a set period of time, lasting from a few to several months, during which the games of a football league are played.

season ticket *n.* a type of ticket for football games that guarantees the buyer the same seat at all the home games a team plays during one season.

second half *n.* the third and fourth quarters of a football game.

secondary *n.* all the defensive backs in a defensive unit.

second-string *adj.* describing players who are behind the starters on a team's depth chart.

sellout *n.* a football game for which all the tickets for seats have been sold.

semifinal (game) *n.* a playoff game whose winning team advances to a championship game.

shoot the gaps *n.* to have a defensive player in a position to cover any of the holes between the offensive linemen that a running back could run through.

short-yardage situation *n.* when the conditions on a certain down—for example, if it is second or third down and only a few yards are needed for a first down—require that the offense try a running play that will probably result in a gain of a few yards.

shotgun *n.* an offensive formation in which the quarterback lines up in the backfield about 5 yards behind the center.

shoulder pads *n.* a one-piece assembly of padding made from hard plastic and other materials with an opening in the middle that fits over a football player's head and rests on his or her shoulders.

shovel pass *n.* a pass that is thrown with an underhand motion, and usually with both hands, to another player.

show blitz *v.* to give signs that one or more players are going to blitz.

shutout *n.* a game that ends with one or both teams not having scored any points.

side judge *n.* an official who watches for penalties on passes and kicks and who also counts the number of defensive players.

sidelines *n.* two lines that extend the length of a football field and, with the end lines, set off the boundaries of the field.

silent count *n.* when the quarterback doesn't shout signals before the snap of the ball but rather the center hikes the ball whenever he or she thinks the quarterback is ready; or when the quarterback uses a gesture, such as lifting up and lowering one foot that the bent-over center can see, to signal the center to snap the ball.

single *n.* in Canadian football, 1 point that is awarded to a team if, after this team kicks or punts a ball that enters the goal area, the receiving team does not return the ball past the goal line.

single-elimination *adj.* referring to playoff games whose winner will play in another game but whose loser will not (in other words, is eliminated).

situation substitution *n.* when a defense takes some players off the field and puts players into the game who are better at defending against the type of play the defense thinks is coming from the offense.

snap *v.* See **hike**.

snap *n.* when the center hikes the ball to the quarterback and a play officially begins.

spearing *n.* when defenders dive straight at the ballcarrier, thrusting their helmets into the ballcarrier's body.

specialist *n.* in arena football, a quarterback, placekicker, long snapper, wide receiver/kick returner, or the player who replaces the quarterback on defense.

special-teams unit *n.* the players on a football team who are used during kicking plays.

spike *v.* to throw the football hard down onto the ground.

split backfield *n.* an offensive formation in which two halfbacks line up in back of and one on each side of the quarterback.

split end *n.* in arena football, a player who lines up on the line of scrimmage but no closer than 5 yards to a player on one end of the line.

squib kick *n.* a kickoff that does not go high in the air, as usual, but flies low near the ground and lands not near the kick returner but among the up men.

standings *n.* an official record that indicates how many games have been won, lost, or tied by each team in a football league.

stands *n.* the seating areas for spectators at a football game.

starter *n.* a player who plays on a team's offensive or defensive unit at the beginning and throughout most of a game.

straight-arm *v.* to use one's outstretched arm to push away defensive players who are trying to make a tackle.

strip the ball *v.* to take the football away from the hold of a ballcarrier.

strong safety *n.* the safety who lines up opposite the strong side of the offense.

strong side *n.* the side of the offense on which the tight end lines up.

sudden death *n.* a type of overtime period in which the game is over as soon as one team scores any points; that team wins the game.

suspend *v.* to prohibit a player from playing for a certain period of time.

sweep *n.* a running play in which the running back runs far outside the offensive line, almost as far out as the wide receivers are lined up. Other running backs and wide receivers may run ahead of the rusher and block.

tackle *n.* an offensive lineman who lines up outside of the guards.

tackle *v.* to run into or in some other way force a ballcarrier to fall to the ground, ending the current play.

tackling dummy *n.* an object, approximately the size and weight of a football player, that is hung by rope and that players run into to practice tackling techniques.

tag *v.* in touch football, to touch a ballcarrier with both hands.

tailback *n.* in offensive formations with only one running back, what the running back is often called, especially if the back lines up far to one side of the quarterback to be in a good position either to get a handoff or to receive a pass.

tailgate *v.* to hold or participate in a tailgate party.

tailgate party *n.* a gathering of fans outside of a stadium, often near their cars in a parking lot, before a football game.

take the lead *v.* to score points that give a team a higher score than that of the other team.

takeaway *n.* when a team forces its opponent to turn over the ball.

team area *n.* the marked-off area along the side of a football field where the coaches and personnel of a team, including players who are not playing in the game at the moment, must remain during the game. In the NFL, the team areas extend 24 feet (7.32 m) behind the sidelines from one 32-yard line to the other. Players and team personnel must stay in this area during a game, and in addition a team may allow up to 27 other people, such as representatives of the media or special guests, into the bench area as long as they are wearing badges that read "BENCH." In Canadian football, the team area is 20 yards

(18.29 m) long, running 6 feet away from the sideline. Only coaches and game officials are allowed in the 6-foot-wide area between the bench areas and the sidelines. In college football, the team area starts behind the coaching line and 6 feet inside of the limit line, and it extends between the 25-yard lines. The NCAA specifies that up to 40 members of a team's personnel besides players may be in the team area during a game, and players out of uniform and guests are allowed in the area as long as they are wearing some sort of identification, such as a badge with their name and picture on it. In high school football, the team areas are between the 30-yard lines. As with the high school football goal line, the lines forming the boundaries of the team areas are often a different color than white, and the field inside these areas is marked with diagonal lines or is occasionally solid white. (The interior of team areas on college fields may also be marked with diagonal lines.)

tee *n.* a small plastic object that holds the football upright for the kicker on kickoffs.

territory *n.* the 50 yards extending from the end zone that is defended by one team.

third-string *adj.* describing players who are behind the second-string players on a team's depth chart.

three-point stance *n.* See **down position**.

throw the ball away *v.* to pass the football out of bounds or to a spot on the field where no defensive player can intercept it.

tie *n.* when both teams in a football game have scored the same number of points.

tight end *n.* an end who lines up on the line of scrimmage next to a tackle.

time-out *n.* when the game clock is stopped by the request of one of the teams or the officials.

touch football *n.* a type of nontackle football in which a ballcarrier is ruled down when a player on the other team tags the ballcarrier.

touchback *n.* a kick that goes out of the end zone.

touchdown *n.* a play in which a ballcarrier crosses the opposing team's goal line, a player catches a pass while standing in the other team's end zone, or a defensive player recovers a ballcarrier's fumble in the end zone defended by the ballcarrier's team. This play earns 6 points for the team whose player has the football in the opponent's end zone.

traditional rivals *n.* teams that have belonged to leagues for a long time and have played many games against each other over the years.

trail *v.* to have fewer points than the other team.

training camp *n.* a period before the beginning of a professional football season in which players and coaches gather in one location and prepare for the season.

trash talking *n.* when a player degrades or baits players on the other team; this is done not just as a challenge but for subtle psychological reasons, especially to get the players on the other team angry and make them concentrate less on actually playing the game.

true freshman *n.* a college football player who plays during the first year in college.

turn the ball over *v.* to enable the other team to get possession of the football, as through an interception, fumble, or failure to convert on a fourth down.

turnover *n.* an interception or a fumble by the offense that is recovered by the defense.

25-second clock *n.* See **play clock**.

two-minute drill *n.* an offensive strategy in which a team tries to get as much yardage in as little time as possible, mostly through passing plays that end with the receiver going out of bounds, thereby stopping the game clock.

two-minute warning *n.* in professional football, a time-out that is called by the officials near the end of each half when there are two minutes left on the game clock.

two-point conversion *n.* an extra-point attempt in which the offense tries to run or pass the football into the end zone to earn 2 points.

two-way *adj.* describing a football player who regularly plays both an offensive and a defensive position. In the early days of football most of the players were two-way players, and in high school football many players still are.

umpire *n.* an official who stands four to five yards behind the defensive line at the beginning of every play, counts the number of offensive players, and watches for offsides penalties and for ineligible receivers coming downfield.

under pressure *adj.* with onrushing defensive players getting near.

underdog *n.* a team that is not believed to have much chance of beating another team in a game.

underneath *adj.* describing a pass thrown to a receiver who tries to stay between the quarterback and any defenders.

uniform *n.* special clothing worn by a football player consisting of a jersey worn over the top of the body and special pants and socks, or by a football official consisting of a shirt with black and white vertical stripes, white pants, long socks usually with black and white horizontal stripes, and black athletic shoes.

unload the ball *v.* See **dump the ball off**.

unnecessary roughness *n.* a personal-foul penalty that is called when a player uses excessive force on another player.

unsportsmanlike *adj.* showing little respect for players and the idea of fair competition.

up for *adj.* mentally and psychologically prepared for.

up men *n.* the members of the receiving team who position themselves upfield from the kick returner in order to block.

up position *n.* a slightly crouched stance not requiring that a hand touch the ground.

up the middle *adv.* toward and through the offensive line.

upright *n.* one of two poles that extend vertically from both ends of the crossbar on a goalpost.

upset *v.* to defeat unexpectedly.

varsity *n.* the unit of a high school or college football team that consists of the oldest and the best players and is the unit that competes during the team's regularly scheduled games.

visiting team *n.* the team playing a football game that had to travel from another city or school to play in the game. Also called *visitors*.

visitors *n.* See **visiting team**.

waive *v.* to release (a player) and offer him to each of the other teams in a league, any one of which can claim and sign the player.

walk off (a penalty) *v.* to pick up the football from where it ended up at the finish of a play and move it either forward, for penalties against the defense, or backward, for penalties against the offense, the appropriate number of yards for the specific penalty called.

walk-on *n.* a college football player who was not awarded a scholarship but has tried out for and made a team.

walk-through *n.* a rehearsal of the motions players will go through during the various plays expected to be run in a football game.

warm the bench *v.* to remain on the sidelines and not get to play in a football game. Also called *ride the bench.*

wave *n.* when several spectators in a narrow vertical section of the crowd, from the ground level seats to the top of the stadium, all stand up together with their arms in the air and then sit back down, sometimes while shouting. In the next instant, the spectators sitting on one side of these fans also stand up with their arms raised, then sit down, and the fans next to *them* get up. This continues until spectators in all parts of the stadium have risen and the "wave" is back to the section of the crowd where it was begun; then it repeats several times until the crowd gets tired of it or until action on the field recaptures their interest.

wedge *n.* a formation used by some of the blockers of a receiving team on a kickoff in which the players move forward in front of the returner while standing close together.

West Coast offense *n.* a type of offense that relies on passing plays that are short and underneath.

wide receiver *n.* an end on the offense who lines up several yards to the left or to the right of the linemen on the line of scrimmage.

wild-card *adj.* describing a team that has earned a playoff spot even though it wasn't a division champion, or a playoff game between two such teams.

winning streak *n.* when a team wins several games in a row.

wounded duck *n.* a football that hasn't been thrown with the right passing motion, making it wobble and possibly go end over end and not travel very far.

zone coverage *n.* a coverage scheme in which the territory on the defense's side of the line of scrimmage is divided into zones that are patrolled by one defender so that receivers running their routes through more than one zone will be guarded by more than one defender.